International Manual
of Planning Practice

Judith Ryser and Teresa Franchini
Editors

CONTENT

USB card: full country contributions, accessible through interactive
lists by authors and by countries

Acknowledgments

First and foremost, we wish to express our gratitude to the many authors who have made this book possible. For a successful publication of this kind we depended on the generosity, professional knowledge and insight of planners in their respective countries. Only with such cooperation were we able to update the existing entries and add new ones with accuracy and to high standard. We are particularly grateful for the loyal authors who updated their contribution, sometimes over several editions. We are pleased to welcome new authors who have accepted our invitation to widen the scope of the previous edition. We also appreciate those who were willing to update contributions of the 2008 edition whose authors were no longer available.

We are particularly keen to thank our former president, Max van den Berg for inviting us to produce a new edition of the International Manual of Planning Practice towards the 50th anniversary of ISOCARP, building on the great undertaking of Adriana dal Cin and Derek Lyddon who initiated this publication together with Javier de Mesones. We also appreciate the great support of Jef van den Broeck who chairs ACC50 in charge of the anniversary celebrations. We were assisted generously by Gaby Kurth, Eline van Haastrecht and others of the ISOCARP secretariat with logistics which was extremely challenging, and we are grateful to Vice President Gabriel Pascariu for managing the printing. We are very pleased that Paula Blanco Ballesteros who designed the 2008 IMPP edition and Dino Juloya who produced the CD have agreed to contribute their imagination and talent to the design and technical preparation of this new edition. We are indebted to Sonia Freire Trigo for working with us on the synthesis of the country contributions.

Again, we have been supported by colleagues and friends, too many to mention individually, who were instrumental in keeping our spirits up at times we were overwhelmed with the task of gathering articles and convincing authors that their efforts were for a good cause. It was tempting to write a companion book about the process and human dimension of producing IMPP. Conversely, we see great potential for future networking between the authors who have offered to be involved in this common pursuit and that would suit also the aspirations of ISOCARP to develop into an international networking society able to deliver concrete results.

There is great potential to develop IMPP in new directions making use of mobile technology and virtual space, something that should interest planners for their own work, but the process of producing this compendium revealed many institutional and behavioural hurdles which may hinder such a pursuit. What counts are the generous and knowledgeable contributions without which a compendium of such scope would be impossible to produce and inspire the younger generation of planners. That may well be the reason why IMPP is unique and therefore a precious instrument for all those involved in planning to make our world more sustainable.

The editors, *Judith Ryser & Teresa Franchini, London and Madrid, September 2015*

This publication is an account of a two year study focused on planning paradigms and practices in hundred and thirty five countries worldwide. It is a restructured and expanded version of the IMPP 2008 edition, with the new and updated reports, and a series of new entries exclusively prepared for this volume presenting planning practices of the countries for the first time in IMPP. The volume comes with an enriched and expanded content incorporating the thematic topics of sustainability, governance and use of ICT in planning. These subjects are timely and appropriately selected among the most challenging questions planning is facing at present.

Fundamental to every exploration of planning in use is the question of what constitutes good planning practice in the wider context of planning theories and assumptions about their application. With regard to that relationship IMPP appears a valuable source for learning and comparison and is a promising and rewarding reading. The cases present diversity, reflecting different approaches to planning and understanding the role it plays in time and space. Conversely, they exemplify closeness in thinking and action concerning issues of sustainability, urban resilience, climate change or ICT expansion. The case-studies talk about the growing understanding of a need for planning and about planning at city or national scale within the global scene. Today, planners view the local setting as a part, or a place of reflection of much broader development transformations whose effects become best visible and comprehensible at the scale of a city, a town or a region. Yet, their linkages to the global level or a wider perspective remain a constant of their development trajectories. It is from that perspective that the country profiles on planning assembled in this publication contribute to a better understanding of the meaning and importance of sharing knowledge and experience regardless of geography.

Writing a book or assembling a compendium like this one is never a lone venture. Many colleagues and friends from all over the world contributed generously with their articles, case studies, ideas or advice. We gratefully acknowledge their work and the contribution they made. Very special thanks go to the editors Judith Ryser and Teresa Franchini for their excellent work in putting together this publication, and their guidance and patience in working with the authors. Last but not least, the words of appreciation go to Paula Blanco Ballesteros whose inspiring visualisations gave an added value to this volume.

Milica Bajić-Brković
President of ISOCARP 2015

Once again a new edition of IMPP, the International Manual of Planning Practice lies before you. Once again it is a unique product of the highest quality. Read it, study it to enrich your knowledge about planning worldwide. Above all use it during planning practice and in education as a tool to learn about and understand the great differences and similarities of national planning systems and goals in the world.

I have been a great supporter of the International Manual of Planning Practice ever since Javier de Mesones, Adriana dal Cin and Derek Lyddon launched the idea of this project at the 1988 ISOCARP congress in Taormina during the discussion on the future orientation of the planning profession at which many members from outside Europe participated. Following the simple premise that "planning is making arrangements for the future", the question arose: "what type of arrangement and for the future of what?" IMPP was conceived to garner answers to these questions from all ISOCARP member countries and to compare their respective approaches. IMPP has evolved since then, broadened its scope of content as well as the number of countries and followed the geopolitical context affecting planning continuously. How lucky we are with an actualised and expanded IMPP containing 135 countries.

IMPP is not only a publication that provides comparable inside information on planning systems, procedures, methods, cultures around the world and, most importantly, a critique of the gap between planning systems and their application in practice. The richness of similarities and scope of differences is astounding me. I am also very surprised about rapid changes in spatial planning systems in many countries all over the world.

In my view IMPP enriches your knowledge about spatial planning and is of immense importance for practising and teaching. I have promoted it and I encourage you to promote the new edition all over the world in offices, planning institutions and education establishments. Colleagues will be glad to know that a new edition is available.

I have used IMPP with my students at the University of Utrecht and advising internationally in Europe and above all in Syria. I let students analyse key planning results in other countries and design and improve planning products with the help of IMPP. The real value of IMPP is working with it.

As everybody can imagine the realisation and production of such a Manual is huge and intensive work. So many countries, regions and authors had to be encouraged to join a cooperative setting inspired and guided by the editors. They developed a concept for the manual, its content and form, contacted authors, had to cagole them to write (in time), gave comments and prepared the results for production. ISOCARP, the National Delegations and the members should thank the editors for their commitment and for the result which delivers basic knowledge for planners, urbanists, politicians and everybody dealing with spatial development. Your achievement is fantastic and I admire you both, Judith and Teresa, for all the creative work you have done for Isocarp.

Max van den Berg
Former ISOCARP President 2015

Classical music buskers, London, UK, photo Judith Ryser

About this book

This book is a compendium on planning of use to practising planners in both the public and the private sector, as well as to other built environment professionals. It also constitutes a reference book for academics and students and provides basic information for planners, developers and investors who intend to operate in countries beyond their own. Besides a succinct background on each country and its planning system, the focus of the Manual is on planning practice. The format is a small book with summary pages of each country and an incorporated USB card with the country profiles as part of this publication, in interactive mode similar to the 2008 edition. In the editors' essay we attempt to highlight the communalities and differences of planning practices around the world based on the information provided by the authors.

IMPP gives readers a comparative overview of planning worldwide provided by experienced practitioners and academics in five continents. The aim of the 135 case studies is to give a comprehensive panorama of the regulated development process and puts it into the perspective of real world experiences. For that reason the editors devised a template for the country contributions:

- General country information
    description of the general country information (text, diagrams, maps, dealing with location, size, characteristics of the country, population, GDP, government, etc.)

- Planning framework
    political and institutional structure and organisation, administrative competence for planning, main planning legislation. planning and implementation instruments and development control mechanisms.

- Planning process
    planning system and plan making, development control procedures, participation and appeal, other initiatives.

- Sustainability and governance
    environmental protection, Agenda 21, specific complementary legislation; main stakeholders in the spatial physical development process, urban management and maintenance, and relations between built environment users; use of ICT in the planning, information dissemination and participation process

- Evaluation
    planning system in practice, critical analysis of the application of the planning system in practice, focusing on the gaps between planning legislation and physical spatial development and the future prospects of the planning process, besides other relevant comments.

The template was not always followed nor was information supplied on all aspects. The editors restructured the information when possible according to the template and completed it from public sources for easier comparison to the best of their ability. The book is published in English, but English is not the first language of many authors and the texts were subedited for comprehension. As the whole book is produced entirely with free contributions there was no possibility of complete translation. The full subedited papers are on the incorporated USB card with illustrations produced by their authors who have the rights and responsibilities for the contents of their contributions. The previous authors whose papers have been updated by others are cited in the text, and other mentioned collaborators are included in the indices on the USB card and in the book.

'Planning System at a Glance' contains a concise synthesis of each country, together with an international list of planning contacts produced by the editors Judith Ryser and Teresa Franchini. The facts about the countries, their institutions and settlement structures are provided by the authors and completed by the editors when necessary. The CIA FactBook is used as primary source for the summary facts, together with information from official government sites when available, and complementary information from the web.

The one page country profiles include maps, fast facts, settlement structure, institutional structure, web addresses of key planning agencies and summaries of:
- administrative competence for planning
- main planning legislation
- planning and implementation instruments
- planning process and development control
- sustainability and governance
- planning system in practice.

'The World of Planning and its Future', the essay written by the editors Judith Ryser and Teresa Franchini completes the compendium. The essay evokes the context of planning focusing on the 50 years of ISOCARP's existence. It discusses the interaction between complex forces in creating contradictions between formal planning systems and their application in practice as well as development processes occurring outside these controls. It attempts to highlight general features of planning with their origins and mutual influences across countries and to show country or region specific characteristics. However, the scope of the essay is limited as the editors focused on obtaining as many country contributions as possible while in-depth research would be necessary to do justice to this rich material.

The World of Planning and its Future

The World of Planning and its Future

Purpose of the essay

The essay of the 2008 edition was putting the content of the country contributions into a brief historic context of planning which was traditionally based on a European point of view and opposed that to the Latin American perspective before moving onto a tentative review of 21st century changes relevant to planning. Among the common findings from the 101 countries was the shift from government to governance in planning and especially implementation. They included trends towards devolution, often in the form of regionalisation, and the emergence of cities as drivers of development. However, the promises of public participation - even enshrined in law - remained unsatisfactory for the 'planned' who claimed a greater share in the planning process. A second aspect was the growing importance of environmental concerns in planning, often driven from the bottom up, and both these issues were taken on board more explicitly in the framework of the country contributions for the 2015 edition. Then as now lack of planning skills are seen by many as contributing to poor planning. The position of design and aesthetics among planners remains an unresolved debate whilst the dichotomy of planning as politics or technical expertise seems to weaken.

The 2008 edition was based on contributions emanating from a period of consistent physical growth in the developed world and urbanisation in the developing world. This was putting pressure on the planning system which was often overtaken by these forces, leaving scars on both the built and the natural environment. The contributions were not yet affected by the global financial crisis, ensuing austerity measures and stagnation which are important factors for the 2015 edition as they challenge planning as a hindrance to recovery and claim presumption in favour of development. Globalisation has accelerated speed of communication and worldwide interdependence. It turned what were traditionally national or local incidences, such as volatility of financial markets, unstable raw material and oil prices, but most alarmingly armed conflicts and terrorist attacks and in their wake catastrophic human tragedies that lead to massive population displacements and migration into grossly amplified fluctuations with direct repercussions on human settlements and spatial development. These changes became apparent to many contributors despite inherent inertia in planning and many suggested new measures in the evaluation chapter.

A systematic comparative analysis of the planning processes in the participating countries is beyond this essay. Nevertheless, an attempt is made at a conceptual framework to initiate such comparisons to enable planners from different contexts to learn from each other's responses and explore new avenues collectively. The essay attempts to identify long term planning principles which may remain pertinent and set them against place-specific short term reactions and their effects on the sustainability of the development process. Some trends may arise from putting these examples into the context of social and spatial cohesion as well as competitiveness, and relating them to alternative models of cooperation and complementarity. Finally, the essay will connect these deliberations to the role and responsibilities of planners in an uncertain and erratically changing world.

Cycles in Antwerp, Belgium, photo Judith Ryser

1 | Context of the spatial development process

Planning entails a lot of inertia by its very nature. Thus many deliberations of the essay in the 2008 IMPP edition based on contributions from 101 countries remain pertinent[1] and are briefly reiterated below. Yet, momentous events have taken place since then which have sent shockwaves through society and paralysed the planning process in many places.

1.1 Geo-political transformations

Occupy London 2011, photo Judith Ryser

TThe global financial crash - unexpected and intense - shook the capitalist economic edifice at its roots, bringing hardship to a vast number of people who continue to endure austerity. Social movements proposing alternatives to the neoliberal austerity measures have emerged throughout the world like 'Occupy' and some have made it into mainstream politics where they advocate social and spatial justice beyond the old left-right dogmatic divide. To name but a few: in Europe they are 'podemos', 'indignados' and 'democracia real ya' in Spain; 'tempo de avancar' in Portugal, 'syriza' in Greece; 'citta slow', 'sollevazione generale', 'rete habitare nella crisi' in Italy; 'transform' in Denmark; and the orange revolution in Ukraine; in Latin America 'piqueteros', 'autoconvocados' in Argentina; Zapatistas in Mexico; in Asia the red shirts in Thailand; the movement for consumer rights in India; as well as the Arab Spring in North Africa and the Middle East. While some are protest movements like the one in Brazil against the world cup and the many protest marches against military intervention in third countries, many others are seeking positive alternatives to the austerity model in favour of more sustainable alternative lifestyles built on solidarity, democracy and autonomy.

Social media and support by eminent establishment figures like Josef Stiglitz[2] may signal a more successful future for these movements than previous ones, such as the environmentalists, May 68' and similar in the nineteen-sixties. Sadly, the hope and optimism which these movements had stimulated were often short lived and followed by backlashes, political chaos, armed conflict or downright oppression, alongside fundamentalist movements, the most extreme being the jihadists, Isis in the middle east and Boko Haram in Africa. Quasi fascist movements are also gathering momentum, often underground accompanied by outright criminal gangs. Pulling in opposite directions these movements indicate that the world is again at a crossroads between civilisation and barbarism.

A brief summary of the longer term history of planning was given in the 2008 essay. It showed that the binary world of market and planned economies secured some perverse stability and certainty which the demise of communism had not reinforced as expected, quite the reverse. Suffice to say that since the end of the cold war, the world has become much more unstable and the future very unpredictable. Being about the future planning has not excelled in producing new scenarios of change.

Since the last IMPP edition a shift has taken place of geo-political power relations and domination with direct repercussions on planning. While the USA remains the dominant world force, the rise of the 'Asian tiger' revealed the new powers of China and India, the two most populous countries of the world at the head of other fast developing Asian countries of ASEAN. Russia remains an important player, determined to increase its role in geo-politics by exercising greater influence over the new independent republics from soviet times, as well as over selected Middle Eastern, African and Asian countries. Conversely, Europe is on a considerable slow down and facing mass immigration from war-torn countries in sub Saharan Africa, central Asia, the Middle East and North Africa. Split over sovereignty and solidarity, the European Union seems to fail in its role of cohesive joint force on the world stage. Africa has the fastest growing population which will put pressure on Europe, and Islamic countries aspire to world power, better still domination by other means.

Makeny, Sierra Leone, photo Luis Perea

In economic terms China is forecast to overtake the United States by 2017[3] and other BRIC countries (India 3rd, Russia 5th, Brazil 7th) will have moved ahead of traditional European 'world powers' (UK 8th, France 9th) by 2020. Yet, GDP per capita (PPP) ranking[4] gives a rather different picture of average living standards. Except for the United States which ranks 10th, none of the high ranking countries in terms of GDP are among the top ten GDP per capita, which encompass small countries like Luxembourg (1st), Qatar (3rd), Macao (4th), Singapore (9th), the Scandinavian countries (Norway 2nd, Sweden 7th, Denmark 8th), and Australia (6th).[5] In 34 years (1980-2014) China's GDP per capita increased from US$ 313 to US$ 7,589 (expected US$ 11,449 by 2020); India's from US$ 266 to US$ 1,627 (expected US$ 2,672 by 2020) both showing steady growth. Russia's GDP per capita rose from US$ 576 to US$ 8,184 (expected US$ 14,480 by 2020) after steep decline following the demise of communism, then steady growth until decline started again recently. Australia (from US$ 10,999 to US$ 61,219) also shows rocky changes while Singapore (US$ 5,004 to US$ 56,319) experienced stepped but steady growth. UK grew from US$ 10,039 to US$ 45,653 (expected US$ 55,576 by 2020) but with enormous fluctuations on the way; France from US$ 13,111 to US$ 44,538 (expected US$ 45,861 by 2020) seems now in slow but steady decline. What these spot examples demonstrate are very uneven economic processes, despite globalisation. Due to the intricate link between planning and the economy, periodic local financial crises have a direct impact on the planning process in these countries.

Another perspective of the relative prosperity and quality of life of countries is the GINI index[6] which measures the gap between rich and poor. According to World Bank data[7] the GINI index was for China 37.0 (2011), USA 41.1 (2010), India 33.6 (2011), Russia 42 (CIA WFB), UK 38 (2010), France 30.9 (CIA WFB), Singapore 46 (CIA WFB).[8] According to these figures USA have greater polarisation than China, India and the UK, but there is no data to show evolution over time. According to the CIA World Factbook[9] the rank order of the GINI index shows enormous discrepancies between developing countries where the index is up to 63% and Russia, the USA (42% and 45% respectively) and the European Union with an average of 30.6%, ranging from Sweden's 23%, the lowest recorded, to Bulgaria 45.3%, with France 30.9%, Germany 27%, and the UK 32.3%.

Looking at longer term trends (1960-2012)[10] while absolute inequality had slightly declined overall, it has increased over recent years, even among the most egalitarian nations. While living standards had risen absolutely in most parts of the world, this did not happen in relative terms, and average living standards per country do not translate the gap between the rich and the poor discussed above.[11] The premise that (economic) growth needs to take priority over all else, assumed to trickle down to the poorer parts of society lacks evidence and is challenged by many IMPP contributions. Other values such as human rights and fairness come into play and the continuum between the poor and the very rich matters less than eradication of seemingly intractable extreme poverty which is evoked by many IMPP contributors, especially from the developing world.

1.3 Changing role of planning

Kowloon, Hong Kong, source:
https://commons.wikimedia.org/wiki/File:Kowloon_Panorama_by_Ryan_Cheng_2010.jpg

Where does that leave planning? Recent events in Europe send out pointers to two contrary futures: a world of fortresses and exclusion with razor wired walls, water cannons and autocratic repression by force, as opposed to solidarity and compassion of a 'one world' future which aims to find solutions at either end of current mass migration across continents. Movements of people are an integral part of human history with its counterparts of violence and killings, underlying the present swell of displacement as so often before. What is the role of planning in all this? To date, the planning systems appear completely powerless in dealing with essentially spatial, but also economic and social accommodation of the many displaced people, fleeing destitution and death or simply seeking a better life in a peaceful environment. It is significant that all the aggressive advances toward power and domination are resorting to old fashioned territorial land grabs, a far cry from mediation and negotiation, the direction advocated for the future of planning. Current retrogression is in danger of eradicating emancipatory gains, not least for women. It also undermines recent efforts of reliance on more indigenous, local voluntary resources without abandoning an overall planning framework supported by the public sector and accompanied by some redistribution of resources.

Perhaps time has come to look for new avenues of planning in response to the global financial crisis and its aftermath, beyond short lived promises of more inclusive alternative social models which lack adequate clout. Among the 136 countries included in the 2015 edition of IMPP many critical comments are voiced about the powerlessness or down right dysfunction of existing planning systems. None of them though advocates to abandon planning altogether and a number of constructive proposals are put forward to improve and even strengthen planning. They are taken up in the succinct comparative analysis which constitutes the core of the essay.

1.4 Recent evolution of planning and its context

Transformation of a Haussmann quarter in Marseille, France, photo Judith Ryser

Very briefly, the origin of planning practice is seen in the mid 19th century with European industrialisation and urbanisation. The dual approach of urbanism either as art or as a technical & hygiene issue (e.g. Garnier, Sitte, Burnham, Haussman) gave rise to planning legislation and building regulations. In turn, continuous growth and sprawl due to transport innovation led to new urban models. Modernism on the one hand and urban ecology on the other hand led to concepts of garden cities, New Towns, green belts and regional planning.

Planning remained caught in a constant interplay between opposites: futuristic utopias vs emphasis on local needs; spatial physical vs socio-economic and/or environmental planning; infrastructure driven growth vs heritage conservation. The energy shock marked a post-industrial era and globalisation. Preoccupation with regional imbalances ran alongside urban dynamics expressed in brownfield development, gentrification, transformation of local economies, as well as bottom up citizen initiatives and aspiration to better quality of life. This mobilised a paraphernalia of planning approaches, including urban management, local governance and self-reliant public participation, as well as recognition of cities as economic drivers. Climate change awareness introduced the notion of sustainable development and measures to deal with environmental, and to a lesser extent, social imbalances besides spatial ones.

In the 1980s 'new urbanism' emerged in the USA, a new form of regulatory planning in response to post-modern, over-flexible planning. New urbanism underpinned the belief that planning could lead to an ideal state of the city based on scientific, economic and demographic projections, counteracting manipulation and control by public administrations. In that view, achieving the ideal state of cities to the benefit of the public good was essentially in the gift of planners who would influence the nature of communities through design guided by collective preferences. Designing cities would amount to a sort of neo-modern environmental determinism, while running and managing them would be left to other professions.

Historically, models of euro-centric or 'first world' planning were diffused through colonialism, scientific and educational institutions, as well as professional associations and planning journals and, more recently, through international development agencies, as well as internationalisation of planning practices. This led to the adoption of an ubiquitous model of spatial development, either imported or imposed. More focused on process than outcome, this model was often inappropriate for local contexts, ignoring land ownership, materials, forms of construction and customs. Unable to meet the needs of informal settlers it was contributing to their spatial and social marginalisation. Ineffective in coping with rapid growth driven by globalising pressures, unresponsive to climate change issues, sustainability, demand for public participation or transparency, and incompatible with administrations acting as facilitators and promoters, this model was essentially privileging private interventions. It lacked features of contemporary planning: strategic instead of comprehensive planning; flexible instead of focused on fixed end states; community and stakeholder oriented rather than run by experts. Above all it was unable to respond to objectives that reflect overall urban interests: positioning of the city, environmental protection, sustainable development, social inclusion, local identity, quality of urban spaces, integrated urban policies, spatial and sectoral coordination. IMPP evidence shows that this global planning model is not a solution either and planning is again in need of defining its own future.

Ecoquarter Vallecas, Madrid, Spain, photo Teresa Franchini

As in 2008, the bulk of the country contributions of the 2015 IMPP edition deal with the planning system, administrative competence and the planning process, often with emphasis on physical planning. Environmental issues had been evoked before but are occupying a much more prominent place now under the term of sustainability. Natural hazards and risk management are evoked by countries exposed to them which try to incorporate risk management more explicitly into the planning system. Nevertheless, preventive measures related to risks of earthquake, flooding, drought, soil erosion and desertification are not taken up explicitly, let alone strategies to adapt safer structures during reconstruction, and related lifestyle issues. When mentioned, risk management does not include hazardous civil use of nuclear power, notwithstanding the issue of long term nuclear waste which is also omitted in the argument for CO_2 emission reduction. Rarely are long term strategies against natural risks or anticipatory measures incorporated in the planning systems described here, despite more fluctuating and intensive weather conditions. Although sensitivity to climate change issues has increased, many undertakings stimulated by intergovernmental agreements and initiatives, such as Agenda 21, were not kept up and rarely materialised in concrete interventions.

War torn countries describe their planning systems despite their complete irrelevance during the devastation these countries are enduring. Some remain optimistic, expecting the planning system to be of use for reconstruction. The effect of displaced people on planning is rarely touched up, even by small and not very developed countries which are accommodating them in large numbers without a clear outlook of a longer term solution. Little reference is made to cultural aspects of planning, including protection of historic and archaeological sites from barbaric destruction.

Poverty is mentioned but not necessarily as a planning issue, while aspects of health or life expectancy are omitted, despite the notions of healthy and liveable cities. Although precarious living conditions are improving in absolute terms the gap is widening in relative terms, within many countries, as well as between developed and developing countries. Epidemic outbreaks are intense and many curable diseases are not attended to in poor developing countries for lack of redistribution of global resources.

Most surprisingly, land and land ownership do not figure in the IMPP contributions on the whole, except where all land is owned by the state. This despite the fact that planning is recognised essentially as a tool to deal with land use, and thus with land as a finite and precious resource. No explicit measures are stated to deal with adverse effects of land ownership. Sprawl is sometimes seen as wasteful in terms of land use, but often the way conceived to curb it is to build vertically regardless of impacts on daylight and sunlight provision, or turbulence created by very tall buildings at ground floor level which jeopardises the liveability and use of even modest spaces left for public use there.

1.6 Informal cities – and planning responses

Informal settlements on the fringe of Annaba, Algeria, photo Judith Ryser

Informal settlements assume an important part in the 2015 contributions to IMPP. They are widespread in developing countries, although various forms of informal development take place also elsewhere, often in terms of squatting in existing premises.

In Asia on average between 24% and 43% populations live in slums (Thailand 26%, Cambodia 79%), mainly in large metropolitan regions. Planning regulations are obviously ineffective, whether top down or bottom up. Having to rely on out-dated cadastral databases the planning systems produce unrealistic general plans without necessary resources for implementation, moreover handled by inefficient local administrations.

In Latin America and the Caribbean on average 27% of the urban population lives in slums although this varies widely (Chile 9%, Jamaica 60%). Informal settlements are created by organised invasions, informal subdivisions and strong community leaders in large metropolitan regions. These settlements emerge due to inappropriate public housing policies, unrealistic planning regulations and technocratic regulatory plans. Some cities have adopted new innovative approaches: Curitiba, Porto Alegre, Bogota, Medellin, Quito, Lima, Mexico city.

In Africa 62% inhabitants live in slums in sub-Saharan regions and 15% in North Africa. Slums occur in most cities at low density, in terms of peripheral dispersion and large informal settlements, while administrations inherited from colonial times are concentrating on the central cities and rich neighbourhoods, most of them heavily gated.

Responses to informal settlements tend to remain stereotypical. Private owners take invaders or precarious lessees of land or housing to court or use harassment tactics, including eradication. Public administrations are neglecting informal settlements, often through non-intervention, except sporadically, in terms of relocation and more rarely by upgrading such informal settlements. International agencies, such as UN-Habitat and the World Bank are undertaking many interventions in informal settlements in the developing world, but they can only do so with the approval of sovereign states.

Alternative visions to conventional planning for informal settlements exist but remain tentative. There are no simple models, as planned or public intervention depends on the legal framework of the countries, their political culture, as well as readiness for action of governments. Collaborative initiatives and participatory approaches are invoked but rarely implemented and leave planning with an enormous burden and a great need for innovation.

2 | Common ground of planning and practice and innovative departures

Based on the 136 contributions to IMPP from all continents and most regions, this chapter is an attempt to highlight what countries have in common in terms of context, competence and institutional arrangements for planning, what planning issues they share and where their approaches to planning differ. Due to the complexity of the information and the great variety of planning and its context, the choice was made to compare planning and its practice within each continent, and its sub-regions. The comparisons are structured according to the subheadings used by the authors for their contributions. The countries mentioned in parenthesis are not exclusive or exhaustive and are meant as indications only. The editors are aware that this very rich material warrants much greater study in depth.[13] What this essay endeavours is to produce some initial highlights.

AFRICA

Country contributions
East: Burundi, Ethiopia, Kenya, Madagascar, Malawi, Mozambique, Sudan, Tanzania, Zimbabwe (9)
Middle: Angola, Cameroon, Gabon, Sao Tome & Principe (4)
North: Algeria, Egypt, Libya, Morocco, Tunisia (5)
Southern: Botswana, Lesotho, Namibia, South Africa, Swaziland (5)
West: Benin, Cote d'Ivoire, Ghana, Nigeria, Sierra Leone (5)

Independence and constitution
Except for Ethiopia, which is the oldest independent country in Africa and one of the oldest in the world, the inner political division of this vast continent was the result of a long process of territorial structuring by the native societies. This process was altered by the colonial activities of the Western European powers during the 19th century. Although South Africa (1921) and Egypt (1922) were the first countries to get their independency from the UK, the decolonisation of Africa took place gradually after the Second World War, in a process that started in the 1950s in North Africa (Libya 1951, Morocco 1956, Tunisia 1956), West (Ghana 1957) and East (Sudan 1959).

The 1960s witnessed the emancipation of many countries, starting with Benin, Cote D´Ivoire, Madagascar, Cameroon, Gabon and Nigeria in 1960, followed by Sierra Leone

1961, Algeria and Burundi 1962, Kenya 1963, Malawi and Tanzania 1964, Botswana and Lesotho 1966 and Swaziland in 1967. Mozambique, Angola and Sao Tome & Principe got their independency in 1975, Zimbabwe in 1980 and Namibia in 1990.

Except for Morocco, Lesotho and Swaziland which are constitutional monarchies, the countries adopted republican systems and all of them operate in the market economy. Some established socialist regimes since their independence but abandoned them by the 1990s (Angola 1975-1992, Ethiopia 1987–1991, Mozambique 1975-1991 and Tanzania 1967-1986).

Although some countries established their own constitutions immediately or a few years after independence (Algeria 1963, Botswana 1966, Lesotho 1967, Sao Tome & Principe 1975, Namibia 1990), others had undertaken a process of updating during the 1990s (Benin, Gabon, Sierra Leone, Ghana, Cameroon, Ethiopia, South Africa, Nigeria), while most did it in the new millennium: Cote D´Ivoire 2000, Mozambique 2004, Sudan, Swaziland and Burundi 2005, Angola, Madagascar, Kenya 2010, Libya and Morocco 2011, Tanzania 2012, Malawi and Zimbabwe 2013, Tunisia and Egypt 2014.

The chronology of the constitutions´ approval is important regarding the legal and administrative structure, as some countries maintained to some extent the organisational structures inherited from the colonial era, while others, especially the ones which have amended their constitutions during the last decades, have assumed the sustainability principles set up in the Rio de Janeiro Summit in 1992.

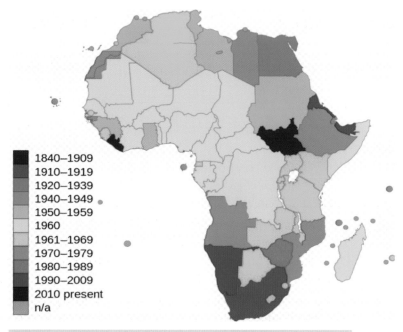

1840–1909
1910–1919
1920–1939
1940–1949
1950–1959
1960
1961–1969
1970–1979
1980–1989
1990–2009
2010 present
n/a

Africa with dates of independence
source: http://jimchampa.tripod.com/oliverssitecontinued/id2.html

General characteristics

Countries in Africa are very diverse in terms of geography, people and economy and a closer look of the IMPP countries data by regions portrays this diversity.

In terms of population, the IMPP countries in Africa vary widely from about 180,000 inhabitants in Sao Tome & Principe to about 180 million in Nigeria. Density is another demographic issue, but not so relevant since it depends on the size of the country, and ranges from 1 pop/km2 in Namibia to 190 pop/km2 in Nigeria.

Maputo, Mozambique, photo Luis Perea

Freetown, Sierra Leone, photo Luis Perea

The African continent has a high rate of population growth, up to 2%. At regional level, the Western region has the highest rate (Zimbabwe 4.4%, Burundi, 4%), the Southern region, except for Swaziland (1.2%), has a lower rate, less than 1%, and Botswana records a negative growth and the Northern region shows a remarkable difference, from 0.9% in Tunisia to 3.1% in Libya. According to these rates of growth, it is estimated that a quarter of the world population will live in Africa by 2050.[14].

Overall urban population is 37% in Sub-Saharzan Africa and 60% in North Africa.[15] The rural conditions of some countries determine a low rate of urbanisation. This is the case of the Eastern countries, where the highest urbanisation rate (33%) is recorded in Zimbabwe, Madagascar and Mozambique. A similar situation is registered in the Western countries, with a figure inferior to 50%, except for Nigeria and Ghana (51% and 55% respectively). Northern, Middle and Southern regions show a different reality: some are highly urbanised countries (Libya, Algeria, Gabon, South Africa, with more than 70% urban of the total population), in comparison to Sudan 33%, Lesotho 21% or Swaziland 28%.

Capitals[16] and their metro regions have very high population concentrations far ahead of second cities. In overall terms, macrocephaly based on rural population migration characterises the urban systems in Africa. Usually, the majority cities are the capital cities (Luanda, Angola, 3.1 million; Harare, Zimbabwe 2.3 million; Lagos, Nigeria, 21 million, Cairo, Egypt, 11 million), although others are not administrative capitals (Johannesburg, South Africa; Dar es Salaam, Tanzania; Casablanca, Morocco; Manzini, Swaziland).

Economically, the gap is very high between the poorest and the richest countries. Looking at GDP in $US per capita, the following ranking portrays the situation: less than 1,000 $US Madagascar, Benin and Sierra Leone; 1,000-2,000 $US Zimbabwe, Morocco, Lesotho, Cote D´Ivoire; 2,000-5,000 $US Swaziland, Ghana, Cameroon; 5,000-10,000 $US Botswana, South Africa, Angola; 10,000 - 20,000 $US Libya, Namibia; +20,000 $US Gabon.

Administrative competence in planning
In most countries the administrative competence at national level is under one or several ministries in charge of different sectoral policies. In general, spatial planning is included among other related matters of national interest.

Except for Sudan which has a Ministry of Physical Planning and Public Utilities, in most countries one ministry (Ethiopia, Kenya, Madagascar, Mozambique[17]), commission (Kenya, Tanzania), council (Sudan) or two ministries regulate planning (Burundi, Malawi). Sometimes several ministries are responsible for planning, housing, construction and environmental matters. Sometimes ministries are unique autonomous entities (Burundi). Some Ministries are vested to deal with economic and social development (Mozambique),

Soweto, Johannesburg, South Africa, source:
https://commons.wikimedia.org/wiki/File:Soweto_Housing,_Johannesburg.jpg

local government (Malawi, Zimbabwe), environment (Sudan) or housing (Malawi), including planning responsibilities. Conversely ministries of planning can be responsible for economic development (Mozambique). Separate Ministries can be responsible for physical and national spatial planning, even if plans are prepared at a lower level (Sudan). Some countries have regional bureaux with planning competence (Ethiopia, Kenya, Madagascar) which also provide technical support for the local level, and sometimes enforce development control (Kenya). Sometimes regional levels are arms of the state and oversee lower tier plan making. Even in centralised countries, large cities may have delegated planning powers (Malawi).

A top down planning system is prevalent in the Northern countries, whereby the state is responsible for national and regional plans and the municipalities for ultra vires local land use and detail plans as well as development control.

In Southern and Western countries, the dualism of democratically elected representatives and chieftainship is ingrained in planning development. Chieftaincy rules planning alongside the state in Botswana (Kgotla system), Lesotho, Swaziland, Ghana, Sierra Leone, Namibia (chieftainship) and South Africa (Traditional Affairs).

Nominally, in most countries municipalities are in charge of local plans, but subject to compliance with upper tiers (Tanzania, Sudan, Malawi, Zimbabwe) which have powers to change such plans. In the absence of specific planning acts, national frameworks, standards and regulations rule spatial planning.

As many countries are undertaking decentralisation processes the administrative competence in planning is facing a particular period of change. Trends to promote decentralisation are included in various constitutions and numerous legislations.

Main laws related to planning
Planning laws and sometimes separate building laws regulate planning. Often there is a single law for land and planning codes (Burundi, Madagascar); others have comprehensive legislations (Ethiopia, Malawi, Tanzania), even prompted by the constitution (Mozambique, Kenya).

A wave of upgrades occurred in Africans countries since the mid 1990s, the majority of them from 2005 on. This is of particular importance for those countries with nationalised land (Mozambique, Tanzania), affected by problems derived from that land tenure, which are seriously affecting rural areas and food security.

Only few countries still regulate planning practice with old legal structures, including from colonial times (Cameroon, Nigeria, Sierra Leone, Cote d´Ivoire, Nigeria). The rest have updated their planning legislation, or are under preparation to include new planning approaches (Egypt, Building Law 2008 including strategic urban planning approach; Gabon, New Urbanism Law 2013; South Africa, Development Facilitating Act 1995 setting out the principles of integrated, compact, liveable settlements without sprawl and the Municipal Systems Act 2000 introducing the integrated development plan as the instrument to be adopted by metropolitan, district and local municipalities).

Decentralisation has been introduced recently (Tunisia, Algeria, Cameroon, Gabon, Benin, Kenya, Madagascar, Sudan, Mozambique, Ethiopia, Tanzania, Zimbabwe) with varying effects.

In spite of this array of legislative bodies related to planning instruments and development control, little attention has been given to rural planning matters, an important aspect for countries with large agricultural activities.

Regeneration of Tunis, Tunisia, photo Judith Ryser

Planning instruments and development control
All countries use the traditional hierarchical planning systems, from national to regional and local levels.

National planning administration is in charge of long term development instruments, such as Tanzania Development Vision 2025, Kenya Vision 2030, Nairobi Metro 2030, Benin National Spatial Agenda 2030, Agenda for Prosperity Sierra Leone, Lesotho Vision 2020, Namibia vision 2030, Cameroon Development Vision 2035, Strategic Plan Emerging Gabon 2025.
At local and regional level, some countries have no planning instruments at all (Sao Tome &

Principe, Gabon), while others have few (Burundi masterplan for the capital city). In Egypt, strategic plans for regions and governorates focus on mega projects and inter-regional and regional interventions. Nonetheless, the majority of countries has a panoply of plans adopted to deal with different purposes: national urban development schemes, regional urban development plans, strategic and land use plans at local levels; national spatial policies, national and regional spatial development strategies, detailed urban plans, sub regional plan and local physical development plans, master plans, local plans, and others.

Regional plans are rare (Egypt), or produced by the central government (Tanzania). Sectoral plans are also produced separately (Malawi). Local development plans include structure plans, district plans, masterplans, local plans, detail plans and urbanisation plans (Mozambique), sometimes infrastructure and maintenance plans (Sudan). Some have city plans (Burundi, Madagascar, Ethiopia) and special plans, as well as land use guidance (Cameroon).

Development control is mostly carried out at the local level, except in these countries where paramount chiefs hold the land in trust (Sierra Leone, Lesotho, Namibia, Swaziland). Some countries produce neighbourhood plans and local plans to incorporate projects of national interest (Madagascar) and others are regulated by supra levels: provinces (Angola), central administration (Cote d´Ivoire, Nigeria, Sierra Leone), every administrative level with different actors (Benin and its principle of "Results based on management"), Town and Country Planning Department regional offices and districts to operate their respective mandatory functions (Ghana).

Luanda, Angola, source:
http://venturesafrica.com/wp-content/uploads/2015/06/HARD_BAIA-DE-LUANDA_AMPE-ROGERIO.jpg

Sustainability

Two milestones have guided the national approaches towards sustainability: the UN Stockholm summit 1972 and the UN Rio de Janeiro summit 1992.

The effect of these international meetings on the African countries has been varied. Most of the countries adopted the environmental approach proposed in Stockholm and have set up environmental charters or environmental action plans. Several countries created environment ministries (Madagascar, Kenya, Zimbabwe, Mozambique, Cote d´Ivoire, Angola, Cameroon), are using EIA (Environmental Impact Assessment) and SEA (Strategic Environmental Assessment) and have introduced environmental legislation already after the Stockholm conference or the Rio Summit.

Conversely, very few have adopted the sustainable approach. However, in some countries, sustainability is embedded in their constitutions (Kenya, Mozambique, Egypt), some adopted the Agenda 21 (Benin South Africa, Gabon). More agricultural countries are not concerned about the environment, and some more about rural human development (Burundi). Sierra Leone has an Agenda for Prosperity which assumes sustainability as second pillar of its natural resources strategy. Ghana has created the Sustainability Ministry of Environment and Science, Technology and Innovation with Paramount Chiefs.

Climate change is an issue of national interest in Mozambique, Botswana, Namibia and South Africa, which adopted different strategies to cope with natural risks. Angola has a great concern for the situation of nomadic peoples.

In some countries all cities and urban administrations have to ensure that urban plans evaluate their social, economic and environmental impacts (Ethiopia). Some countries use public private partnerships to foster sustainability (Madagascar). Some also explicitly promote environmental education (Mozambique). Often sustainability is reduced to environmental criteria though. Sometimes sustainability objectives contradict other existing laws (Tanzania) sometimes they are cast very widely to incorporate reduction of poverty (Zimbabwe).

Governance

Efforts are made to improve transparency (Angola, Botswana, Ghana) and decentralisation (Morocco, Egypt, South Africa, Sierra Leone). Benin has created the Ministry of Decentralisation and Local Governance as well as the Ministry of Territorial Administration and Decentralisation, and the Good Governance Committee is put forward in Cameroon. However, these steps seem to be difficult to achieve and especially in most countries where hierarchy prevails (Tanzania, Zimbabwe, Mozambique). Leaving all to the lowest tier has produced haphazard development (Tanzania). Some countries have produced specific tools, such as an urban good governance package (Ethiopia) which consists of seven sub-programmes: land development and administration systems improvement; public participation; urban planning improvement; urban infrastructure and service improvement; organisation and human resource management reform; urban finance and financial management improvement; and justice reform. Federal and regional governments have to provide support to cities to achieve these goals.

Decentralisation is taken up by many African countries but it is rarely working in practice, except in a few places where constitutional reform has been supported by decision makers (Cameroon, Malawi) and led to active public participation, or where local communities have been actively intervening. Policies on decentralisation and strengthening of local authorities have led to continued haphazard development of urban land. The conventional planning procedure for public requirements is slow and unpopular. Tanzania recognises that reforms are needed on decentralisation, participation, partnerships, community empowerment, transparency and accountability.

Even when a decentralised model of governance is adopted local governments may remain highly dependent on central government (Zimbabwe) and even when participation channels are legally articulated is their usage being debated (Zimbabwe). Decentralisation seems to work better where chieftaincies exist and where it is enshrined in law (Benin, Cote d'Ivoire).

Alger Kasbah, Algeria, photo Judith Ryser

Some countries struggle with the workings of the planning system and politicians who use power to access land and get plans approved irrespective of legality (Malawi). Planners have no say in their implementation. Most developers construct informally due to weaknesses in the development control process. Corruption is widely suspected. There is a large number of land lords and none of them, including the central government, has respect for approved plans. The general public also opts for building informally.

Use of ICTs
Overall in Africa ICTs suffers from limited access to the internet due to high user prices and subscription costs (Sierra Leone, Mozambique). Mozambique has become a member of the Affordable Internet Alliance to improve its situation. ICTs are being introduced in the planning process, sometimes only for staff (Cote d'Ivoire, South Africa, Madagascar, Egypt). Other counties consider it important to introduce ICTs into the planning system as it is believed to increase efficiency (Ethiopia).

General introduction of ICTs is often done through new ministries (Namibia, Zimbabwe) or national ICTs plans (Gabon, Zimbabwe). Egypt established a national urban observatory and local development observatories. Mozambique promotes affordable internet. Madagascar is using GIS for urban services and its planning is digitised. In some countries public participation is taking priority (media libraries in Angola).

Planning practice
Urbanisation is taking place even in relatively rural countries and cities are expanding most and informally regardless of planning (Burundi, Sao Tome & Principe). African countries are among the most rapidly urbanising in the world (Ethiopia) and planning has difficulties to keep up with the urbanisation process. They find that economic and social plans are needed alongside physical spatial plans. There is a lack of public awareness of planning activities which may lead to poor public participation and support (Ethiopia) and deliberate awareness raising is needed. Implementation is a generalised problem, not confined to Africa though.

Some countries resort to new towns to cope with urban migration (Angola where China is helping to build the Kilamba Kiaxi new town) but most of the time cities develop in haphazard and uncontrolled fashion and most of them have no formal planning arrangements (Kenya). Some adopt new constitutions to introduce structural measures to cope with unfettered urbanisation. There is also a need for professional expertise and staff. For a few countries, planning is relatively new (Madagascar) while informal urbanisation continues its trend. Many countries struggle with plan making, either because the law is out-dated (Gabon), the planning system unrealistically complex (Ethiopia), ambiguous (Benin), or with incomplete coverage (Sudan). All this leads to large scale informal settlements (Kenya, Madagascar, Sudan, Tanzania, Mozambique, Sierra Leone and most others) which can reach up to 80% of all settlements.

Laws may give full powers to municipalities for planning and urban land management (Mozambique), but the local authorities do not have the capacity to implement them and often these laws are neither known nor respected. Also the pace of 'natural' urbanisation is such, that local authorities are overwhelmed.

Even if plans can be prepared, by the time they are ready they are out of date (Tanzania), enforcement is weak and implementation non existent (Tanzania). Bureaucracy is eroding local authority powers (Zimbabwe), together with preferential foreign investment (Tunisia). Even when the planning system is somewhat working, plans may not be ratified and it is hampered by corruption, land owner interests, lack of respect for approved plans even by central government, system of tenure, customary laws, lack of fiscal devolution, and planning blight for lack of infrastructure (Madagascar). The political crisis which followed the Arab Spring has brought planning to a standstill in a number of countries and is expected to change fundamentally (Libya). In some countries, despite democratisation and decentralisation important problems of political responsibilities persist, illegal development and activities proliferate and development control is ineffective (Malawi). In many countries corruption is a major obstacle of planning and regulated development.

Good urban governance is considered essential to poverty alleviation (Malawi, Mozambique). Sometimes incomplete coverage by the planning system is seen as a cause for poor development control (Sudan) and inappropriate locations of new development are using up rich agricultural land or are situated in areas of natural risks. Spatial justice and social integration remain key challenges (Sudan). Sometimes changes of regime, for example from socialism to mixed economy have adverse effects on public participation and involvement of civil society (Tanzania). Alternative bottom up initiatives may take place in such countries, especially in existing cities to improve local conditions (Tanzania).

Finally, lack of human resources in planning and especially at the lower tiers, poor planning skills (Nigeria), inappropriate or non existent planning education (Nigeria, Mozambique, Sudan), absence of appropriate local resources and finance for implementation, and lack of public awareness of planning are all invoked as obstacles to proper planning. Other hindrances are due to cultural factors, such as the role of language, gender, age and status (Swaziland). Even if planning is able to regulate land use, it is incapable of contributing to eradicate poverty or even to improve living conditions in the informal settlements which are still often earmarked for demolition rather than regeneration. New forms of planning are not necessarily more successful either (South Africa), especially when they do not address the need for coordination between spatial, economic and social objectives (Ethiopia). Nevertheless, urban development programmes have been able to improve land management, water and food insecurity somewhat, as well as socio-economic growth (Swaziland).

Overall, implementation and enforcement of policies and regulations is the greatest challenge in many African countries. The over-dependency on the central government and the unavailability of resources, especially in local authorities, inhibits the practice of sustainable development. Bureaucracy and political interference have eroded the powers of local authorities. Public participation has not been adequately institutionalised despite legal and political efforts. Most planning instruments are based on zoning which prevents the system from coping with the high levels of urban growth, most of it informal.

AMERICA

Country contributions

North: Canada, Mexico, USA (3)
Central: Costa Rica, El Salvador, Guatemala, Honduras, Nicaragua (5)
Caribe: Barbados, Dominican Republic, Haiti, Jamaica, Trinidad & Tobago (5)
South: Argentina, Bolivia, Brazil, Chile, Colombia, Ecuador, Guyana, Paraguay, Peru, Suriname, Uruguay, Venezuela (12)

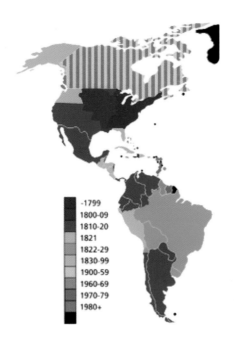

America with dates of independence
source: https://commons.wikimedia.org/wiki/Atlas_of_South_America

Independence and constitution

Different from Africa, the American countries got their independence at the beginning of the 19th century, after five centuries under the domination of some Western European crowns.

The discovery of the existence of another continent West of Europe in 1492 gave place to feverish competition between Empires of Spain and Portugal for the distribution of the new lands. The Treaty of Tordesillas resolved this situation in 1494, splitting the continent into two territories: the Portuguese - which led to the current Brazil - and the Spanish, corresponding to the rest of the continent, including the Caribbean islands. The administrative structure of their new domains designed by the Spanish empire from a distance gave rise eventually to the formation of the current countries of Central and South America, Mexico in the North and some Caribbean islands.

In parallel, the colonial activities of other European colonial powers - UK, France, the Netherlands - gave rise to the formation of the USA, Canada, some Caribbean countries and the enclaves of Belize in Central America and Guyana, French Guyana and Suriname in South America.

The process of independence of the American colonies began with the USA (1776), followed by a current of liberalisation through most American countries between 1800 and 1820. Canada (1867) and Cuba (1895) were the last countries to become independent in the nineteenth century. During the twentieth century Guyana and Barbados (1966), Suriname (1975) and Belize (1981) became independent. At present some islands are still administered by the original European colonial countries and by the USA.

Whilst several original constitutions (USA 1781), adopted during the 19th century (Argentina 1853, Canada 1867) or during the 20th century (Mexico 1917, Costa Rica 1949, Uruguay 1966) are still in force, new constitutions were adopted mainly between 1980 and the mid-1990s. The last countries to approve a new constitution were Bolivia (2009), Ecuador (2008) and Venezuela (1999), which adopted new forms of government and administration, as shown later.

In political terms, all countries adopted republican systems which operate in the market economy,

Manhattan transformation, New York, USA, photo Judith Ryser

except for Cuba and Venezuela, which embraced the socialist model in 1959 and 1999 respectively.

General characteristics

Countries in the Americas are very diverse in terms of population, economic development and urban aspects. Populations vary from the little Caribbean islands (Barbados 280,000) to 6.1 million in El Salvador in Central America, 320 million in Mexico and 200 million in Brazil.

Contrary to the African continent, population growth is less than 1% on average; exceptionally the rate is higher than 2% (Costa Rica and Haiti). Some countries are losing population due to migration to more prosperous countries and to birth control.

One aspect that characterised the continent is the high rate of urbanisation of the South American region (Uruguay 96%, Venezuela 94%, Argentina 93%, Chile 90%, Brazil 85%) and the North region (Canada and USA 81%). Very few countries are less urbanised than 50% (Honduras, Guyana, Trinidad & Tobago). The high percentage of urban population does not imply the existence of a balanced settlement structure though; quite the reverse. Except for the islands and the Central American countries, densities are in general low due to the geographic extent of the countries (Colombia and Canada 4 pop/km2, Chile 9, Argentina 14, Paraguay 17).

Population is concentrated in large cities. The capitals, often megacities, range from 12 million (Buenos Aires) to 19 million (Mexico City) and 20 million (Sao Paulo). They have by far the largest population and are leaving a great gap with the second city; macrocephaly characterises the urban settlements system there, except for Bolivia and Ecuador.

Buenos Aires, Argentina, photo Teresa Franchini

Economically, the gap is very wide between the richest country (USA, GDP per capita $US 53,042) and the poorest country (Haiti, GDP per capita $US 790).

Administrative competence in planning

All countries have state administrations for national spatial policies; some have a single All countries have state administrations for national spatial policies; some have a single one, the majority has two or more institutions while some share spatial policies between different ministries, institutes, national councils and technical secretariats (Costa Rica).

Brazil is the unique case that has created a Ministry of Cities in 2003. The case of Venezuela is a particular one since the country has devised several ministries to follow the principles of the 'Bolivarian socialism': Ministries of Popular Power for Planning and Development, Ministry for Communes and Social Movements, Ministry for Eco-socialism and Water, and Ministry for Housing and Habitat.

In many countries upper tier levels are dominating spatial policy making and local governments are considered as policy takers (Canada). Indigenous self-government is weak and indigenous peoples have very little control over their own land. This issue is of special interest in many countries (Ecuador, Venezuela, Bolivia, Costa Rica, Colombia, Canada, Guyana).

Cancun, Mexico, photo Teresa Franchini

Main laws related to planning

American countries have a proliferation of laws related to spatial development. Some have kept legislation from colonial times (Surinam, Guyana, Barbados, Jamaica) while others have developed special frameworks for planning: municipal codes, building codes, urban subdivision laws, urban planning laws, standards and guidelines, etc. In some cases, planning directives are included in the national constitutions (Guatemala, Ecuador, Mexico).

The opposite is the case in countries without a national planning legislation to guide urban development, such as Surinam, Haiti, Paraguay and, incomprehensively, Argentina, a highly urbanised country.

Brazil is the unique case to have approved the federal law known as Statute of the City in 2001, which led to the creation of the Ministry of Cities in 2003. On the other hand, Venezuela removed the existing legislation between 2008 and 2012 to give way to the "21st Century Socialism".

The disastrous effects of natural hazards (tropical storms and earthquakes) in Central America and Caribe and the environmental problems that some continental countries are facing, have led to the adoption of national systems of risk management and national climate change policies, with influences on spatial planning (Honduras, El Salvador, Jamaica, Trinidad & Tobago, Ecuador, Peru, México).

Uruguay and Chile still maintain the legislation approved in the 1970s; Colombia has been inspired by the Spanish legislation and approved its Law on Territorial Planning in 1997; Peru updated its legislation in 2003 and Trinidad & Tobago in 2014. The countries with new constitutions have focused their legislation on governance matters: Bolivia (Governmental Administration and Control 1990, Popular Participation Act 1994, Administrative Decentralisation Act 1995 and Municipalities Act 1997) and Ecuador (National Decentralised Participatory Planning System, Decentralised Autonomous Governments constitutional mandate, 2008).

Planning instruments and development control

All countries have planning instruments for the traditional territorial levels: national regional, urban. Except for the countries which delegate planning to states or regions (Canada, USA), the majority has national strategies aimed to promote economic and physical development and to guide public investments. These sectorial policies include urban and regional proposals to be developed by the corresponding authorities. This kind of development plans is widespread through the continent (Barbados, Haiti, Costa Rica, Jamaica, Trinidad & Tobago, El Salvador, Bolivia, Colombia, Ecuador, Paraguay, Peru, Suriname, Uruguay).

Although the regional level is adopted in the majority of planning structures which state that regional governments have to prepare and approve regional development plans in agreement with the municipalities, this level of planning is barely used, unless it refers to metropolitan regions (Costa Rica, Guatemala).

The main objects of planning are the cities and for this level the planning instruments adopt different modalities: masterplans, municipal land use plans, designation of built up areas, land subdivision zoning laws, building regulations, etc. Moreover, some have special plans for historic districts (Honduras, El Salvador, Brazil). On the other hand, some countries have no well-defined zoning ordinances or legislation (Guyana, Paraguay).

A special case is Colombia, where the effects of the armed conflict led to the creation of new political institutions and planning mechanisms: the relocation of 5 million displaced people has been tackled by the Victims and Land Restitution Act 2012. This challenge demands different roles and responsibilities, particularly at municipality level, for which it is necessary to clarify processes and procedures.

In all countries municipalities are responsible for development control, authorising building and planning permits. For the treatment of the illegal settlements several mechanisms have been devised. They run from municipal amnesty to legalising illegal plot division or buildings to neighbourhood upgrading. Local organisations, such us the Local Grassroots Organisation in Bolivia, are important agents for the promotion of these activities.

Sustainability

In terms of nature preservation, Surinam was the first country to launch its legislation early in 1954. The influence of the two milestones – Stockholm in 1972 and Rio de Janeiro in 1992 – can be traced following the creation of a special institution – all at the highest administrative levels, the approval of related legislations and the launching of strategic lines of action. Except in a few cases, all American countries have responded to the UN demands.

Guatemala was the first country that approved an environmental protection law in 1986 and created the Ministry of Environment and Natural Resources while the majority reacted after the Rio summit with new ministries (El Salvador, Dominican Republic, Colombia, Brazil, Argentina), special offices (USA, Guyana), environmental acts (Chile, Barbados, Paraguay, Peru, Bolivia), sustainable development act (Canada), standards, guidelines and criteria for

San José, USA, photo Judith Ryser

territorial planning (Nicaragua), green laws (Mexico, Barbados). Costa Rica is a particular case, since it has become a lead country in placing a natural capital at the centre of development, promoting a green growth strategy. This success is based on its Biodiversity Law 1998. Honduras, meanwhile, is promoting sustainable cities with international cooperation.

Other countries included the sustainable principles in their constitutions (Ecuador, Venezuela) while others assume the Local Agenda 21 principles (Jamaica, Trinidad & Tobago). The case of Brazil is worth mentioning since after a strong impulse determined by the Rio summit, the Agenda 21 subject has been gradually abandoned. The Commission for Policy and Sustainable Development prepared the Brazilian Agenda 21 in 2002, however little has been achieved to implement it and few cities have a local Agenda 21. Therefore environmental measures like Agenda 21 exist only in the political discourse. The same analysis can be done for Argentina where the legislation passed has not guaranteed the sustainable management of natural resources, and the adaptation of Agenda 21 has had little impact.

Overall, actions developed by national governments for environment protection and sustainability promotion have been extensive and profuse: all countries have created special bodies and legislation to deal with these matters. However, the effects have been uneven, since the main focus is placed on the protection of natural resources, leaving aside the two remaining factors of sustainability: social welfare and economic efficiency. Although the care of the environment and the concern about sustainability is well rooted in local societies, at political level the actions reside more in discourse rather than in actions on the ground (Uruguay, Argentina).

Governance
Governance is a topic which is still in its infancy in most American countries, after the many centuries of operating under highly centralised political and administrative systems. In a way or another, countries are moving towards decentralisation, some by launching partial measures and others by adopting formal measures: project for strengthening local government (El Salvador); national decentralised participatory planning system (Ecuador); inclusive state apparatus based on municipal, departmental, regional, and indigenous-peasant autonomies (Bolivia); multilevel territorial governance (Venezuela). In any case, the economic weakness of the majority of the local governments reinforces the central government role, thereby maintaining the previous status quo to different degrees.

Although the participation of the community in governmental planning affairs is formally promoted in several countries, it is widespread only in very few of them (Canada, USA, Suriname, Trinidad & Tobago). Some countries are promoting a participatory bottom-up planning approach providing channels for public participation (Jamaica, Venezuela). Others formally endorse the principles of decentralisation, administrative coordination, public and private partnership and citizen participation, however it is only partially applied (Peru).

On the whole, public participation is very low, citizens have little room for intervening and lack of transparency is an endemic problem subject to constant criticism. In the absence of institutional frameworks for territorial planning, citizens´ participation movements have emerged with the aim to modify and/or stop large plans and projects (Chile). In other cases, major real estate companies have developed large projects under legal determination and subject to public hearings, but the different aspects of the negotiations between the government and the private entities are not always very clear to the population (Brazil).

Use of ICTs
Gradually, e-communications are incorporated in the planning process to varying degrees and ICTs use is adopted by public administrations which facilitate communication with the citizens also about planning.

Although in some countries the introduction of ITCs is still low (Haiti, Suriname, Paraguay, Guyana) in the rest of the continent the process is progressing. In other countries the issue was tackled at the highest level: Directorate of Innovation and Information Technology of the Presidency of the Republic (El Salvador); National Office for Electronic Government and Information Technology and Digital Agenda (Peru), or by approving special laws on Access to Public Information (El Salvador, Chile). Ecuador is building Yachay city of knowledge, a new town which considers the ICTs as one of the main drivers of national economic development.

The dissemination of ICTs technologies in local administration is progressing fast: in Brazil approximately 250 cities are transforming themselves into Digital Cities, in Venezuela the majority of municipalities have websites to perform e-government, in Chile the Ministry of Housing and Urban Development has created the Urban Observatory website containing the plans produced for the whole country. In general, most local governments have webpages with basic information about their areas. The largest ones have achieved positive results regarding queries, claims, tax payments, publication of local laws, etc. but the challenge is to expand this service to other cities and municipalities.

The use of ICTs has allowed a significant

Posadas, Argentina.
photo Teresa Franchini

empowerment of local communities (Dominican Republic) and improved the general communication capacity (Haiti).

Planning practice
In political and administrative terms, the importance of physical planning is not questioned, although in practice planning still remains little known to the general population and even to some parts of the public administration.

This is particularly true in Argentina, one of the largest countries in the region, where planning exists only in political, social and professional discourses, while market forces are shaping the cities due to the inefficiency and inequity of the administrative system. Conversely, several countries improved their structures in order to reinforce the role of planning (SISPLAN in Bolivia, SEDATU and SEMARNAT in México, PNDU in Costa Rica, PNODT in El Salvador) although their performances are, in general, still low and the centralised planning model remains in place. In between these two extreme situations, planning practice is achieved by using an array of instruments and legislation with many overlaps and duplications of competences, as well as contradictions.

In spite of the efforts made by numerous countries to get planning instruments to guide urban development, the main hindrance is located at the implementation level, inexistent in many cases or only partially achieved in others due to several factors: the incapacity of the decision makers to conceptualise high-priority projects, the politicisation of the urban issues, difficult inter-institutional coordination and the lack of agreements among partners which tends to favour clientilism and corruption.

The existing urban and regional planning legislation does not clarify the role of the municipalities. Local governments are responsible for planning enforcement, but they are affected by lack of resources, equipment and qualified personnel and lack of specific rules to draw up and implement plans. Moreover, legislation tends to be over-complex, general and vague and regulations are usually not hierarchical, which gives raise to misunderstandings and contradictions among institutions, people and investors. Very often local plans follow a national blueprint rather than local requirements or use planning methodologies that prevent the inclusion of specific local aspects. The rigidity of plans allows many exceptions, many of them related to public projects, which compromise the planning system and prevent it from being effective. While this aspect refers to the limited capacity of the existing planning systems to control urban expansion, this situation is quite different in Canada, were the system is not really able to deal with declining regions or shrinking cities.

In sum, lot of efforts and innovative steps have been taken, including decentralisation and more local self-determination to create basic conditions for territorial entities in providing goods and services to reduce poverty. But it is necessary to prepare the ground for a more sustainable way of dealing with the urban problems related to poverty, lack of housing, infrastructure and public facilities, rural migrations, urban sprawl and environmental deficits that affect many cities. The proactive role of planning needs to be triggered by a planning system that incorporates strategic and integrative roles into the development process and greater transparency into the planning process, increasing the opportunities of public participation. For a better future of planning, it is also necessary to resolve the general complaint about lack of technical and professional planning competence.

Los Angeles, USA, photo Judith Ryser

ASIA & PACIFIC

Country contributions
Central: Bangladesh, India, Kazakhstan, Kyrgyzstan, Maldives, Pakistan, Sri Lanka, Uzbekistan (8)
East: Cambodia, China, Hong Kong, Indonesia, Japan, Malaysia, Myanmar, Philippines, Singapore, South Korea, Taiwan, Thailand, Vietnam (13)
Australasia: Australia, New Zealand, Papua New Guinea, Samoa (4)
Middle East: Iran, Iraq, Israel, Lebanon, Palestine, Qatar, Saudi Arabia, Syria, United Arab Emirates (9).

Independence and constitution

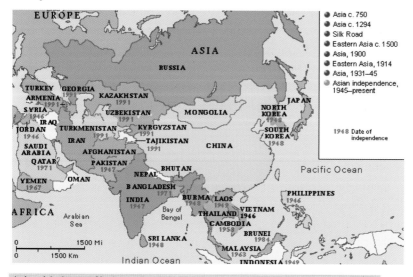

Asia with dates of independence
source: http://jimchampa.tripod.com/oliverssitecontinued/id2.html

Colonies in Australasia started to be liberated from their many diverse colonial masters, many Many colonies in Australasia started to be liberated from their many diverse colonial masters after the second world war.

Independence from the UK: Jordan (1946), India (1947) - then creation of Bangladesh and Pakistan after Indian partition (1971/1973); Sri Lanka (1948); Burma (1848) now Myanmar; Malaysia (1957)' Singapore (1965); Israel (1958); some earlier like Australia (1931 with the Statutes of Westminster and finally 1986 with the Australia Act); Iraq (1932); some later like Maldives (1965); Bahrain (1971); South Yemen (1976) - then merged with North Yemen (1990); Qatar (1971); New Zealand (circa 1973 when UK entered the EU); Brunei (1984).

Independence from other countries: France: Lebanon (1943) when occupied by Germany; Syria (1946); Vietnam (1946); Cambodia (1952); Laos (1953); from the Netherlands: Indonesia (1949); from Japan: Korea (1945); from the USA: Philippines (1946); from New Zealand Samoa (1962); from Australian administration: Papua and New Guinea (1975); much earlier from Portugal: Bahrain (1602); from the Soviet Union after its demise in 1991: Kazakhstan (1991), Uzbekistan (1991), Kyrgyzstan (1991), Tajikistan (1991), Turkmenistan (1991), Georgia (1991), Armenia (1990).

Conversely, China, Japan, Nepal, Bhutan, Afghanistan, Thailand, Iran, Saudi Arabia, Kuwait were not colonised, while Mongolia and Taiwan remain disputed.

Unlike Africa, countries in Asia were colonised or occupied by outside powers worldwide - Europeans, USA, Soviet Union, Japan – Australia, New Zealand, some by different ones at different times. Some Asian countries were colonised over many centuries by other powers while others endured new waves of colonisation or occupation recently, and others still slid from dominion status to self-rule (New Zealand). This made for unstable boundaries, decolonisation in phases, further secessions, new federations and alliances, etc. Most British ex-colonies chose to belong to the Commonwealth with the UK Queen as head of state, as did Australia and New Zealand in Australasia.

Most constitutions in operation in Asia are recent, or were amended recently. Japan got a new constitution in 1947 after allied occupation, India in 1949, Brunei in 1959, Bangladesh in 1971, Pakistan in 1973 and Sri Lanka (then Ceylon) in 1944, reformed in 1972 with latest amendment in 2015. China amended its 1982 constitution (people's congress) in 2004. The Central Asian countries which gained independence after the demise of the Soviet Union adopted constitutions in 1991. The Middle East region was structured during the 20th century and is undergoing a new wave of change at present. Most constitutions were written just before (Iraq and Saudi Arabia (1932), (Lebanon 1926/1943/1995) and after the Second World War (Israel 1945, Syria 1946). The others date from the 1970s (United Arab Emirates 1971, Qatar 1971, Iran 1979). Many of them were amended recently (United Arab Emirates 1996, Iran, Iraq 2005, Qatar 2005, Syria 2012 – Israel has no formal constitution).

Middle Eastern countries have different forms of government: monarchies, (theocratic, Islamic, multi-confessional, etc.) republics and parliamentary democracies. Most countries in Asia are (presidential) republics or unitary parliamentary democracies. A number are member of what has become the Commonwealth of Nations (former British Commonwealth) and the ex-soviet republics are becoming market economies but remain economically tied to Russia with remittances making a large contribution to their economies.

General characteristics
The characteristics of this vast region vary widely and are presented in sub-regions. The Middle East has a very turbulent recent history and suffers from civil wars which emaciated planning. The IMPP countries are densely populated with varying population growth (it more than doubled from 1990 to 2010). Qatar had the highest population growth with 3.5% (2015 est.). Urbanisation is high, ranging from 57% (Syria) to 98% (Qatar). However, recent events have slowed down population growth with changes due to massive displacements and migration. Capitals (or sometimes other first rank cities) dominate city sizes, ranging from 8.2 million (Teheran Iran) to less than 1 million in the small gulf states and Israel.

Economically, IMPP countries in the Middle East vary from GDP per capita of $US 192,900 (Qatar) to $US 3,600 (Iraq) (non oil based Israel $US 31,000 – Palestine $US 2,900). Wars and lowering oil prices have affected this.

Central Asia consists of large sparsely populated countries (35% urbanised, except for Kazakhstan 55%). Population growth is between 1% to 2%. Capital cities dominate over second cities, and range from 2.3 million population (Tashkent Uzbekistan) to 1.4 million population (Almaty Kazakhstan).

In contrast, Southern Asia is far more populated. India is the second most populated country in the world with 1,252 million population and a population density of 381 pop/km2, although urbanisation is still low at 33% but rapidly increasing. India has megacities: New Delhi the capital of 24.953 million population is followed closely by Mumbai with 20.741 million; Pakistan Karachi has 14.664 million, with Islamabad coming second as a small administrative capital 1.264 million; Bangladesh's capital Dhaka has 5.378 million and Chittagong 3.760 million while cities in Sri Lanka (642,163) and Maldives (103,693) are much smaller.

(left) Sana´a, Yemen, photo Teresa Franchini / (right) Mumbai, India, source: http://graphics8.nytimes.com/images/2013/09/12/world/asia/12-slum-mumbai-indialnk/12-slum-mumbai-indialnk-superJumbo.jpg

Economically, Central Asia and Southern Asia vary in similar ways. GDP per capita in $US spans from $US 12,118 in Kazakhstan to $US 5,600 in Uzbekistan and $US 2,400 in Kyrgyzstan; and in Southern Asia from $US 5,973 in Maldives to $US 5,900 in India, $US 2,399 in Sri Lanka, and much less in Bangladesh $US 848, Pakistan $US 802.46. Economic growth rates are high and vary from Uzbekistan 8.1%, Sri Lanka 8%, India 7.2%, Bangladesh 6.3%, Kazakhstan 4.2%, Kyrgyzstan 3.9%, Pakistan 3.6%, and Maldives 3.4%.

East and South East Asia are similar as they are very populated and urbanised. China dominates the continent as the largest country with a population of 1,360 million and the largest economy (GDP $US 9.17 trillion). At 0.49% it has a much slower population growth rate than India which is expected to overtake it by 2030. Urbanisation is still low at 41% compared to Hong Kong and Singapore (100% which are small Islands though), South Korea (93%), Taiwan (80.3%), Malaysia (71%), Indonesia (54%), while Philippines 44.5%,

Thailand 40%, Vietnam 34%, Cambodia 30% Myanmar 28.6% are below 50%. China has many megacities (capital Bejing with 21.15 million and the largest city Shanghai 24.15 million), but Japan has the largest megacity Tokyo (metro) with 38 million population, followed by the Osaka-Kobe city region with 20.2 million. Other countries have multi-million first and second cities: Manila with 21.2 million and Quezon with 2.8 million (Philippines); Jakarta with 10.2 million and Surabaya with 2.8 million (Indonesia); Hong Kong with 7 million and Kowloon with 2 million; Bangkok with 6.9 million and Chiang Mai with 170,000 (Thailand); Seoul with 10 million and Busan with 3.4 million (South Korea).

The gap between the first and second city is generally wide, contrary to Taiwan with Taipei with 2.6 million population and Kaohsiung 2.8 million; Vietnam with capital Ha Noi with 6.9 million and Hi Chi Minh with 7.8 million; Myanmar with Nay Pyi Taw with 1.2 million and Yangon with 2.98 million; Malaysia with Kuala Lumpur with 1.67 million and Subang Jaya with 1.6 million. Singapore is a city in itself of 5.5 million population.

GDP per capita in $US varies from very high and equal to developed nations, to very low: Singapore $US 81,300, Hong Kong $US 42,000, Japan $US 36,225, Malaysia $US 24,500, South Korea $US 22,670, Taiwan $US 20,900, Indonesia $US 10,600, China $US 6,760, Thailand $US 5,340, Philippines $US 3,300, Vietnam $US 1,700, Myanmar $US 1,113, Cambodia $US 1,036. GDP growth rates vary also widely but from very different bases: Myanmar 8.3%, China, 7.67%, Cambodia 7.6%, Philippines 7.2%, Hong Kong 5.8%, Malaysia 5.6%, Vietnam 5.6%, Indonesia 5%, Thailand 3.4%, Singapore 3%, Taiwan 2.2%, South Korea 2%, and Japan 1.6%.

IMPP countries in Oceania are sparsely populated (Australia 2.9 pop/km2, New Zealand 15.8 pop/km2, and Papua New Guinea 20 pop/km2), except for Samoa where population is concentrated on the main islands (density 64.7 pop/km2). Urbanisation is high in developed Australia 89.3% and New Zealand 86%, and very low in Papua New Guinea 12.5% and Samoa 20%. The gap between the largest and second cities is high: Sydney with 4.7 million population and Canberra (administrative capital) with 374,912 (Australia); Auckland with 1.44 million population and Wellington with 197,019 (New Zealand); Port Moresby with 364,145 population and Lae with 100,677 (Papua New Guinea); Apia with 7,237 and Salelologa with 6,062 (Samoa).
GDP growth varies across economic rank order and size: Papua New Guinea 4.6%, Australia 2.3%, New Zealand 1.4%, Samoa 0.85, while GDP per capita in $US is high in the advanced economies Australia $US 19,243 and New Zealand $US 39,450, and low in Samoa $US 6,200 and Papua New Guinea $US 1,759.

Administrative competence in planning
In most of Australasia planning is centralised except in federal states. Authority for planning is mainly held by central state planning, environment or economy ministries. In federal

countries, the centre has low or no planning competence and (semi-) autonomous entities are in charge of planning law and plan making (Australia). Some capital and large cities have either own planning capacity (Iraq and UAE) or are planned centrally (China, Bangladesh) including new towns (Taiwan), while some have elected city development committees (Myanmar) or devolved powers (Israel, Myanmar). Planning competence is either with a single ministry - planning, economy (Central Asia), or environment (New Zealand), or with a number of them (Israel, Kyrgyzstan, Malaysia, Myanmar, Hong Kong, Taiwan, China, India, Maldives) and run vertically from the state (Pakistan, India, Sri Lanka). Plan making and development control is often devolved to the lowest tier, albeit mainly under the ultra vires principle.

Main laws related to planning

The colonial power relations had direct repercussions on the planning system as many have inherited their systems from their colonisers, did not always shed them and are retaining them to this day (Hong Kong, India, Sri Lanka, Palestine). Some countries do not have explicit planning legislation (Qatar, Maldives), others have a proliferation of laws, regulations and standards (Kyrgyzstan, Uzbekistan), others still have just a single planning law (Sri Lanka, Taiwan, Cambodia, Thailand, and Philippines the latter still to be approved); some focus on city development (South Korea). Laws are either specifically directed to spatial planning (Papua New Guinea) or of a more general nature incorporated in environmental legislation (New Zealand) or focused on the urban level and its management (Samoa). Very few include rural planning explicitly (China, Japan, Myanmar). In federal states planning laws are drawn up by the state authorities (Australia).

Planning instruments and development control

In most of Australasia planning instruments are hierarchical, at state, rarely regional and local levels. Types of plans vary widely at national level from national long term visions, spatial frameworks, development strategies (Samoa), to national plans including the economy (China) and/or the environment (New Zealand), encompassing all levels at the centre (Papua New Guinea), or none in federal countries (Australia). The regional level is generally weak (Australia), controlled from above or used as an arm of the state, or its plans are not implemented (Palestine). Local plan making is left to municipalities, usually under supervision of the state, rarely with autonomy. Development control is usually left to the lowest tier, but sometimes controlled from the centre (Qatar, Saudi Arabia, Myanmar), sometimes by separate agencies linked to the courts; in some countries it is negotiated (Taiwan) and in a few cases there is no formal development control (Malaysia). In some countries the development industry or the private sector are playing an important role by proposing large projects (China). Very little is mentioned about land ownership issues, except for China where the state owns all land, as well as in Hong Kong to the chagrin of the development industry.

Sustainability

Progress depends on country circumstances. Fossil energy rich countries have a greater dilemma than energy poor countries which seek energy security through sustainable energy policies (Kyrgyzstan, Uzbekistan). However, more recently many countries have adopted sustainability in their national development strategies, environmental or resource management laws (New Zealand), focusing on nature conservation and climate change issues, and sometimes in their constitutions (Bangladesh). Following the Kyoto and other

Doha cornice, Qatar, source: https://commons.wikimedia.org/wiki/File:Doha1908.jpg

UN agreements, many have adopted EIAs, SEAs sometimes in cooperation with the private sector (Cambodia, United Arab Emirates), incorporated sustainability principles in local planning (Qatar, Malaysia, Singapore), and through Agenda 21, the latter not often with implementation success, and sometimes sustainability is driven by civil society (Palestine). China adopted eco-city principles and is taking measures to curb environmental pollution especially in cities, and Japan has adopted a low carbon city promotion act. Some countries raise consciousness of sustainability (Thailand, Bangladesh) while others do not enforce it (Maldives) or simply ignore it (Myanmar, Iraq, Saudi Arabia, Iran).

Governance

Decentralisation, self-government and participation aspects of sustainable development are attempted in many countries (South Korea, Japan, Taiwan), informally (Vietnam) or through new laws (India, Cambodia) but not necessarily succeeding well (Philippines) and planning is not always targeted directly. The understanding of 'governance' varies widely, and even where existing planning systems are considered too rigid and top down, no concrete measures are implemented to change this. Planning seems often divorced from civil society and its wishes and perpetuated as a formal exercise. Reality is overtaking it, visible in the growth of informal settlements. The need for planning overhaul is expressed by a number of countries, yet without concrete proposals other than a need for more flexible, adaptable, integrated and proactive planning. They tend to ignore key obstacles like lack of human and economic resources though.

Rapid urbanisation remains a challenge and new ways of cooperation need to be invented between a wider range of stakeholders. A number of countries are set to include the development industry (China, Indonesia), and some involve the social sector and citizens in the improvement and management of the built environment, not least to increase risk sensitivity (Iran, Palestine). However, there are tensions between these two groups of stakeholders. They reflect the contradictions of planning itself which aims to establish a balance between the public good and private property rights. Some countries are working on self-governance at local and regional levels (Kyrgyzstan), but more often to attract inward investment generally and not necessarily for urban planning and development. Efforts to decentralise are considered to fail due to lack of awareness of the planning process among the population.

Dubai, United Arab Emirates

Use of ICTs
The use of ICTs is closely related to the stage of country development, except when it is driven by international subsidies and the digital industry. It varies from non existent (Myanmar) to high penetration (Thailand, Kazakhstan, Uzbekistan, UAE, Qatar). While the use of digital communication is increasing everywhere it has not necessarily found its way into the planning process. A number of countries have digitalised planning and made planning instruments available on websites (Bangladesh), others use it to improve planning staff proficiency (Maldives, Australia). However public participation has not increased noticeably as citizens may lack tools of access and know-how to use this medium.

Planning practice
Centralised countries voice criticisms about excess complexity, rigidity (Israel), statism (Saudi Arabia), confinement to physical controls (Israel), lack of transparency of hierarchic planning systems and their inability to engage with, and empower civil society. Conversely, federal countries are considered to suffer from lack of both horizontal and vertical coordination (Australia). Whether imposed or desirable decentralisation or regionalisation are perceived as leading to uncontrolled (Cambodia) and uneven (Indonesia) development, without acknowledging that this is equally widespread under centralised planning systems. National infrastructure plans designed to assist equitable economic development are unlikely to be implemented when left to the private sector (Indonesia). Moreover, centralised planning systems are noted to lead to lack of implementation powers at the lowest tier, although other reasons are also put forward, such as lack of local resources, finance, planning skills and executive support, clientelism, political instability (Iraq, Libya) and corruption (Iraq), but also over-emphasis on property rights, local economy and budgets at municipal level (Israel). Centralised planning is considered unable to cope with continuous turbulence and rapid urbanisation partly due to migration (Lebanon), nor with the deterioration of natural resources that this entails (Indonesia). Sustainability is added to the planning system but rarely with necessary readjustment of traditional approaches. However, an original initiative is the focus on environmental and resource management as a basis of all planning (New Zealand).

Too many bureaucratic layers and preoccupation with implementing rules and regulations hamper promotion and guidance of planned development (Saudi Arabia). However, in certain regimes rigid planning systems are adaptable to developers' request (Taiwan), as are 'laissez faire' market oriented policies which expect the public sector to play a mere facilitating role (Malaysia). Gaps are wide between long term national investment plans and decentralised objectives or local visions (Syria) and physical master planning is not able to interact with local economic and social interests. Nor can it provide for specific needs of women, children and the elderly (Japan). However, planning is expected to become instrumental in preparing reconstruction of damaged countries (Syria, Libya, Iraq).

Old planning methods, together with very out of date plans (Teheran Iran) may hamper urban development. Attempts are made to evolve the planning system by including qualitative dimensions (Iran), less prescriptive or prohibitive features and greater flexibility and a more organic approach (Maldives), also in countries which have inherited soviet planning culture. This cannot be achieved without re-educating planners to cope with contemporary reality (Kyrgyzstan, Uzbekistan, Kazakhstan). Ownership rights are an issue in these countries, as well as overpowering state control, blurred responsibilities and corruption which thwart attempts at self-government (Uzbekistan). Devolution of powers to districts has promoted numerous planning initiatives elsewhere (Pakistan) yet implementation does not often follow. There may also be direct contradictions between national objectives and regional and especially metropolitan development aims which may exacerbate spatial inequalities (Sri Lanka). Planning needs to remain responsive to geo-political dynamics (Palestine) and in certain circumstances planning can only be practised voluntarily awaiting clearer competences (Palestine).

Where there is no national body responsible for national physical planning the regional and metropolitan tiers also tend to be weak. Consciousness of the need for urban planning arises when cities show acute problems (Bangladesh). Informal settlements are not only an urban but also a rural problem in less urbanised countries (India) where environmental degradation is acute. Lack of institutional capacity and technical tools hamper sustainable development alternatives. Even if the planning system is functioning somehow enforcement is often weak and leads to infringements (Pakistan).

Where land remains in the hands of the state and is leased to developers central government keeps control but this is disliked by global property investors and provokes competition between cities (China). The shift from planned to market economy renders existing plans inefficient and inappropriate (China, ex-soviet countries). Ultra-rapid development pace is creating socio-economic spatial divides in the settlement structure between state managed, large scale housing blocks and demonstration of opulence (China), and leads to poor environmental conditions which may hamper the development momentum. Similarly, more attention is attributed lately to the value of cultural heritage and urban identity (Singapore). Another role of the state is to deal with unforeseen and unforeseeable needs for which pre-emptive measures need to be in place, including land reserves.

Pollution remains a problem at very high densities (Hong Kong) as well as rapid motorisation (China, South Korea). Conversely, ageing and shrinking populations may lead to lower urban densities although they need to remain sufficient to maintain levels of services and quality of urban life (Japan). Planning is subjected to different and contradictory regulatory systems (Taiwan) in countries with special status (Hong Kong) and centralisation of controls may affect the property market adversely which requires flexibility. Officially plan-led planning systems may end up in reality favouring development (Taiwan). Centrally steered post industrial countries need to modernise urban governance and improve participation. Planning needs to be vision oriented and qualitative instead of hierarchic and prescriptive and adapt to newly decentralised municipal structures. Only when planning is progressing at all levels simultaneously does it permit incorporation of short term outside demands (Taiwan).

While many countries aspire to decentralisation this needs to be accompanied by democracy and inclusive urban governance, community empowerment, environmental sustainability and cultural conservation (Taiwan). Those countries who do not have any or only a succinct formal planning system are aspiring to one (Cambodia, Vietnam, Myanmar) as they are confronted with wild land and property speculation and wish to redistribute value added of development to the community at large (Cambodia, Vietnam). Implementation remains an intractable problem (Philippines) regardless of planning regime as it depends on the contradictory forces of private investment and public custodianship of the common good (Vietnam). Often the gap between very elaborate planning systems and realisation seems unbridgeable (Cambodia), not least in countries which depend on financial assistance (Papua New Guinea). Part of uneven development are overgrown capital cities (South Korea) which absorb inordinate national resources and concentrate wealth, talent and economic activities to the detriment of other cities and most of all rural areas. Sometimes other measures than physical planning are advocated to deal with uneven development, such as fiscal arrangements, taxation and incentives, and optimistically some expect NGOs to step into 'laissez faire' situations to redress inequality (Philippines).

Tokyo, Japan, photo Sonia Freire

Country contributions

Europe (48)

European Union, EAA, and similar: Andorra, Austria, Belgium, Bulgaria, Croatia, Cyprus, Czech Republic, Denmark, Estonia, Finland, France, Germany Greece, Hungary, Iceland, Ireland, Italy, Latvia, Liechtenstein, Lithuania, Luxemburg, Malta, Monaco, Netherlands, Norway, Poland, Portugal, Romania, Slovakia, Slovenia, Spain, Sweden, Switzerland, UK (34)

Other Europe: Albania, Armenia, Azerbaijan, Belarus, Bosnia & Herzegovina, Georgia, Kosovo, Macedonia, Moldova, Montenegro, Russia, Serbia, Turkey, Ukraine (14)

GreaterEurope
source:nhttp://mapofeurope.com/wp-content/uploads/2013/07/map-of-europe.jpg

Independence and constitution

Most European countries have been in existence as sovereign states for a long time: Denmark (ca. 960), Sweden (11th century), Switzerland (1291), Norway (Kalmar Union 1397, 1905), Quite a few were colonial empires: UK, France, Spain, Portugal, Netherlands, Belgium, Germany, Italy, Austria-Hungarian, Russia, and many of them have left planning legacies in their former colonies. A number of these ex-empires remain constitutional monarchies while others have become unitary republics.

Other countries have gained, lost and regained independence more recently in the 20th century. They include Finland (1917) and later the Baltic states: Estonia, Lithuania, Latvia (1991); the Republics which had formed part of the former soviet union: Azerbaijan, Armenia, Belarus, Georgia, Moldova and Ukraine (1991); as well as the constituent republics of ex-Yugoslavia: Bosnia and Herzegovina, Croatia, Kosovo, Macedonia, Montenegro, Serbia and Slovenia (1991). Although nominally independent, the states of the then COMECON were also under soviet influence which had repercussions on their planning systems: Poland (1989), the Czech Republic (1989), Slovakia (1992), Hungary (1989), Bulgaria (1990),

Romania (1989), whilst Albania (1912) was a one off under Hoxha's communism. Some very small countries have special status: Monaco, Andorra and Liechtenstein, while others gained independence from Western European colonialists: Malta (1964), Cyprus (1960). Turkey became a modern republic (1922) after the First World War when the Ottoman Empire was dismantled.

Accordingly all European countries established their constitutions and only few got amended

recently. 28 European countries are members of the European Union. A few others are applicant EU members while others have more long term aspirations for membership. Except for Belarus and Monaco, all IMPP European countries are members of the Council of Europe.

Malta, tourist development sprawl, photo Judith Ryser

General characteristics

Contrary to countries of the other continents Europe has a slow population growth rate and some regions are actually shrinking. Urbanisation is very advanced in many European countries whose area tends to be densely populated. However, European urbanisation varies widely from 100% in Monaco (an exception as it is a city state) and 97.9% in Belgium, to 45% in Moldova and 14.3% in Liechtenstein (another small state exception).

The settlement pattern contrasts between the central European countries and those in the West, East and North. For historic reasons, the former have a very polycentric urban structure with no dominant capital or first city (defined by at least double the population than the second city), while France, the UK, Russia, Sweden, Norway, Finland, Denmark, Iceland, Ireland, Austria, Belgium, Luxemburg, Greece, Portugal, Spain, Bulgaria, Czech Republic, Hungary, Poland, Romania, Slovakia, Croatia, Macedonia, Montenegro, Slovenia, Albania, Armenia, Georgia, Russia, Ukraine, Turkey have a dominant capitals or first cities. However, cities in Europe, even capitals, are relatively small, and only the UK has a megacity (London with 8.63 million population) besides Russia (Moscow 12.1 million) and Turkey (Istanbul 14.2 million). Population densities vary enormously from 3 pop/km2 in Iceland to 1,321 pop/km2 in Malta (except for Monaco which has a density of 19,000 in de facto one city).

Economically, Europe is very diverse. Western Europe is considerably wealthier than Eastern Europe (respectively around $US 40,000 and $US 46,000) and also southern Europe (between $US 25,000 to $US 30,000). In Europe, the highest GDP per capita is found in Luxemburg ($US 92,000) and the lowest in Moldova ($US 5,000). The central

European countries which have joined the EU have improved their economies (around $US 24,000 - $US 28,000 except for Romania and Bulgaria which remain below $US 20,000). In the Caucasus and ex soviet countries income per capita remains low (below $US 10,000), except for oil rich Azerbaijan ($US 17,600), akin to Belarus which also has oil ($US 18,200). The non EU ex-Yugoslav countries have also a low GDP per capita (between $US 8,000 and $US 15,000).

Administrative competence in planning

Administrative structures range from a single ministry responsible or bespoke for planning (France, Ireland, Romania, Poland) or the environment (Latvia, Lithuania, Estonia, Denmark, Czech Republic) to shared planning powers between ministries (Bulgaria, Hungary) of the environment, public works, local government economic development or transport, to sometimes up to six institutions (Sweden). In ex-Yugoslav countries planning competences are bundled with competences for other sectors in the same ministry.

The unitary states have national planning powers, strategies, and sometimes national plans and visions. Most planning systems are hierarchic with all levels holding planning competence subjected to the upper tiers and eventually the central state. In many countries the state assumes de facto all planning powers (Cyprus, Greece, Malta, Monaco and Portugal, Azerbaijan). Other countries are sharing planning competences between different levels (Italy and Ukraine with three levels and Spain with two levels). Most ex communist countries have split competences between the national and the local levels reflecting the desire to move away from previously centralised planning systems.

While the heritage of formal hierarchic planning systems persists (France, Ireland), potentially contradictory changes are occurring under pressure from

Paris, France, photo Judith Ryser

both the development industry and civic society. While most unitary states practise the ultra vires principle others operate according to the subsidiarity principle, whereby decisions should be made at the lowest political level possible (Sweden, Finland, Denmark). In some decentralised countries, the ultra vires principle is adopted alongside the subsidiarity principle (Austria). When municipal planning authorities coexist with mutual influence, it means that the upper tiers cannot withdraw rights from the lower tiers, but the lower tiers have to consider guidelines and principles devised by higher levels (Germany). The federal or devolved states (mainly in central Europe) have few or no planning powers at federal / central level. Planning is devolved to lower tier levels of government, (more or less autonomous) 'states', regions, provinces, cities and municipalities. Where countries have three tiers of administrative levels, national/ federal, state/regional/cantonal, municipal, the upper one has very few planning competences, the middle one is setting the planning framework and the lower one has full planning powers (Norway, Finland).

In all cases, the lowest level is usually responsible for local detailed plans and development control. Nevertheless, planning of capital cities and sometimes large second cities tends to be closely controlled from the centre, not least through its fiscal powers (Budapest Hungary, Belgrade Serbia). Conversely, reforms have led to genuine devolution of even fiscal powers (Denmark) which has led to genuine localism. Devolution is expected to work in small countries where the levels are close to each other. However, various countries have attributed greater autonomy for planning to municipalities,

Helsinki, Finland, photo Judith Ryser

sometimes with a monopoly for planning (Sweden). Social democracies have long constitutional traditions of local government as most important systems of self government (Finland). There the local level has great relevance, either because it has traditionally been very autonomous (Iceland) or because countries are in the process of decentralising (Russia, Turkey), although some have reversed this trend (Russia). Special cases are the UK which has devolved planning powers to its constituent 'nations' Scotland, Wales and Northern Ireland (to their respective parliament or assemblies) and Belgium with planning powers respectively devolved to the Flemish, Walloon and Brussels-Capital regions. Some countries are sharing planning between local government and quasi governmental agencies ('Agences d'urbanisme' in France) or city managers (Ireland).

Although the regional level is usually weak, it is introduced in some countries as suitable structure to receive EU funding (Romania, Bulgaria). This may lead to horizontal contradictions of competences (Moldova) due to overlapping planning competences.

In more neo-liberal countries the development industry is successfully lobbying for less planning (UK, Netherlands). A way round traditional planning was to set up development corporations, para-public bodies ('quangos') with no local and little central accountability, but with compulsory purchase power of land and real estate (UK, Ireland). Their political purpose is to stimulate development, especially regeneration of large scale brown field sites, often in public ownership (utilities, railways, etc.). Land passes through the ownership of these corporations to be sold off to private developers who determine future land use through their investment powers. These operations are long term, reach over several business cycles, including bankruptcies (property developers going into receivership or administration), and over several generations, and they are likely to face change of policies, development objectives and priorities (UK, Netherlands).

Main laws related to planning

All European countries have specific laws of planning, except for Hungary and Monaco, the latter having an 'Ordonnance Souveraine' instead. Some have an overarching planning mandate for the whole country (Germany, Switzerland), while federal states have different laws in their constituent parts (Russia, Austria, Switzerland). In Spain each region ('comunidad autónoma') has its own planning law, compatible with the land use and planning laws at the national level. In the UK, the four 'nations' have their own planning laws, but there still exists a national planning policy framework. Such devolution may create difficulties for countrywide coordination.

In the ex-soviet countries planning law is very basic. Except for Moldova which has a comprehensive territorial approach, planning law has a clear urban focus. Some countries restrict planning to physical or building aspects (Czech Republic, Slovakia). This differs from centralised planning under soviet times when territorial planning was just a projection of state controlled economic planning and planning and urban design were regulated by the soviet union in occupied territories (Estonia). Planning culture of central and eastern European as well as some Mediterranean countries retains power-based command and control solutions for conflicts instead of resorting to communication and mitigation of conflicts to reach generally acceptable deals. Elsewhere, rational settlement structures were sought by means of central place theory as leading concept at regional level which resulted in the centralisation of all investments in central places and suppression of small villages (Czech Republic). Sometimes contradictions take place between different laws related to planning, for example in disaster prone areas where the state can overrule all planning laws and centralise decisions, including land appropriation while excluding public information and participation (Turkey).

In Nordic countries (Norway, Sweden and Finland) all nature areas are considered public space by law, safeguarding the right of public access ('allemansrätten'). This 'everyman's right' provides access for everybody to privately owned land for recreation, etc., as long as

Trnava, Slovakia, photo Judith Ryser

no damage and pollution are caused. This right has its roots in the sparse population and large nature areas and is highly valued among citizens. Urban sprawl is actively fought be legally prohibiting development in rural areas altogether favouring very concentrated large scale agro-businesses, as well as by restricting development of second home zones and concentrating them into built up areas (Denmark).

Planning instruments and development control

Neo-liberalism has become the mainstream context of planning in Europe. Planning has shifted from being the central instrument of securing the public interest to seeking a balance between the public interest and private property rights, moving gradually toward presumption in favour or development. A way round traditional planning which is considered a hindrance in liberal economies, was to set up development corporations, para-public bodies expected to achieve large leverage from private sector investment through public-private partnership arrangements (UK, Netherlands, Ireland).

Property rights and land ownership are strong drivers of the development process, including in Eastern Europe where these rights have been reinstated after the demise of communism in 1989. They play also a role in the European Spatial Development Strategy and its non statutory guiding principles which aim to reconcile economic competitiveness with social cohesion and spatial justice and thus to reduce regional disparities by means of EU regional policies (related to EU NUTs) and their instruments, the strategic funds. Sustainability is introduced into planning in this process, especially in Eastern Europe. Poly-centricity was another planning tool to work towards greater spatial and social equality. This method suited the existing settlement structure mainly of the central part of Europe while implementation of this policy was more difficult in the West and the East due to their legacy of larger empires, centralised powers and dominant capitals. Complementary to poly-centricity are the European TENs (Trans European Networks, including transportation by rail and road, air, gas, oil and energy supply networks). They are completed with EU subsidies and influence the European settlement pattern and its development arguably more than national, regional and local planning.

Characteristics of plans

Many countries apply a strictly hierarchical system of plans (mainly ex-soviet, COMECON influenced countries and ex-Yugoslavia). They concentrate on essentially physical, land use plans. A distinction prevails between (sometimes non physical) strategic and operational planning, but some countries use both modes at all levels (Croatia) or at several levels (Slovenia). Long term horizons are incorporated in structure plans which are not always a statutory instrument though. In some countries no plans have statutory powers (Russia). For development plans, land use plans, or masterplans the time horizon is some ten years. However, in many countries updating does not occur regularly and is overtaken by the reality of development pressures. The development industry denounces planning as an impediment of progress which it perceives as development without regulation, a view often endorsed by politicians as well. In many places, this raises bottom-up protest and resistance to development, often by 'Nimbys' (not in my backyard) who are educated, middle class and able to influence the system.

A number of countries have adopted integrated comprehensive planning to overcome sectoral fragmentation and lack of coordination (Norway as precursor, followed by Finland and Denmark). Such planning has also been described as 'framework management'[18], meaning that spatial planning aiming to achieve spatial coordination is conducted through a systematic and formal hierarchy of plans from national to local level. This tradition is associated with mature planning systems and requires responsive and sophisticated planning institutions, as well as political commitment to the planning process. Such planning also lends itself to cross border planning which is important in very small countries (Liechtenstein, to connect railways between Switzerland and Austria, several countries to share sustainability strategies in the alpine region, Luxembourg to integrate traffic flows with the surrounding countries). Another means of cross border planning is a voluntary association of regions. For example CENTROPE is a politically led communal cross border region between eastern Austria, southern parts of the Czech Republic and western parts of Slovakia and Hungary. One of its aims is to coordinate the twin-city-situation of Vienna and Bratislava –two national capitals only 60 km apart from each other.

Many countries distinguish between strategic and operational planning (Moldova) and carry them out at different levels (Germany, Austria, Belgium, Switzerland, UK). Planning claims to follow the hierarchic subsidiarity principle, but often ultra vires prevails at least in parts (Luxembourg). While strategic spatial planning is postulating general and abstract principles, concrete physical planning aims to be interactive with influences working in both directions, from regional planning to local planning and vice versa (Estonia). However, such plan making requires cooperation (UK planning law prescribes a duty to cooperate horizontally between planning authorities).

Rarely, national planning objectives are set at regular intervals to correspond to the electoral cycle (Norway). Planning is also a tool of sectoral coordination between physical, social, cultural and economic objectives (Norway), as well as a means of vertical communication and mutual added value gains between planning levels, providing that the system is not

Wroclaw, Poland, photo Teresa Franchini

adversarial (Norway). Some countries produce national visions or concepts (Austria, Switzerland) but, on the whole, federal countries tend to have few or no planning competences at national level. Conversely, in strongly centralised countries most planning is concentrated at national level. In both cases, vertical coordination is seen as a problem. In Europe, the regional level (sub-regional in federations) tends to be weak. Reasons for their weakness are that regions are not often directly elected and are dependent on central state and municipal funding (Denmark, Sweden, Norway, Austria). Often regions are competent only for specific sectors, such as health, education or sometimes regional economy which, moreover, are only loosely related to spatial planning. Nevertheless, regional planning has great potential to operate as a useful buffer between the central and local levels and as a mediator to avoid direct confrontation. It has also gained importance with EU structural funding. Voluntary cooperation has been set up at regional level to overcome the urban rural dichotomy. It can encompass local authorities of different levels (SCOT- 'schema de coherence territoriale' - in France where it has become almost the prime level of strategic planning). Other forms of loose associations have been introduced for planning purposes (in France groupings of municipalities in urban areas – 'communautés urbaines') or for functional cooperation, such as regional transport, etc.

A major reason for setting up formal regions in European countries is to have appropriate channels to receive EU-structural funds, as they are based on the structure of regional spatial entities (NUTS-areas). Therefore regions which basically represent the NUTS III-areas, have strengthened their relevance during the last years (Austria, Romania). In many EU countries, and especially in the more recent member states, the principles of planning, environmental standards and transportation have been adjusted to the EU, its spatial objectives and its procedures.

More specifically, where planning has competences at regional level, coordination between vertical levels and horizontal cooperation across administrative borders seem to work well (France, Netherlands Baltic and Nordic countries - except Sweden and Denmark). Elsewhere, in the absence of regional planning competence operational planning which is usually confined to the local level (England, except for greater London, Iceland, Ireland) is used as a planning tool at regional level (Luxembourg) while strategic planning is carried out at central level.

At the local level a standard discourse is to 'get planning closer to the people'. In some countries this meant the introduction of formal neighbourhood plans, led by local communities (UK, Norway). On the whole though local community plans cannot overrule the higher order plans and need to fit into spatial and other strategies of local and/or regional authorities. Neighbourhood plans which incur costs and require time and some expert knowledge seem to be drawn up mostly in affluent areas by affluent people. It could be argued that this leads to increasing polarisation (UK). From a technical point of view, there are good examples of graphic representation of hierarchic plans (Belarus, Germany).

Local planning is often limited to specific areas and detailed plans (in most countries). While planning instruments vary between implementation-oriented tools, such as agglomeration programmes to improve horizontal local collaboration throughout 'functional spaces' (Switzerland), others impose a duty of cooperation (UK), others still focus on urban development (Cyprus, Greece, Malta, Turkey), but rarely on rural development (Russia). Most have a mainly territorial approach based on land use and plot subdivision, and in some countries preparatory land use plans are the main planning instrument (Germany). Some countries do not have any formal planning instruments and use rules and regulations instead, but the local level does not seem able to convert them into local plans (Georgia).

Development control
Development control is understood in two ways in the contributions on Europe: the control and participation mechanisms during the plan making process, and the issuing of permits to develop and build. Rarely is there an independent body to which objectors can appeal (except in Ireland). Sometimes there are separate planning permits (location, use) and building permits (construction, plot ratio, coverage of area, safety, sustainability).

London, UK, photo Judith Ryser

Intervention by the public are getting increasingly restricted to directly interested parties, land owners, developers, immediate neighbours while the public interest is losing importance in this process. Land use plans with strong legal powers are applied sparingly in the case of conflict of interest (e.g. between land owners) and for specific areas only (e.g. Luxembourg airport). Planning conditions are often weak, arbitrary and easily overridden by developers (e.g. proportion of social housing in new residential developments and provision of amenities, open spaces and infrastructure).

Although development control is usually entrusted in the local level, there are wide ranging differences in application (Russia). Central governments are often involved in large scale projects and projects of national importance (ex-Yugoslav countries) overruling local priorities. Sometimes large interventions are entirely in the hands of central government (Slovenia). In some countries development control is shared between all planning levels (Bosnia, Kosovo, Montenegro and Serbia) or between the national and the local level (Armenia).

Sustainability

Sustainability, in terms of what were previously ecological and environmental concerns has been taken into consideration for a long time (Germany, Nordic countries, Switzerland). More recently, sustainability has been incorporated more formally into the planning process in most countries, either pragmatically (Baltic and Nordic countries) or through legislation, or through merging competences of planning and environmental legislation (Netherlands). Coordination between planning and environmental objectives remains an issue (ex-Yugoslav countries). Some countries focus specifically on CO2 reductions and environmental risk planning practices when they suffer from high environmental pollution (central and south eastern European countries, Azerbaijan, Bosnia, Croatia and Slovenia). While natural and built environment resources are seen as the largest economic and social assets for future development (Croatia), the social dimension of sustainability is not prominent and only addressed in selected 'mature' countries, although others are aware of it (ex-Yugoslav countries).

Sometimes the incorporation of sustainability principles happened through supra-national environmental legislation. This includes United Nations led conventions with incentives to accelerate the uptake of sustainability principles. The UN initiative of Agenda 21 which promotes bottom up and local initiatives aimed to be practical. It had some positive impacts on environmental awareness and change of behaviour, and lack of more successful implementation was attributed to poor monitoring processes.

A series of European Union directives fostered the introduction of sustainability into planning law and practice. This included making EIA (Environmental Impact Assessments) and SEA (Strategic Environmental Assessments) compulsory in EU countries for large developments, infrastructure projects and related protection measures of the natural and historic built environment. However, they tend to be rather abstract bureaucratic exercises with little practical implications. Nevertheless they have been adopted by non EU countries, alongside Agenda 21 principles, albeit without necessarily meeting the EU targets (Russia, Turkey, Armenia, Azerbaijan, Georgia, Ukraine, and ex-Yugoslav countries). EU environment directives also influence the natural environment through programmes like 'Natura' (Italy).

In Europe, some countries use sustainability principles in a more abstract mode, for example for 'beautification' purposes, or by creating numerous green areas to increase biodiversity (Monaco), However, the sustainability of growth policies may be questionable when they require tunnelling and reclaiming land (Monaco) due to development pressures. In some countries environmental concerns have been taken up by landscape planning (Italy), in others environmental planning is reaching out to the sea (Norway), and some countries include climate change considerations formally in local plans (Denmark).

Vienna, Austria, photo Judith Ryser

Nevertheless, environmental, ecological or climate change issues are not necessarily integrated into spatial planning and may be dealt with in parallel by other ministries and executive institutions. Sometimes there exist internal conflicts regarding sustainability within ministries (e.g. Environment and Urbanisation Ministry in Russia which entails difficulties in balancing the development pressures with environmental regulations). Sometimes countries concentrate on environmental protection without embracing the wider concept of sustainability (Russia). Despite increasing attention to sustainability, pressures for trade-offs between the environment and the economy remain high during financial crises, or are justified by climate change sceptics (Netherlands).

Regarding better public participation, a key aspect of sustainability - local and municipal planning with more devolved powers from the centre - is seen as the key instrument for planning to foster strong public participation. Sometimes reorganisation of local government precedes devolution which often consists of a considerable reduction of the number of local authorities. It is arguable though whether such concentration is enhancing empowerment of local communities, although it may be feasible in small countries (Denmark).

Governance

Decentralisation is seen as a major issue of modern governance and sometimes planning powers have been genuinely decentralised (Finland). However, decentralisation of responsibilities and increased participation are not only due to democratisation but also to diminishing resources and finance at local level. Even if self governing local councils are in charge of EU structural fund programmes and implementation they are burdened with growing demands for welfare and public services which they have to finance increasingly through municipal taxes. More local autonomy is going hand in hand with more local responsibilities (Slovakia). As local authorities wish to preserve their autonomy and refuse mergers, decentralisation leads to poorer coordination. Universal right to public access to land is more difficult to enforce with devolution (Denmark).

Decentralisation and devolution are not straight forward. Devolution of planning powers should follow subsidiarity principles but national and sometimes autonomous regional governments retain ultra vires powers (Netherlands, Slovenia, Spain, Greece, Ireland). In reality, the national level reserves planning powers for projects of national importance, as well as those relating to security and national interest. Nowhere are real bottom up planning powers enforced vertically. The nation state remains the locus of ultimate power even if the structure of planning power does not always consist of a direct line from the centre to the various lower tier levels and can take place laterally through central (specialised) agencies. Most importantly, devolution of responsibilities is not usually followed by resources and finance (Moldova, Kosovo, UK). However genuine devolution exists when there are practically no planning powers in the centre (Germany, Switzerland). Decentralisation has led to various forms of restructuring lower tier levels and changes of administrative boundaries to reflect the real settlement structure of conurbations (Ireland). Decentralisation can lead to a combination of spatial planning and environmental powers as a means to simplify the planning process (Netherlands). Even where a three tier administrative structure is responsible for planning ultimate government powers for planning remain in the centre (Norway).

Public participation varies throughout Europe and follows different motivations. A distinction has to be made between participation and consultation. What matters is the timing and access to active involvement in the planning process. Although embracing sustainability the notion of governance does not necessarily guarantee effective participation for a number of reasons. Even when participation is embedded in planning law many hurdles may prevent

Madrid, Spain, photo Teresa Franchini

it from happening in practice. Invoked are planning 'language', remoteness of the process, lack of access to digital technology and to information generally, restriction of participation to only the last stages of the plan making process, cumbersome procedures, lack of transparency of planning objectives, lack of understanding of effects on the 'planned', or simply lack of public interest.

In many countries participation is open, throughout the planning process, democratic and strong (Nordic and western countries, Moldova), but effective participation does not always follow (Iceland). Others practise only consultation (Estonia, Latvia, southern countries, ex-Yugoslav countries), but social movements have started to protest and to claim a more transparent democratic process (Spain, Italy and Greece). Participation remains weak in many places, possibly due to recent history where lack of planning culture is invoked (Russia, Eastern Europe, ex-soviet countries, ex-Yugoslav countries). Experiments with new tools of participation are piloted, such as visioning (Kosovo). Some countries are not including participation in the planning process at all (Monaco), or have introduced it only recently (Turkey). Sometimes participation is aimed exclusively at internal procedures, and sometimes only well resourced and knowledgeable stakeholders as well as local authorities are able to participate in the planning process.

Use of ICTs

Countries make general comments on progress of ICTs penetration, as well as the specific use if UCTs in planning, but many do not attribute it prime importance and some do not mention it at all. Most widespread is the use of GIS for on-line planning information. Planning authorities also have set up websites with specific pages for planning, but this presupposes that the general public has ICT skills and affordable access to ICT tools, together with a belief in the effectiveness of their digital participation. The more developed the countries the higher the ICTs incidence, including e-governance, e-planning, e-environmental and nature information (Denmark). However, occasionally, less developed countries have leap-frogged in incorporating ICTs in planning. Some consider the introduction of ICTs as a prerequisite of effective public participation (Eastern Europe). The effect of digital media has not been invoked, but EU requirements and incentives have contributed to a greater use of ICTs within the EU and also among applicant countries.

Planning practice

The selection of, and emphasis on specific aspects of planning practice depend on the authors and their preferences and preoccupations. In their own view, many ex-soviet countries in Europe are still carrying along a heritage from communist times, including tendencies to centralisation and ultra vires systems of planning. They often remain very bureaucratic, with many stages between the decision to plan and to adopt a plan (Montenegro, Macedonia, Serbia). However, when planning is mainly plan-led it can lack national coordination which may also hamper balanced spatial development (Denmark).

Even liberal planning cannot guarantee politically desirable development in the right place at the right time, as planning intentions are mainly realised by private developers and investors (Denmark). However, with the necessary legislation municipalities themselves could act as quasi developers by compulsory purchasing land and developing it (Denmark). Neo-liberal countries are demanding to simplify planning procedures and to shorten the time it takes to draw up plans, as it would accelerate planning permits for private developers and investors (Netherlands, UK, Hungary). However, this should only take place if environmental protection can be properly assured (Lithuania). Some see planning as a cost rather than an asset (Denmark). Others see a greater need for public private cooperation with the development industry from the outset through negotiated planning and commonly reached detailed plans and projects (Finland). Some regret the lack of longer term responsibility of developers for their interventions, for example those which resulted in post boom empty properties in tourist areas (Spain, Greece). The same argument applies to empty speculative offices (Netherlands) and to 'buy to leave' speculative housing sold for mere capital investment (UK). A more optimistic view is that planning in the new millennium has been improved and consolidated and is gathering new momentum and importance all over the world (Croatia).

An important aspect of planning in practice is the influence of outside bodies (World Bank, IMF) as they tend to impose their own objectives and values, especially in countries which are relying on loans to implement spatial development (Croatia). EU accession conditions also shape planning procedures in applicant countries. They are seen to be biased towards marketisation to the detriment of local and especially social development objectives (Albania,Serbia).

EU funding is the main motivator for new EU Member states to adjust their legislation and change their spatial policies in Eastern Europe. The same applies to UNECE assistance in greater and South East Europe (Armenia); as well as to UN Habitat and PNUD programmes.

Fiscal aspects and effects of money transactions were deliberated widely in many country contributions. Money does not follow responsibilities (Georgia), therefore devolution of powers should be matched with finances (Latvia). There is a need for public authorities to be able to purchase land at current use value, not expectation market values (Ireland) to be able to implement planning strategies aimed at the public good. Land is a national treasure and there is a need to develop mechanisms which support public interests in market conditions (Bulgaria). This may be achieved by well defined and properly allocated public property rights (post-communist Eastern Europe).

Regarding tax incentives their long term benefits were questioned and they were seen as a means of distorting the planning process. Subsidised projects tend to be abandoned as soon as subsidies dry up. Alternatively they can lead to oversupply or distortions with long term effects (e.g. only wind energy subsidy among renewable technologies). Responsibility for the impact of unforeseen and unforeseeable economic change was also discussed. This included impact of economic decline on overoptimistic development expectations incorporated in plans, but also impacts of context bound phenomena, such as widening economic gap and polarisation which led to population emigration as partial cause of shrinking cities in many European countries.

Suburbanisation due to growth of car use remained a trend and hollowed out compact European cities despite sustainability policies. The car was still dominating planning in many countries despite their adoption of sustainability principles (Estonia), leading to urban sprawl and suburbanisation despite planning to the contrary (Greece, Luxembourg).

Although planning goals were not explicitly included in the template for the 2015 IMPP, they were apparent in the critical comments on planning practice. An implicit assumption was that if planning does not shed its past command and control structure it will be considered backward and unable to cope with the pressures of the market led development industry (Czech Republic). This has led to a shift from spatial planning to flexible urban management and governance on a case by case basis. Democratisation was seen to go hand in hand with privatisation of land and property (Croatia) and speculative pressures (Albania). However, the most adverse effects could be mitigated by incorporating needs and preferences of the local players into planning conditions (Croatia). Moreover, obligation to pay market price compensation for planning decisions was deterring strategic long term planning objectives, including change of use designation for the public good and could act against compact contiguous development and related efficient public services (Croatia).

Many contributors commented on the link between planning and settlement structure. Even in very populated European countries, land coverage by the built environment is not very important, but often occurred in unsuitable areas on fertile agricultural land or in high quality natural areas (Germany, Austria, Slovenia). This reinforced the argument in favour of concentrated settlements (Norway) which would lead to reduced energy consumption for transport and housing, more play and recreation facilities in built-up areas and other common services within the local area, as well as more efficient arrangements for water, wastewater and waste. Concentration could work well where it was balanced with enough natural resources outside urban areas. However, the countryside was not necessarily free from all development which amounted to decentralised concentration, a strategy which guided spatial planning based on the concepts of central places and development axes (Germany). This approach was able to fit close knit polycentric settlement structures and had inspired the EU spatial planning vision, but was more difficult to realise in large countries with greater urban concentrations and vast sways of hinterland (Russia). This approach was not necessarily able to remedy very fragmented territories and their adverse effects on efficient management of resources and infrastructures. Due to enforced separations whole infrastructures tended to be abandoned (e.g. Nicosia airport) and led to political conflicts over the use of trading ports (Cyprus).

Informal settlements and illegal construction were widespread in the southern and eastern Europe (Turkey, the Balkan and Caucasus countries, and to a lesser extent East Europe). The poorer the country the more informal settlements seemed to be putting the effectiveness of planning into question. There may be a need of other measures to deal with excess housing demand over formally planned supply. Minority groups with good local support were experimenting with alternative approaches to urban development, such as slow cities. Unfortunately, the official planning system does not seem to recognise it as a feasible development process (Italy).

Many comments concerned the role and responsibilities of planners. They attributed deficiencies of planners to inadequate planning education (France, Norway, Eastern European countries), lack of planning research (Slovakia) and the position of planners generally. In the south planning remained dominated by architects. Very few still considered planners as neutral public servants who offer their technical skills. Many saw planners as builders of community consensus, negotiators and mediators, political advisers, entrepreneurs, or advocates and agents of radical positive change. Although, none of them conceived planning overtly as politics, many hinted at a political role of planners with social responsibilities instead of mere technical skills providers.

From this rich collection of country observations and succinct comparisons many potential correlations appear to emerge between planning systems and other characteristics, such as level and type of economic development, institutional structure and governance, geography, history and culture but, most of all, political regimes and motivation of stakeholders who include planners. From this initial overview it could be argued that planning is essentially political and planners need to adjust to this notion if they want to play an important role in the development process in future.

Berlin, Germany, photo Judith Ryser

Relentless urbanisation

Most countries included in IMMP are urbanised, albeit some remain still very rural (Burundi (10.6%) and others are de facto city states (Monaco (100%). Most countries continue to urbanise, some like in Africa and Asia at a very fast pace, others at a slower pace (Latin America), while some countries in Europe have shrinking cities. All countries have a physical spatial planning system, only few since recent times. The aim of planning is to regulate land use, albeit with varying objectives, the most widespread being for the common good, to safeguard property rights, to create harmonious communities, and to protect the environment. These objectives are rarely explicit, and no country singles out land as a precious finite resource in the custody of democratically elected political bodies. Market mechanisms are at work in all IMPP countries. Some are treating land and real estate as pure commodity, even where all land remains in the hands of the state or absolute rulers. Vertical expansion is offered as a solution to combat urban sprawl considered a damaging land consumer, leading to ubiquitous skyscraper city centres facilitated worldwide by new lift technology. This includes hyper-density, high rise housing likely to become the slums of tomorrow.

Urban and rural - complexity and reality

Two aspects are striking. One is that planning focuses predominantly on cities while mostly ignoring rural settlements. Often separate environmental measures are in place to protect nature, fauna and flora, forests and coasts. They are not always effective though and none deal directly with rural ways of life. The other aspect is the gap between often incredibly elaborate, complex and bureaucratic planning systems and their effectiveness in the real world. Informal settlements are rife not only in the developing world where they constitute up to 80% of the built fabric usually in the poorest countries, but they occur in different guises in the developed world as well. Often IMPP contributions state that the planning system is not working in practice and planning seems to be in crisis in many places.

Implementation: between a rock and a hard place

Concrete reasons given for difficulties with implementation are the lack of planning skills and education, lack of professional planners as well as lack of resources attributed to planning. This is especially acute in smaller and more remote municipalities which are carrying the brunt of everyday planning responsibilities, including enforcement and control. The greatest obstacles of planning when seen as a tool of spatial and social justice are market driven development processes on the one hand and persistent adverse existential conditions, poverty above all, on the other hand.

These conditions have not changed since the 2008 edition of IMPP, nor have new measures been put into place to improve them. Quite the reverse. The recent global financial crisis has led to austerity measures in many countries which have slowed down the economy, lowered average living standards, accelerated privatisation of public goods and curbed public investment in physical infrastructure, not to mention social improvements. This has affected implementation of planning and, in particular, large long term projects which are often left to the private sector. The same decline occurs with projects fostering sustainable development brought into being by intergovernmental bodies, such as Agenda 21, or the application of EIAs and SEAs, increasingly left to private industry enabling it to push its 'smart city' technologies or building certifications (LEED, BREEAM).

Regionalisation

Attempts at more balanced regionalisation floundered at the weakness of intermediary levels between the state and the local level. Regional planning is weak or non existent, even in more or less autonomous entities of federal countries, despite the great potential of regional levels to mediate between lower and upper tiers and to create allegiances across planning levels. Countries with a federal structure fare slightly better at pertaining more balanced polycentric development. However, lesser polarisation is essentially due to a welfare approach to society and to planning which even the most equal countries seem to abandon though. Innovative voluntary regional agreements to tackle polarisation, excess gentrification, as well as land flight and shrinking cities lack institutional anchorage in existing power bases to sustain their momentum in the longer term. Alternatively they are internalised in the mainstream planning system regrettably to the detriment of their innovative power.

Governance

Governance is changing, although countries do not share their understanding of this concept. Popular demand for decentralisation and more local autonomy is a prime contributor to changing governance. In reality decentralisation remains an illusion as long as the centre retains fiscal powers and planning is subjected to the ultra vires principle, with ministers having the last word and the private sector the privileged ear of government. Conversely, bottom-up autonomy brings with it responsibilities as well as powers, need of self-reliance as well as top down assistance. IMPP examples show many innovative bottom up initiatives, but even cumulatively, they cannot replace some form of institutional planning and a comprehensive framework of future spatial reality.

Public participation

While public participation has been incorporated into the planning system often as While public participation has been incorporated into the planning system often as condition for external loans and grants it is ineffective in practice, and often practised only at the end of the plan making process. It remains weak owing to the disinterest of the public which cannot understand the planning process for lack of clear communication. The use of ICTs has been promoted to assist planning and development. However, its use is uneven and arbitrary, most practised in advanced countries, introduced more widely with intergovernmental incentives, but not necessarily enhancing public involvement in planning. For many countries, governance means greater involvement of the private sector, not only in the development process but in plan making itself. Nevertheless, no country proposed to abolish planning altogether as it has its uses in creating and protecting added value during the development process.

Evolution of planning

Where is planning going from here? Can it evolve from autocratic or ultra-liberal modes to sustainable forms, from capitalistic or social market models to sustainable development or, in more conceptual terms from absolute space and relative space-time to relational space? How would alternative planning look? It cannot be the 'third way' which was a failed attempt at a compromise between liberal and state planned models, nor can it rely solely on bottom-up autonomy. All countries affirm the need for national and possible super-national coherence, as only thus it is possible to achieve coordination or cooperation across horizontal borders and vertical sectors within the current systems of governance.

Options for planning

IMPP evidence confirms that planning remains intrinsically linked to the state, national economic development strategies and political vision. Saddled with intrinsic inertia of physical transformation and legislation, spatial planning retains nevertheless a prominent role and remains a legal force. However, it divides increasingly into three modes:

- prescriptive, restrictive, centrally controlled;
- laissez faire, assisting economic liberalisation and privatisation, as well as decentralisation except for purse strings;
- guidance based on a vision embedded in societal and political goals, translated into flexible spatial frameworks to integrate, or at least coordinate environmental constraints, economic means and cultural aspirations.

Transformation of planning and education

Planning has changed dramatically since its heydays of the nineteen-sixties and -seventies when it was dominated by physical development. The private sector is playing a much greater role in the development process, alongside rising preoccupation with the environment, due to the debate on climate change and the incorporation of 'sustainability' in the planning system. So far, sustainability was used as an all encompassing concept, but its meaning and operational competence have to be much more clearly defined to be of use to planning. Would these changes have to be accompanied by a shift from formal education and qualification to include experience from practice-based commitment and lifelong learning?

Role and responsibilities of planners

The changing object of planning has continuously animated debates on planning and how it conditions the role of planners albeit rarely their responsibilities. By its nature, planning had always to deal with uncertainty and the unknown future. The current dynamic of change, volatile economic regimes, rebellion of civic society, together with terror and fear of terror with its consequences of mass migration and new settlement demands seem to overwhelm both those who plan and those who are planned for. Perhaps planning needs to move from its premise to create certainty and long term stability and accept its role as active partner in coping with uncertainty. Many authors from the 136 contributing countries raise doubts about the pertinence of their existing planning systems including the role of planners. Time may have come for planners to query their attributed role and assume full responsibility as active stakeholders in the political process of spatial transformation.

NOTES

1. A short history of contextual changes responses of planning are given in Judith Ryser (ed), 2015, "ISOCARP, fifty years of Knowledge Creation and Sharing", ISOCARP.

2. Josef Stiglitz, e.g. Globalisation of Protest. 4 November 2011. http://www.project-syndicate.org/commentary/the-globalization-of-protest

3. http://blog.euromonitor.com/2010/07/special-report-top-10-largest-economies-in-2020.html. based on IMP, International Financial Statistics, and World Economic Outlook/UN/national statistics

4. http://knoema.com/nwnfkne/world-gdp-ranking-2015-data-and-charts

5. http://knoema.com/sijweyg/gdp-per-capita-ranking-2015-data-and-charts

6. Gini index measures the extent to which the distribution of income or consumption expenditure among individuals or households within an economy deviates from a perfectly equal distribution. A Lorenz curve plots the cumulative percentages of total income received against the cumulative number of recipients, starting with the poorest individual or household. The Gini index measures the area between the Lorenz curve and a hypothetical line of absolute equality, expressed as a percentage of the maximum area under the line. Thus a Gini index of 0 represents perfect equality, while an index of 100 implies total inequality.

7. http://data.worldbank.org/indicator/SI.POV.GINI

8. https://www.cia.gov/library/publications/the-world-factbook/rankorder/2172rank.html

CIA World Factbook, Definition: Distribution of family income - Gini index measures the degree of inequality in the distribution of family income in a country. The more nearly equal a country's income distribution, the lower its Gini index, e.g., a Scandinavian country with an index of 25. The more unequal a country's income distribution, the higher its Gini index, e.g., a Sub-Saharan country with an index of 50. If income were distributed with perfect equality the index would be zero; if income were distributed with perfect inequality, the index would be 100.

9. https://www.cia.gov/library/publications/the-world-factbook/rankorder/2172rank.html

10. http://stats.areppim.com/stats/stats_ginixparam.htm evolution of GINI index 1960-2012

11. https://www.equalitytrust.org.uk/about-inequality/scale-and-trends

12. Tony Garnier, Une Cite Industrielle, 1917; Camillo Sitte, City Planning According to Artistic Principles, 1889; Daniel Burnham, Plan of Chicago, 1909; Georges-Eugene Baron Haussmann renovation of Paris 1853-1870

13. The editors realise that relevant comparisons would require information beyond contributions of selective authors as well as the use of new paradigms of comparison, e.g. Jennifer Robinson, Cities in a World of Cities, The Comparative Gesture, In: IJURR Vol 35.1 Jan 2011. Both are beyond this essay.

14. http://www.cnbc.com/2015/07/30/world-population-quarter-of-earth-will-be-african-in-2050.html

15. http://data.worldbank.org/topic/urban-development

16. https://en.wikipedia.org/wiki/List_of_metropolitan_areas_in_Africa

17. Countries in brackets are indicative, not exhaustive.

18. EU compendium of spatial planning systems and policies, comparative review, CEC, regional development studies, regional policy and cohesion 1997.

Planning systems at a glance

Africa

BURUNDI

FAST FACTS

- **Total Area:** 27,830 km²
- **Total Population:** 10,888,321
- **Population Growth:** 4%
- **Unemployment Rate:** 14%
- **GDP:** $1,700 billion
- **GDP per capita:** $600
- **GDP growth rate:** 4.7%

SETTLEMENTS STRUCTURE

- **Capital City:** Bujumbura
  331,700 pop
- **Second City:** Gytega
  23,167 pop
- **Density:** 391 pop/km²
- **Urban Population:** 10.6%

INSTITUTIONAL STRUCTURE

Republic composed of 17 provinces, 129 municipalities, 375 zones and 2908 rural areas (collines) and urban neighbourhoods.

Read on: www.burundi-gov.bi

Administrative competence for planning

The Ministry of Water, Environment, Regional Planning and Urbanism through different entities: FPHU, Funds for the Promotion of Urban Housing; SIP, Public Lands Company; ECOSAT: Supervision of Construction and Landscaping Grounds and INCEN; National Institute for Environment and Conservation. Provinces are governed by governors appointed by the central state and provide regional plans. Municipalities are the sole decentralised territorial entities with legal personality and financial autonomy.

Main planning legislation

The main laws are Law N° 1/008 Land Code of Burundi 1986 and Law N° 1/13 2011 revising the land code of Burundi.

Planning and implementation instruments

The Master Plan of the city of Bujumbura is expected to be approved. The Government will provide a set of guidelines and principles regarding land use to raise investors' confidence. Key factors for the success of this project will include the support and commitment at the highest level of the Government of Burundi and Bujumbura.

Development control

Municipal councils are responsible for the implementation of the City Council deliberations.

Sustainability and governance

Agriculture and livestock play an important role in the Burundian economic system. Human development will improve progress in some social sectors, such as education and health. Health has undergone dramatic improvement due to the decision to subsidise maternity care, and children under 5 of people living with HIV (PLHIV), those with tuberculosis, as well as a strong anti-malarial grant. Governance is essential for reflection and proper implementation of sustainable development issues. Governance is a new form of participatory democracy. It requires dialogue, cooperation and partnership between all stakeholders in sustainable development.

Planning system in practice

The generalisation of the urban process is a fact: even if only one in ten Burundians lives in cities and despite the low rural-urban migration and the low rate of urbanisation, the city of Bujumbura encompasses nearly three-quarters of the urban population. The main challenge is to manage the development of the capital city. The Ministry responsible for planning within its remit has just introduced a new strategic development plan for the city of Bujumbura for the period up to 2045. The plan was inspired by top planning experts. The master plan calls for building spaces for recreation and spaces for social facilities, such as schools and health centres. This master plan, which has just been published, is not definitive because it could include some changes.

ETHIOPIA

FAST FACTS

- **Total Area:** 420,000 km²
- **Total Population:** 87,900,000
- **Population Growth:** 2.89%
- **Unemployment Rate:** 17,5%
- **GDP:** $52 billion
- **GDP per capita:** $570
- **GDP growth rate:** 10.9%

SETTLEMENTS STRUCTURE

- **Capital City:** Addis Ababa
  3,040,740 pop
- **Second City:** Dire Dawa
  341,834 pop
- **Density:** 85 pop/km²
- **Urban Population:** 19%

INSTITUTIONAL STRUCTURE

Republic composed of 9 regional states and two administrative states.

Read on: www.mwud.gov.et; http://www. eservices.gov.et

Administrative competence for planning

The Federal Ministry of Works and Urban Development is in charge of defining strategies, policies, and guidelines concerning the urban development and construction sector. Regional bureaus and zone departments of works and urban development are accountable to their respective regional councils and zone administrations and responsible to provide technical supports to municipalities in the preparation and implementation of their urban physical plans.

Main planning legislation

Urban Development Policy 2006 specifies the roles that federal, regional and local governments have to play in order to fulfil integrated urban and rural development goals. Urban Planning Proclamation 2008 replaces the existing urban planning laws with a comprehensive legislation which takes into account the federal structure of government and the central role of urban centres in urban plan preparation and implementation.

Planning and implementation instruments

There is a hierarchical system composed by the National Urban Development Scheme, Regional Urban Development Plan the Urban Plans, which are of two types: City Structure Plan and Local Development Plan.

Development control

No development activity may be carried out in an urban centre without a prior development authorisation based on the urban plans. Cities or urban administrations take appropriate measures if a development activity is carried out without development authorisation.

Sustainability and governance

All cities and urban administrations have to ensure that their urban plans evaluate their social, economic and environmental impacts. The governmental has produced an "Urban Good Governance Package" consisting of seven sub programmes: land development and administration systems improvement; public participation; urban planning improvement; urban infrastructure and service improvement; organisation and human resource management reform; urban finance and financial management improvement; and justice reform. Federal and regional governments have to provide support to cities to achieve these goals. There is a need to enhance efficiency of urban planning through increased use of appropriate information technology.

Planning system in practice

The country has important problems with plan preparation, implementation and evaluation. Ethiopia is now among the most rapidly urbanising countries in Africa, however more flexible strategic plans are needed, including economic and social plans alongside the physical and spatial ones. There is a need to create national awareness of planning activities to ensure its implementation. It is necessary to identify and secure the support needed by the regions and the two autonomous cities from the federal government, as well as those required by the cities from their regional governments.

FAST FACTS

- **Total Area:** 580,367 km²
- **Total Population:** 41,800,000
- **Population Growth:** 2.7%
- **Unemployment Rate:** 17,1%
- **GDP:** $52 billion
- **GDP per capita:** $1,138
- **GDP growth rate:** 6.2%

SETTLEMENTS STRUCTURE

- **Capital City:** Nairobi
  3,138,000 pop
- **Second City:** Mombasa
  1,200,000 pop
- **Density:** 77 pop/km²
- **Urban Population:** 24,78%

INSTITUTIONAL STRUCTURE

Republic composed of 47 counties.

Read on: www.nlc.or.ke; www.nema.go.ke; www.ardhi.go.ke

Administrative competence for planning

The National Land Commission has the mandate over all land use planning in the country and coordinates planning by the counties. The county government is responsible for preparing and implementing physical development plans and the enforcement of development control. City/municipal boards are responsible for the preparation and implementation of town development plans. There is a County Land Management Board (as agent of the Commission) in each of the counties, in charge of overseeing the implementation of county land development plans.

Main planning legislation

The Constitution of Kenya 2010, National Land Commission Act 2012 County Governments Act 2012, Urban Areas and Cities Act 2011, National Land Policy 2009, Physical Planning Act 1996 and Physical Planners Registration Act 1996.

Planning and implementation instruments

The National Land Commission prepares the national land policy and guidelines for planning at the national, county and urban levels. The preparation of county, sub-county, ward, village and city/urban physical development plans is the responsibility of the county government and the city/municipal boards and town committees.

Development control

Development projects and proposals must first be approved by to the county government and/or city/municipal board and town committee. All building construction works are regulated by the National Construction Authority.

Sustainability and governance

The Constitution assumes sustainable development as one of the key principles. The Environment Management and Coordination Act 1999, and subsequent guidelines provide specific legislation on the protection and enhancement of the environment in all development projects. EIA licences have to be obtained from the National Environment Management Board. Presently the country has no national physical development policy, guidelines and strategies. Some policy guidelines can be found in other policy documents: Human Settlements Strategy 1987, Kenya Vision 2030, Nairobi Metro 2030 and National Land Policy 2009. A draft document on urban development policy was prepared in 2010 but it has not be adopted by government or approved by Parliament. ICT has not been effectively incorporated in town and country planning.

Planning system in practice

Development in towns is haphazard and uncontrolled. Very few towns and county governments have established town planning departments and the resources allocated for county or town planning is scarce. The constitutional, legal and policy system is undergoing a transitional and transformation period. At the moment, new and enabling legislation is being enacted in line with the new Constitution, which presents opportunities and challenges for development planning. Town and regional planners need to expand their knowledge and skills into new frontiers.

MADAGASCAR

FAST FACTS

- **Total Area:** 592 000 km²
- **Total Population:** 21,300,000
- **Population Growth:** 2.9%
- **Unemployment Rate:** 2,6%
- **GDP:** $9,94 billion
- **GDP per capita:** $467
- **GDP growth rate:** 1%

SETTLEMENTS STRUCTURE

- **Capital City:** Antananarivo
  - 1.300,000 pop
  - 2,700,000 metro. area
- **Second City:** Tamatave
  - 270,000 pop
- **Density:** 36 pop/km²
- **Urban Population:** 32,9%

INSTITUTIONAL STRUCTURE

Republic composed of 6 provinces, 22 regions, 112 districts, 1548 communes - 45 urban and 1503 rural - and neighbourhoods (fokontany).

Read on: www.mepate.gov.mg

Administrative competence for planning

The Ministry of Planning and Infrastructure is responsible for national spatial planning policy and the national spatial development framework, as well as the national, regional and local structure and land use plans. Regions and municipalities are in charge of elaborating plans at their level and ensure complementarity which coordination is top down.

Main planning legislation

Planning Code 63/1963 was updated in 2010 but not yet ratified. It comprises land management, resource and finance mobilisation as well as coordination of sectoral policies. Law 2014/2014 defines decentralised territorial collectivities and their planning and land management competences. A new planning law is being prepared on the coordination of sectoral policies related to spatial planning.

Planning and implementation instruments

The strategic and land use plans at local levels (PuDi) translate national spatial policies (PNAT) and national spatial development strategies (SNAT) as well as regional ones (SRAT). It includes building regulations as well as communal spatial development plans (SAC). The structure plans cover demography, social policies, the environment, and infrastructure networks. Detailed Urban Plans (PUDe) complement these at the level of neighbourhoods, together with zoning plans, location and construction plans. The local plans have to incorporate projects of national interest. Plans are elaborated in cooperation with the state and the region on demand which ratify local plans. They have to be updated every ten years.

Development control

Municipalities are responsible for development control through the road inspectorate. The urban municipality of Antananarivo, the capital, has set up a notification system whereby citizens can inform on illegal constructions. Other municipalities have put in place informal communication systems which enable citizens to participate in urban management. Appeals are possible and are dealt with by the judicial services of the municipality but they are not frequent.

Sustainability and governance

The law 90-033/ 1990 has set up a charter for the environment and the decree request to check whether investment proposals are compatible with the environment. The decree 99-94/ 1999 requests an EIA for all public investment projects and for large private projects depending on their location and a permit is required from the National Environment Agency. Planning is often contracted out to consultants and public private partnerships are becoming more widespread. GIS is used for urban services and planning is digitised.

Planning system in practice

Planning is relatively recent in Madagascar. The first plan for the capital was drawn up in 1926. Many plans were never ratified. People are not very involved in planning while informal urbanisation (80% in the capital) is increasing. Planning blight is widespread as finance is lacking for infrastructure projects.

MALAWI

FAST FACTS

- **Total Area:** 118.484 km²
- **Total Population:** 16,310,431
- **Population Growth:** 3,2 %
- **Unemployment Rate:** -
- **GDP:** $4.408 billion
- **GDP per capita:** $800
- **GDP growth rate:** 5.7%

SETTLEMENTS STRUCTURE

- **Capital City:** Lilongwe
  1,037,294 pop
- **Second City:** Blantyre
  884,497 pop
- **Density:** 138 pop/km²
- **Urban Population:** 16,1%

INSTITUTIONAL STRUCTURE

Republic composed of 3 regions in line with tribal groupings, and 40 districts, 12 urban and 28 rural. Districts are divided into Traditional Authority Areas, wards and villages.

Read on: www.malawi.gov.mw; www. lands.gov.mw; www.mlgrd.gov.mw

Administrative competence for planning

The Ministry of Lands, Housing and Urban Development (MLHUD), is responsible for physical planning at the national level. The Ministry for Local Government and Rural Development channels central policies to the local level. The Commissioner for Physical Planning, under the MLHUD prepares plans for districts and towns, performed through four regional offices. Lower levels than districts have no planning responsibilities except for information dissemination or participatory processes. The three largest cities have obtained delegated planning powers to draw up their physical development plans.

Main planning legislation

The Town and Country Planning Act 1998 is currently under a revision process (Physical Planning Bill 2012). It is supported by several other statutes related to land, local governance, infrastructure development and environmental management among others.

Planning and implementation instruments

There are four levels of plans: National Physical Development Plan, District Physical Development Plan, Sub Regional Plan and Local Physical Development Plans, including urban structure plan, detailed urban layout plan and urban civic plan. Subject Plan refers to sectoral plans.

Development control

Local governments are responsible for development control. National standards and guidelines, reviewed in 2008, assist in effective implementation of the plans.

Sustainability and governance

The National Environmental Action Plan 1994 provides the environmental protection and management framework. An Environmental Management law and a policy were approved in 1996, revised in 2004. Guidelines for environmental assessment were adopted in 1997, reviewed in 2014. Reports are prepared in strategic district. The high price of internet connection and printing costs limit the use of ICT in planning practice.

Planning system in practice

Despite the process of democratisation and decentralisation, there are important problems related to political responsibilities, fiscal devolution and administrative coordination within the planning system. Informal development, street vendors' relocation, illegal urban farming, waste disposal are some problems that make development control ineffective. Politicians use power to access land and get plans approved irrespective of legality. Planners have no say in their implementation. Most developers construct informally due to weaknesses in the development control process. Corruption is widely suspected. There exists a large number of land lords and none of them, including the central government, has respect for approved plans. The general public also opts to building informally. It is expected that the approval of the new lands law reinforce the capacity of local authorities to face urban needs. Urban governance is crucial for poverty alleviation.

Administrative competence for planning
The Ministry of Planning and Development guides and coordinates the planning process and the economic and social development, but it can intervene directly in some sectors, such as municipal urban management.

Main planning legislation
Constitution of the Republic of Mozambique 2004 which states that land is a state property, Territorial Planning Law 2007 and its Regulations 2008, Urban Land Regulation 2006, and Land Law 1979 and its Regulations 1998.

Planning and implementation instruments
At national level: Strategic Territorial Development Programme, Territorial Plans and Land Classification. At provincial level: Provincial Spatial Development Plan. At district level: District Land Use Plan. At municipal level: Urban Structure Plan, General and Partial Urbanisation Plans and Detailed Plan.

Development control
Local authorities have the responsibility of applying local plans. They are in charge of managing land grants and construction permits.

Sustainability and governance
Ecological balance, environmental protection and quality of life improvement are constitutional mandates. Climate change and its effects on coastal cities is an issue of national interest. They led to the creation of the Ministry for Environmental Action Coordination Programme and provincial offices to give support to municipal departments, traditional authorities and communities. Environmental education is also been promoted. The Institute of Physical Planning and Environment was created in 2008 to provide qualified personnel. The Constitution proclaims decentralisation to strengthen provincial, district and municipal competences and promotes civil society participation, however all goals difficult to achieve. Regarding the use of ICT, 95% of the population has no access to Internet services and the subscription cost for mobile services are so high that they discourage their use. Mozambique becomes a member of the Alliance for Affordable Internet Alliance to improve this situation.

Planning system in practice
Mozambique is fighting for eradicating poverty and for minimizing environmental problems, such as the loss of biodiversity, water pollution, land erosion, lack of sanitation and natural disasters. Although there is a legal planning structure, there are neither policies, strategies or programmes at national level, nor references on the way local authorities have to produce and implement their plans. The Land Law gives full powers to the municipalities for the urban development management, but does not clarify the specifics of the process. The main hindrances for effective local planning management are the lack of trained technicians, material resources and effective tools to control urban growth. Some municipalities have started to produce their structural urban plans while partial urbanisation plans and detailed plans are being developed in cities and towns across the country.

FAST FACTS

- **Total Area:** 799.380 km²
- **Total Population:** 25.833.752
- **Population Growth:** 2.44%
- **Unemployment Rate:** 21%
- **GDP:** $15.329 billon
- **GDP per capita:** $635
- **GDP growth rate:** 8.3%

SETTLEMENTS STRUCTURE

- **Capital City:** Maputo
  1.191.613 pop
- **Second City:** Matola
  684.263 pop
- **Density:** 32 pop/km²
- **Urban Population:** 31,7%

INSTITUTIONAL STRUCTURE

Republic composed of 10 provinces, divided into municipalities and districts, and the Maputo capital city.

Read on: www.portaldogoverno.gov.mz;
www.legisambiente.gov.mz

SUDAN

FAST FACTS

- **Total Area:** 1,861,484 km^2
- **Total Population:** 37,3
- **Population Growth:** 1,9%
- **Unemployment Rate:** 13,6%
- **GDP::** $ 159.1 billon
- **GDP per capita:** $2,600
- **GDP growth rate:** 3,4%

SETTLEMENTS STRUCTURE

- **Capital City:** Khartoum

  639,598 pop

  5,274,321 metro. area

- **Second City:** Nyala

  629,971 pop

- **Density:** 20 pop/km^2

- **Urban Population:** 33%

INSTITUTIONAL STRUCTURE

Republic composed of 18 states (Wilayat), municipalities (Mahaliyat), localities and popular committees (lijan shabiyaat).

Read on: www.sudan.gov.sd; www.sudan. net/government.php

Administrative competence for planning

The National Council for Physical Planning, chaired by the Minister of the Ministry of Environment, Forestry and Physical Development is responsible for national spatial strategies, planning legislation and the approval of the physical or structure plans prepared by the states. The State Ministry of Physical Planning and Public Utilities is responsible for physical planning at regional and local levels. Municipalities make inputs to village plans. Planning ratification depends on the central government.

Main planning legislation

The Physical Planning and Land Disposal Act 1994 is the framework legislation at federal level. The regions and/or states can issue their own building bye-laws, building codes and other related controls. The Local Government Act 2003 specifies the planning powers of lower tier authorities, including the establishment of citizens' popular committees. Several acts regulate settlement rights through land registration and surveying.

Planning and implementation instruments

Long-term strategies define the content of the national socio-economic plans. Regional development plans, planning schemes and development plans for cities, towns and villages are provided by the states. Municipalities are in charge of detailed plans, infrastructure maintenance and subdivision approvals.

Development control

Any building or land development requires licensing by the Town Planning Board at the required level. Licenses are issued conform to the approved detailed or outline Schemes, which must conform to regional and national outline Schemes.

Sustainability and governance

The Environmental Conservation Act was approved in 1975. Sustainability is seen only from the environmental point of view, excluding the social, economic or political ones. The main hindrances are the lack of a comprehensive and participative legislation and the unsustainable land use management and land disposal process. Since 2002, local and international developers are the main stakeholder for the government, particularly for major urban development projects and new housing schemes and infrastructures. The use of ICT in planning decisions dissemination is still too weak.

Planning system in practice

Planning practice is affected by the incomplete coverage of the planning system, the poor level of coordination and the absence of transparency and good governance. It has become a political tool since ad hoc decisions are taken to solve acute problems. Most of the states have not approved their legislations due to the lack of funds and qualified trained personnel and municipalities lack the powers required to undertake their functions. The massive urbanisation is producing unauthorised and squatter settlements, where the major environmental challenges are associated to. Spatial justice and social integration are key challenges to be addressed.

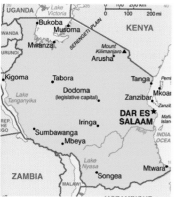

FAST FACTS

- **Total Area:** 963,000 km²
- **Total Population:** 44,928,923
- **Population Growth:** 2,8%
- **Unemployment Rate:** 10.7%
- **GDP:** $36.62 billion
- **GDP per capita:** $1,900
- **GDP growth rate:** 6.9%

SETTLEMENTS STRUCTURE

- **Capital City:** Dodoma
  410,956 pop
- **Second City:** Dar es Salaam
  4,360,000 pop
- **Density:** 51 pop/km²
- **Urban Population:** 29.6%

INSTITUTIONAL STRUCTURE

Republic composed of 30 regions, subdivided into 117 districts which include 37 urban and 92 rural district councils.

Read on: www.mipango.go.tz; www.ardhi. go.tz; www.nemc.or.tz

Administrative competence for planning

At national level the Ministry of Planning and the Ministry of Lands, Housing and Human Settlements Development (MLHHSD) are in charge of the 5 year National Plans and the National Land Use Framework Plan respectively. The Directorate of Physical Planning at the MLHHSD and the National Land Use Planning Commission are in charge of districts, cities and municipal plans. Rural and urban districts identify priority sectors and projects.

Planning legislation

After nationalisation in 1962 land in Tanzania became public. The main legislations are the Urban Planning Act 2007 and the Land Use Planning Act 2007, aimed to enforce the Human Settlements Development Policy 2000. Some of the many related policies and acts are: Tanzania Development Vision 2025; the Local Government Regulations, 2008. Town and Country Planning Regulations, 2001, Land Act 1999, Village Land Act 1999, National Environmental Policy 1997, Local Government Act 1982, Land Acquisition Act 1967, etc.

Planning and implementation instruments

Regional plans, regional integrated plans, regional and district physical plans are provided by the central government, including master plans, interim land use plans, strategic plans, and village land use development plans.

Development control

Local authorities in rural and urban districts have the power to apply planning consent application and appeals and development control.

Sustainability and governance

Sustainable urban development is constrained by the presence of policies and laws that are contradictory to each other. The Environmental Planning and Management approach has been institutionalised at municipal or district levels but the mandates are not clearly defined and the actions are not coordinated. Policies on decentralisation and strengthening of local authorities have led to continued haphazard development of urban land. The conventional planning procedure is slow and unpopular for public requirements. Reforms on decentralisation, participation, partnerships, community empowerment, transparency and accountability are needed. ICT must be applied to ensure that the right information is made available to all stakeholders.

Planning system in practice

Change from a socialist to a mixed economy has had planning implications which are being dealt with by increasing participation of the private sector but not the civil society which develops alternative approaches with greater active participation. Most urban settlements have no planning schemes and regional and district spatial plans are also lacking. Where available they are out of date and rarely implemented, especially in rural areas. Urbanisation continues to produce illegal settlements where 40%-70% of the inhabitants live. Planning remains dominated by experts although civic society based approaches are emerging in some cities.

ZIMBABWE

FAST FACTS

- **Total Area:** 390,757 km²
- **Total Population:** 13,771,721
- **Population Growth:** 4.36%
- **Unemployment Rate:** 95%
- **GDP:** $13.74 billion
- **GDP per capita:** $2,000
- **GDP growth rate:** 3,1%

SETTLEMENTS STRUCTURE

- **Capital City:** Harare
  1,495,000 pop
- **Second City:** Bulawayo
  699,385 pop
- **Density:** 35 pop/km²
- **Urban Population:** 32,5%

INSTITUTIONAL STRUCTURE

Republic composed of 10 provinces -including 2 cities with provincial status - divided into 31 urban and 60 rural districts.

Read on: www.cbnrm.campfirezimbabwe. or; www.environment.gov.zw; www.zimfa. gov.zw

Administrative competence for planning

The Ministry of Local Government, Public Construction and Nationa Housing is responsible for rural and urban local government an development planning. Regional planning councils are responsible fo regional plans but they are not an active part of the planning system Provincial planning structures and planning implementation are in charg of the governors appointed by the president. Ministerial delegation are the competent authorities for urban and rural district councils, loca government and development planning.

Main planning legislation

The Regional, Town and Country Planning Act 1996 vests planning powers land subdivision and acquisition, development control in urban council and rural districts, Provincial Councils and Administration Act 1985, Urba Councils Act 1996, Rural District Council Act 1988.

Planning and implementation instruments

There are basically two types of plans: Master Plans and Local Plans Master Plans are mainly policy documents with development proposal while local plans contain comprehensive proposals for developmen redevelopment or improvement. At times they are supported by Loca Subject Plans.

Development control

Local authorities are in charge of development control. Some application are permitted on the basis of special consent while others are permitte but only with conditions.

Sustainability and governance

The Ministry of Environment and Natural Resources Management i in charge of promoting environmental sustainability. The Nationa Environmental Policy 2003 promotes National Environmental Actio Plans, Local Environmental Action Plans and Environmental Managemen Plans. There are several by-laws and cross-sectoral strategies, such a reduction poverty programmes. Although the decentralised model c governance adopted in 1985, local governments are highly dependent o central government. The participation channels are legally articulated bu their usage is debatable. The use of ICT in government institutions is st limited. The National ICT Policy Framework 2005 was launched to promot its use. A National ICT Authority and a Converged Regulator are expected

Planning system in practice

Implementation and enforcement of policies and regulations is th greatest challenge. The over-dependency on the central governmen and the unavailability of resources, especially for local authoritie inhibits the practice of sustainable development. Bureaucracy an political interference have eroded the powers of local authorities. Publ participation has not been adequately institutionalised. Most plannin instruments are based on zoning which makes the system incapable coping with the high levels of urban growth, mainly informal.

ANGOLA

FAST FACTS

- **Total Area:** 1,246,700 km²
- **Total Population:** 19.813.179
- **Population Growth:** 2,8%
- **Unemployment Rate:** -
- **GDP:** $131.4 billion
- **GDP per capita:** $ 6.508
- **GDP growth rate:** 6%

SETTLEMENTS STRUCTURE

- **Capital City:** Luanda
  5.402.671 pop
- **Second City:** Benguela
  513,000 pop
- **Density:** 15,5 pop/km²
- **Urban Population:** 59,2%

INSTITUTIONAL STRUCTURE

Republic composed of 18 provinces and 164 municipalities subdivided into communes.

Read on: www.minamb.gov.ao; www. portaldeangola.com; www.mincons.gov.ao

Administrative competence for planning

The national institutions in charge of planning matters are the Ministry of Planning and Territorial Development, the Ministry of Urban Planning and Housing, the Ministry of Territorial Administration and the Ministry of Environment.

Main planning legislation

There are the Urban and Regional Planning Act 2004, the Land Act 2004, and the Territorial, Urban and Rural Plans General Regulations 2005.

Planning and implementation instruments

The National Plan of Development 2012-2017 is the fundamental planning instrument for the country and its provinces. At municipal level there are several instruments: Municipal Master Plan, Development Plans, Detailed Plans, Urban Renewal Plans and Rural Regulation Plans. The city of Luanda is currently drafting its General Metropolitan Director Plan.

Development control

Provincial governments manage and control local actions, except the Urban Institute of Planning and Management of Luanda, which controls the activities of individuals in Luanda.

Sustainability and governance

Angola approved the Environment Law in 1998 and created the Ministry of Planning and Environment in 2003, which was divided to create the Ministry of Environment in 2008. The Institute of Planning and Urban Management of Luanda supervises the technical conditions of the new buildings. There is a great concern for nomadic peoples and safeguarding water resources, flora and fauna. Angola implemented a multiparty system in 1992, giving birth to a process of democratisation. The socialist economy became a market economy with a strong government presence. Along with the State, private entities from all sectors have been participating in the national reconstruction. Little by little, greater transparency in public management has been recorded, as required by the World Bank, IMF and the United Nations. ICT's have been used as a means of information and training in the whole country through the Media libraries and centres for digital format consultation.

Planning system in practice

From the 1980's to the 1990's many efforts were made to complete existing unfinished buildings and to produce new social housing particularly for civil servants, low income people and residents from neighbourhoods located in risk areas. With the help of the People's Republic of China, the work of the new town Kilamba Kiaxi started in 2008 and the first phase finished in 2011. Another concern is about the regeneration of urban districts, mainly in Luanda. A master plan for the conversion of some of these districts is in progress. The private sector is contributing to the construction of housing and services.

CAMEROON

FAST FACTS

- **Total Area:** 475,440 km²
- **Total Population:** 23,130,708
- **Population Growth:** 2,6%
- **Unemployment Rate:** 30%
- **GDP:** $ 32.16 billion
- **GDP per capita:** $ 3,000
- **GDP growth rate:** 5,1 %

SETTLEMENTS STRUCTURE

- **Capital City:** Yaoundé
  2,930,000 pop
- **Second City:** Douala
  2,838,000 pop
- **Density:** 48,7 pop/km²
- **Urban Population:** 53,8%

INSTITUTIONAL STRUCTURE

Republic composed of 10 regions, 58 divisions and 360 sub-division (councils).

Read on: www.minepat.gov.cm; http://minatd.cm/gov/site/en

Administrative competence for planning

At the national level, the main institutions are the Ministry of Economy Planning and Regional Planning (MINEPAT), the Ministry of Territoria Administration and Decentralisation and, among others, the Good Governance Committee. At regional level are the decentralised structures of the ministries, the development and approval committees and the regional and local authorities. At local level there are local administrations village development committees and traditional authorities, among others. Although regions and local authorities are decentralised territoria entities, this decentralised structure has not been implemented yet.

Main planning legislation

The Constitution of Cameroon 1996, last amended in 2008, the Act on the orientation of decentralisation 2004 and subsequent regulations for councils and regions, the Law on state-owned land plans, and severa ordinances: on fixing land tenure 1974, on the establishment of the federal system 1974, and on expropriation for public utility 1974.

Planning and implementation instruments

At national level the Strategy Document for Growth and Employment 2010-2014, the Development Vision 2035; regional and local plans. The 'Guide Méthodologique de la Planification Locale' produced by MINEPAT details the planning process to be followed.

Development control

Plans are controlled by their respective administrative level.

Sustainability and governance

Cameroon has committed to implement the UN Conference on Environment and Development principles. The Ministry of Environment and Protection of Nature, 1992, has drafted the National Plan for the Protection of Wildlife and the Plan for National Forest Management, created the Observatory of Climate Change and is working on the National Environmental Management Plan. The Management of the Environment Act 1996 is the main law. National or international NGO's are very active actors. Implementation of environmental protection policies and strategies face several institutional, cultural, educational and financial hindrances. Although decentralisation has been stated, the presence of the state is constant, urban development projects are often coordinated by central ministerial departments and regional delegations. Some city councils have their own website.

Planning system in practice

Until the mid-1980's, the government has guided its policies through five-year development plans but due to the economic crisis, it was forced to adopt short term plans, which reduced the ability of the government to intervene in economic and social sectors. The constitutional reform of 1996 promotes decentralisation, so regional and local planning is progressively becoming an effective modality, including the community involvement in the process. The 'Guide Méthodologique de Planification Régionale et Locale' is intended for local development actors and all those interested in regional and local development issues.

GABON

FAST FACTS

- **Total Area:** 267,367 km²
- **Total Population:** 1,500,000
- **Population Growth:** 1,94%
- **Unemployment Rate:** 21%
- **GDP:** $20.68 billion
- **GDP per capita:** $21,6000
- **GDP growth rate:** 5,1 %

SETTLEMENTS STRUCTURE

- **Capital City:** Libreville
  800,000 pop
- **Second City:** Port-Gentil
  300,000 pop
- **Density:** 5,6 pop/km²
- **Urban Population:** 86,9 %

INSTITUTIONAL STRUCTURE

Republic composed of 9 provinces, 52 municipalities, 29 arrondissements, 26 districts and 152 cantons.

Read on: www.infrastructures.gouv.ga; http://ga.chm-cbd.net; www.en.legabon. org

Administrative competence for planning

Even though there exists a planned process of decentralisation through different proposed legislative Acts, yet to be enhanced, planning policies are still the matter of the central government, implemented by the different entities, mainly the Ministry of Public Works and Territorial Assessment, the Ministry of Housing and Urbanism and the Ministry of the Environment, Forest and Water. Local entities are not in charge of any planning action. Their actions are, at best, confined to their related community infrastructure maintenance purposes.

Main planning legislation

The main laws are Public Land Law 1963, Urbanism Regulations Law 1981 and New Urbanism Law 2013.

Planning and implementation instruments

At central level: strategic orientations at both administrative and infrastructure levels, national infrastructure network and urban planning schemes (local communities are called for advice). At municipal level: approval of the Municipal Master Plans and the Detailed Zoning Plans and Building Codes produced by the central government.

Development control

Performed by the local authorities.

Sustainability and governance

The first sustainability act was the Environment Code 1993 (amended in 2014), which introduced the obligation of environmental studies prior to any major infrastructure project and industries activities. This law was completed by a series of actions: urban waste management code, waste oil management rules, rules for spilling products into surface water, subsoil water and marine water, etc. Environmental impact studies are a routine in the planning process, evaluated by the Ministry of Environment, Forest and Water. The Executive Act of October 2005 intended to meet the Agenda 21 requirements. The implication of ICTs in the planning process is still on the verge. The objective is to set up a National Information Technology Plan with the broader Strategic Plan Emerging Gabon 2025. A National Agency was created in 2010.

Planning system in practice

Since the independence in 1960, the planning process has not taken ground beyond a general legislation process. Being a sparsely populated country, there was no sense of urgency. The first comprehensive urbanism law was adopted in 1981 but maintains the inadequate plans SDAU (Schéma Directeur d'Aménagement et d'Urbanisme) and the POS (Plan d'Occupation des Sols). Infrastructure and urban development have been implemented through punctual projects without a broader vision. Planning instruments remain inexistent, even for Libreville and Port-Gentil, the two major cities, where informal settlements have grown dramatically. One of the most top-down negative aspect is the insufficient involvement of local governments in the decision making process.

SAO TOME & PRINCIPE

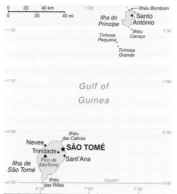

FAST FACTS

- **Total Area:** 1001 km²
- **Total Population:** 178,739
- **Population Growth:** 2,5%
- **Unemployment Rate:** 14%
- **GDP:** $ 334.9 million
- **GDP per capita:** $ 1,692.43
- **GDP growth rate:** 4.2%

SETTLEMENTS STRUCTURE

- **Capital City:** São Tomé
  69,454 pop
- **Second City:** Trindade
  44,752 pop
- **Density:** 179 pop/km²
- **Urban Population:** 67%

INSTITUTIONAL STRUCTURE

Republic composed of one autonomous region (Principe) and six districts.

Read on: www.gov.st

Administrative competence for planning

The Directorate for Public Works and Urbanism implements the territorial management, urban development and national policies for public and private works. Rural land policies are implemented by the General Directorate for Agriculture. In the Autonomous Region of the Príncipe, the Secretary of Infrastructure, Territorial Management and Natural Resources is in charge of planning. Local administrations approve zoning plans, encourage home ownership and self-built programmes and support housing cooperatives.

Main planning legislation

Land ownership regulation has been one of the government´s main challenges since land nationalisation in 1975. The "Law of the Land", 1991, defines the regime for distribution and usage of land by classifying it in four categories: public domain, private domain, private properties and reservations. Successive Decree Laws regulate the distribution of land for agricultural uses.

Planning and implementation instruments

Planning instruments are inexistent. The General Code for Urban Housing Construction was prepared in 2006 but is still waiting for approval. The 1959 General Code for Urban Buildings is still in force.

Development control

Local administrations issue construction permits.

Sustainability and governance

There are several legislative bodies protecting the environment: Environmental Basic Law, Forest Law, Fisheries and Fishing Resources Law, Regulation Environmental Impact Assessment Process Law, Fauna, Forest and Protected Areas Conservation, etc. STP prepared its National Environment Plan for Sustainable Development. Due to its geographic and morphological characteristics, the archipelago has been sought by several investors. The Government has developed initiatives to attract foreign investment, through bilateral cooperation and foreign private companies. To improve the business conditions, there has been a strong emphasis in the implementation of ICT's in order to reduce the bureaucracy of the administration sector and to create a favourable climate for the creation of private sector enterprises.

Planning system in practice

The massive migration from rural areas to the cities has produced the proliferation of precarious construction in the urban centres, defacing these centres and their periphery. With the increase of social polarisation, social diversity and an increase in the claims and new demands of the people that live and work in these urban areas is also felt. Observing this new landscape, where lack of sanitation, increasing degradation of living standards, etc. are notorious, it is essential that the country invests in planning in order to promote an adequate balance between economic development and the exploitation of natural resources. Planning implementation should be supported by the approval of a basic law for territorial management and urban policy, including the legal regime of the planning instruments.

ALGERIA

FAST FACTS

- **Total Area:** 2,381,741 km²
- **Total Population:** 33,200,000
- **Population Growth:** 1.209%
- **Unemployment Rate:** 14.1%
- **GDP:** $270,000 billion
- **GDP per capita:** $7,544
- **GDP growth rate:** 4.6%

SETTLEMENTS STRUCTURE

- **Capital City:** Algiers
  2,559,000 pop
- **Second City:** Oran
  850,000 pop
- **Density:** 14 pop/km²
- **Urban Population:** 70,1%

INSTITUTIONAL STRUCTURE

Republic is composed by 48 provinces (wilayates), 548 districts (daïrates) and 1541 communes.

Read on: www.mate.gov.dz; www.mhuv.gov.dz; www.mtp.gov.dz; www.interieur.gov.dz

Administrative competence for planning

The state is responsible for the national and the regional plans; the wilaya are competent for the provincial plans and inter-communal arrangements. The municipalities are competent for drawing up their own plans, including detail plans.

Main planning legislation

In the absence of a formal planning act (under preparation), a number of complementary regulations determine national, regional and local plan making and implementation. They are the: Framework Legislation for National Spatial Planning 1987, and Land Use Planning Regulations 1990.

Planning and implementation instruments

The planning system is hierarchical with requirement of vertical compatibility between plans.
SNAT: national spatial plan
SRAT: regional spatial plan grouping some 9 wilayas
PAW: structure plan for wilayas
PDAU: municipal or inter-municipal structure and development plan, compulsory for all 1541 communes POS: municipal land use plan, required to be compatible with PDAU, determining COS, CES, formal design and building rules, prepared by professionals
Land subdivision can be initiated by developers.

Development control

Land subdivision, building and demolition permits are the responsibility of the municipalities.

Sustainability and governance

The environment is not a prime concern despite a national fund for the environment and a tax on pollution 2009. The law on the protection of the environment 1983, on waste management 2001, and sustainable development 2001 are not enforced. Pollution and litter are widespread but from 2014 Extranet is in charge waste collection and recycling in the public realm. Free distribution of natural gas contradicts the law on energy efficiency 1999.

Planning system in practice

There is a lack of compatibility between different levels of planning despite legal requirements. This is partly due to an uneven data base and lack of coordinating procedures. Other deficiencies include lack of consultation and insufficient technical competence of decision makers and administrators. Weak instruments of implementation and the lengthy process of plan making and approval require frequent plan revision.

EGYPT

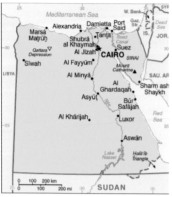

FAST FACTS

- **Total Area:** 1,001,450 km²
- **Total Population:** 85,294,388
- **Population Growth:** 1.88%
- **Unemployment Rate:** 12.7%
- **GDP:** $ 253.3 billion
- **GDP per capita:** $6,500
- **GDP growth rate:** 7,2%

SETTLEMENTS STRUCTURE

- **Capital City:** Cairo
  11,169,000 metro. area
- **Second City:** Alexandria
  4,387,000 pop
- **Density:** 85,2 pop/km²
- **Urban Population:** 43,5%

INSTITUTIONAL STRUCTURE

Republic composed of 27 governorates (muhafazat) included into seven economic regions.

Read on: www.moh.gov.eg; www.mop.gov. eg; www.mof.gov.eg

Administrative competence for planning

The Ministry of Housing, Utilities, and Urban Development is responsible for urban development policies. Socio-economic and strategic planning are led by the Ministry of Planning and the General Organisation for Physical Planning respectively. Economic regions operate under the Higher Committee for Regional Planning. Local Government Units (LGUs) are sub-national entities and includes governorates, Markaz, city, urban district and villages.

Main planning legislation

Law Nº70/1973 refers to the preparation of the national socio-economic plans. Building Law 2008 replaces the traditional master planning for cities and villages by a strategic urban planning approach. Local Administration Law 1979 defines the structure and function of the different LGUs.

Planning and implementation instruments

Long and medium terms national plans do not followed a regular pace. The Information and Decision Support Centre is producing a National Strategic Plan for 2030. Strategic plans are produced for regions and governorates focusing on mega projects and inter-regional and regional interventions. Local governments have to prepare general strategic plans for cities and villages, focusing on allocation of basic services and infrastructure projects.

Development control

Building regulations are applied by the cities and rural councils.

Sustainability and governance

Sustainable development is included in the Constitution 2014. The Building Law 2008 stipulates that strategic plans have to ensure the achievement of sustainable development. Strategic urban plans should be discussed in public consultation with key stakeholders and social representatives. In terms of ICT's, the government has encouraged the use of GIS in urban planning. A National Urban Observatory has been implemented to assist the creation of observatories at governorate level to produce and support production and dissemination of information. The Ministry of Local Development has established local development observatories to provide key indicators related to local governance and development.

Planning system in practice

Planning practice has several problems: top-down approach, centralisation of planning, land management and fiscal functions, inconsistency the legal planning framework and in the territorial definition of government entities, absence of an adequate institutional framework for managing regional and local development, weak capacity to devise national, regional and local polices, etc. The government is developing a strategy based on three objectives: creation of a legal and institutional framework to enable sub-national governments to take a leading role; enhancement of the partnership between regional and local administrations and other actors in preparing strategic plans and budgets, empowering citizens and local and regional actors to improve governance.

LYBIA

FAST FACTS

- **Total Area:** 1,700,000 km^2
- **Total Population:** 6,400,000
- **Population Growth:** 3,1%
- **Unemployment Rate:** 39%
- **GDP:** $9.34 billion
- **GDP per capita:** $16,600
- **GDP growth rate:** -19.8%

SETTLEMENTS STRUCTURE

- **Capital City:** Tripoli

  1.126,000 pop

- **Second City:** Benghazi

  631.555 pop

- **Density:** 3,5 pop/km^2

- **Urban Population:** 78.4%

INSTITUTIONAL STRUCTURE

Republic (in transition) composed of 22 districts (shabiyat).

Read on: www.planning.gov.ly

Administrative competence for planning

The Urban Planning Authority is in charge of producing planning laws and regulations since 1964. Its role is to devise 20-25 years targets for the national spatial development, called "generation": the first generation comprises the period 1965-1985, the second generation was from 1985 to 2005 and the third generation for the 2005-2025 period is under preparation.

Main planning legislation

A high committee was appointed at the end of the 1970's to prepare the local standards aimed to achieve the goals and aims of Libyan society through the planning process. At the outset of the second generation, these standards were ready to be used together with the planning law supporting their use.

Planning and implementation instruments

The Urban Planning Authority starts with general studies towards the National Physical Perspective Plan to define the main national strategies. These outputs are translated into the Regional Plans, which detail the contents of the national plan. The linkage between the Urban Planning Authority and the municipal authorities starts when elaborating the future goals of the region. Municipal authorities are in charge of preparing Master Plans and Layout Plans, using the outputs of the regional plans previously prepared by the Urban Planning Authority.

Development control

The master plans and the layout plans based on predetermined local standards are prepared by a high committee. The Libyan local standards are aimed to achieve the goals of the Libyan society through the planning process. There are standards for the main social sectors. Standards and planning control procedures also exist for other sectors like religion, social and commercial activities. Building licenses are issued after the approval of the local plans. According to the law the local authorities are responsible for their application and the implementation of building regulations.

Sustainability and governance

Libya has problems with long range water transport (GreatManMadeRiver), water pollution and over usage. Libya is installing large solar energy farms. It had initiated eco-tourism before the revolution. The Environment General Authority produced a plan for the urgent transition to environmental sustainability in 2013 with emphasis on ecotourism and the protection of the Mediterranean coast.

Planning system in practice

The history of urban and regional planning in Libya is not long, as it has started in the mid-1990's, after the devastating earthquake that struck the El Marj region. The first planning action taken was the creation of the Urban Planning Authority in 1964. Since then the urban planning process was working smoothly, based on predetermined targets and through the long term planning frameworks 'generations'. After the political crisis that affected the country in 2011, the Libyan society is expecting huge transformations in the existing way of life, including changes in the existing planning system.

MOROCCO

FAST FACTS

- **Total Area:** 710,850 km²
- **Total Population:** 32,600,000
- **Population Growth:** 1.4%
- **Unemployment Rate:** 8.9%
- **GDP:** $127 billion
- **GDP per capita:** $2,999
- **GDP growth rate:** 3.7%

SETTLEMENTS STRUCTURE

- **Capital City:** Rabat
  1,850,000 pop

- **Largest City:** Casablanca
  3,975,000 pop

- **Density:** 45 pop/km²
- **Urban Population:** 57,4%

INSTITUTIONAL STRUCTURE

Constitutional monarchy composed of 16 regions, divided into urban prefectures and provinces, subdivided into districts, municipalities or urban municipalities, and arrondissements in some metropolitan areas.

Read on: www.marocurba.gov.ma; www. mhu.gov.ma; www.hcp.ma

Administrative competence for planning
The General Directory of Urbanism and Architecture under the Ministry of Urbanism and Territorial Planning (MUTP) is responsible for programming, monitoring, approval of planning documents and achievement of technical and legal studies. At the local level the presidents of urban municipalities are empowered to initiate and manage planning documents and issue construction permits, they are assisted by technical urban agencies which are under the MUTP authority.

Main planning legislation
Law N°12-90, approved in 1992, defines the national planning system following the French model. The planning legislation has moved from a repressive and prevention system to a strategic one. The new Constitution of 2011 has increased the capacity of coordination between the state institutions and the local authorities and between them and the local people. A new planning code is expected to be launched during 2015.

Planning and implementation instruments
Strategic planning is of two kinds: optional – the National Scheme of Territorial Planning and the Regional Scheme of Territorial Planning - and statutory – the General Schemes of Urban Planning to structure urban agglomerations for land use and transportation, investment, infrastructure policies, etc. for 25 years, and the Master Plans to define the right of land use at the urban level for a period of 10 years. Development Plans are master plans for rural areas. Subdivision and construction permits are considered local operational instruments.

Development control
Development control is carried out by the municipalities. A new construction code was adopted in May 2013, aimed to easy the building process.

Sustainability and governance
Several strategies have been approved: the National Strategy on the Environment and Sustainable Development, 1995, was followed by the National Action Plan for the Environment, 2002, and the Environmental and Sustainable Development National Charter, 2010. The updating of the previous Communal Charter, 2002, to give more responsibility to the local administration was followed by two Local Governance Programmes in 2005 to 2010. The incorporation of ICT into urban and regional planning practices constitutes an important driving force in the formation of the information society.

Planning system in practice
Planning and urban management problems refer to the lack of an integrated system of urban planning, inadequate provision of documents, planning with local realities and specificities and the adoption of stereotyped development regulations, and documents of immutable and rigid character. A flexible planning system that associates all the partners instead of a rigid and normative system is needed. Territorial strategic planning should care also for rural areas since they were relatively ignored by the planning system.

TUNISIA

FAST FACTS

- **Total Area:** 162,155 km²
- **Total Population:** 10,886,5000
- **Population Growth:** 0,92%
- **Unemployment Rate:** 15,2 %
- **GDP:** $ 45 billon
- **GDP per capita:** $ 4,138
- **GDP growth rate:** 2.3%

SETTLEMENTS STRUCTURE

- **Capital City:** Tunis
  2.500.000 pop (metro. area)
- **Second City:** Sfax
  600.000 pop (metro. area)
- **Density:** 67 pop/km²
- **Urban Population:** 66,6%

INSTITUTIONAL STRUCTURE

Republic composed of 24 provinces (governorate, wilaya), 264 delegations, 2050 communities (imadas) and 264 municipalities.

Read on: www.ins.nat.tn; http://admi.net/ world/tn; www.mehat.gov.tn

Administrative competence for planning

The nation state, through its ministry of works, housing and spatial planning remains responsible for most planning: national, regional, special protection, operational planning. With decentralisation introduced in 1994 municipalities and/or public operators, such as the housing real estate agency, and the land management agencies of tourism and industry, are competent for local land use plans. Private developers have rights to propose land subdivisions, or whoever intends to build housing estates.

Main planning legislation

Planning Act 1994 (CATU: Code de l'Aménagement et de l'Urbanisme).

Planning and implementation instruments

There is regulatory and operational planning. The main plans are: SDATN: national spatial plan; SDA: structure plan for built up areas and sensitive areas; departmental plan; PAU: urban land use plan; PAD: detailed plan; land division plan and operational plan for large projects. Any extension of building land is regulated by the planning system.

Development control

Development control is carried out by technical services of large municipalities; the state is responsible for all other areas, in cooperation with operators (e.g. utilities, transportation). Permits for land subdivisions area issued either by the regional or local authorities. Sustainable economic development is included in spatial planning as well as sustainable management of resources and funds are allocated to the protection of the environment.

Sustainability and governance

The policies of the ministry of environment and sustainable development aim at sustainable urban development, sustainable transport and energy consumption. It is adapting governance for that purpose. Citizens are mobilised to take responsibility for sustainable behaviour. 264 municipalities have adopted Agenda 21 and are preparing guidelines for sustainable development, eco-tourism and air and water pollution control. Sustainability and energy efficiency were incorporated in the education curriculum towards the UN decade of sustainable development 2005-2014.

Planning system in practice

The urban development plans - PAU - tend to be weak. Just over half of them are implemented, while the realisation of planned infrastructure remains below this level. Infrastructure plans are often devised separately from PAU. PAU are essentially tools for development control and land division, not spatial development strategy. They become obsolete quickly as they are overruled by derogations for developers, state public operators and residents. This situation also favours the generation of illegal settlements, which tend to be integrated post hoc by the state. Often not respected due to derogations the PAU tends not to conform with SDAU contrary to what the law requires. Development on the ground often overtakes also the other structure plans which are hampered by weak vertical integration and horizontal administrative coordination at state level. Foreign investment obtains preferential treatment.

BENIN

FAST FACTS

- **Total Area:** 114,700 km²
- **Total Population:** 9,985,000
- **Population Growth:** 3,34%
- **Unemployment Rate:** 25%
- **GDP:** $ 8,150 billion
- **GDP per capita:** $815
- **GDP growth rate:** 4.5%

SETTLEMENTS STRUCTURE

- **Capital City:** Porto - Novo
  280,000 pop
- **Largest City:** Cotonou
  678,000 pop
- **Density:** 87 pop/km2
- **Urban Population:** 46%

INSTITUTIONAL STRUCTURE

Republic composed of 12 departments divided into 77 communes, sub-divided into 546 arrondissements and 3,743 villages or city districts.

Read on: www.gouv.bj; www.decentralisa-tion-benin.org

Administrative competence for planning

The Ministry of Settlement, Urbanisation and Planning (MSUP) and the Ministry of Decentralisation and Local Governance make a decision about planning and nominate ad-hoc technical commissions. The technical commission, the Country Planning Delegation and the local administration draft the plan. The MSUP and the local government ratify the plan.

Main planning legislation

The Declaration of the National Planning Policy 2002 draws up the legal, organisational and practical planning framework for planning and integrated management of the whole national territory. Law 2013-01 2013 defines land and domain code for urban and rural centres.

Planning and implementation instruments

At national level the Town and Country Development Plan and the National Spatial Agenda 2030. At regional level the same national instruments plus Regional Cluster Development Plans. At local level Municipal Development Plans, Local Development Programmes and Local Development Plan (LDP) that includes the Comprehensive Urban and Housing Plan.

Development control

Control is performed following the principles of "Results based on management" and involves diverse actors at every administrative level. The central government mandates the National Council for Planning for the implementation of the plans and the Council, in turn, charges the regional Planning Delegation to supervise and coordinate the implementation process.

Sustainability and governance

Benin possesses a dense and diversified natural inheritance that is however exposed to progressive degradation. Some of the reasons are demographic pressure, a bad use of natural reserves, and an extensive and backward agriculture. Some preventive measures were taken concerning reforestation in 1895, and environmental impact assessments in 1991. After the Rio Summit 1992, the country adopted the National Agenda 21 involving ministries, agencies and communities. Benin has adopted participatory governance in its process of resources mobilisation. Law 98-030 1999 deals with environmental matters and urban plans.

Planning system in practice

Planning has been introduced in Benin after the 1990 constitution which instituted decentralisation as the main framework of sustainable development. The actions relate mostly to urban issues with much less attention to spatial or physical development. After the first municipal elections in 2003 the first plans were produced and today, every commune/ municipality has its LDP. The multiplicity and complexity of the laws, the ambiguity of the land code and the instability of the planning institutions have led to illegal actions carried out by the local and central administration. Consequently, the country is facing an extensive uncontrollable urbanisation process.

FAST FACTS

- **Total Area:** 322,462 km²
- **Total Population:** 23 202 000
- **Population Growth:** 2,4 %
- **Unemployment Rate:** 9,7%
- **GDP:** $28.288 billion
- **GDP per capita:** $ 1,200
- **GDP growth rate:** 8,5%

SETTLEMENTS STRUCTURE

- **Capital City:** Yamoussoukro
  966,000 pop

- **Largest City:** Abidjan
  6,351,086

- **Density:** 72 pop/km²

- **Urban Population:** 43%

INSTITUTIONAL STRUCTURE

Republic composed of 14 districts (of which two are autonomous), 31 regions and 107 departments (prefectures), 510 sub-prefectures, 197 municipalities and 8,549 villages.

Read on: www.ministere-construction.ci;
www.environnement.gouv.ci;
www.fonctionpublique.egouv.ci

Administrative competence for planning

The Minister of Construction, Housing, Sanitation and Urban Development is responsible for elaborating prospective studies, general planning and development policies, strategic projects of national importance. The decentralised administrations - regions and cities - are responsible for planning their respective territories and initiating and conducting urban projects

Main planning legislation

The legal framework comprises five significant laws: Order 508-MCU 1970 on General Planning Rules; Order 1089-MCU/CAB/DUA 1976 on General Rules for Construction; Order No. 1593-MCU 1983 on planning certificate; Law 97-523 1997 on building permit and Decree 2005-261 2005 on implementation rules for town planning and housing.

Planning and implementation instruments

Master Plan is the main urban planning instrument, comprising Detailed Plans to specify land uses. Subdivision Plans defining each single lot and its possible use, based on Detailed Plans. The process of making Master Plans is still highly centralised, particularly for the main cities (Abidjan and Yamoussoukro), which are taken care of by the National Bureau for Technical Studies and Development.

Development control

The Urbanism Certificate is delivered by the Central Administration prior to any project. Technical documents have to be approved by either the government or the local authorities.

Sustainability and governance

The Ministry of Environment and Sustainable Development has to develop and implement the national policy in this field, but it has limited influence on the Government agenda. The compulsory EIA reports are generally not performed. Nevertheless, sustainable development issues are being taken into account by the administration and the citizenship. The difficulty of gaining land ownership and tenure security is the main shortcoming, due to the plurality of documents needed to obtain land titles, the corruption and the chaotic process for granting building permits.

Planning system in practice

The planning system has a limited influence on city development. Defaulting stakeholders and inefficient governance make it difficult to monitor and steer the development of cities. Urban expansion depends on uncoordinated projects of private investors, scarcely integrated with the city and poorly equipped. The Government has to provide sanitation, electricity and water supply. Several factors explain the lack of efficiency of the planning system: the difficulties to obtain building permits; the inconsistent land subdivisions without taking into account the Master Plans provisions, and the uncontrolled proliferation of slums due to the lack of social housing policies. While the principle of decentralisation is firmly enshrined in law the existing planning system is still highly centralised. The challenge is to adopt innovative approaches in planning, relevant to the context and local potential.

GHANA

FAST FACTS

- **Total Area:** 238,539 km²
- **Total Population:** 24,658,823
- **Population Growth:** 2,5%
- **Unemployment Rate:** 11%
- **GDP:** $35.48 billion
- **GDP per capita:** $4,200
- **GDP growth rate:** 6.2%

SETTLEMENTS STRUCTURE

- **Capital City:** Accra
  1,848,614 pop
- **Second City:** Kumasi
  645,100 pop
- **Density:** 103 pop/km²
- **Urban Population:** 53,4%

INSTITUTIONAL STRUCTURE

Republic composed of 10 regions divided into districts.

Read on: www.ndpc.gov.gh;
www.tcpghana.gov.gh;
www.mlgrdghanagov.com

Administrative competence for planning

The Town and Country Planning Department, under the Ministry of Environment and Science, Technology and Innovation, is in charge of land-use plans and proposals for urban and rural settlements. The Ministry of Local Government and Rural Development is responsible for planning decentralisation. The National Development Planning Commission issues national development strategies for district assemblies and approves all plans. The Metropolitan, Municipal and District Assemblies produce development and structure plans and the sub-districts produce local action plans.

Main planning legislation

The main legislations are the Planning Systems Act 1994, the Planning Commission Act 1994 and the Local Government Act 1993.

Planning and implementation instruments

The Town and Country Planning Department sets the standards for planning at national level and provides technical support for structure plans and planning schemes. It has offices in the regions and districts to operate its mandatory functions.

Development control

District authorities approve planning applications and legal sanctions ensure conformity to plans.

Sustainability and governance

Ghana's Environmental Protection Act 1994 mandates the Environmental Protection Agency to be responsible for maintaining the environmental integrity. The National Environmental Policy ensures the environmental management. All spatial and economic development planning processes are subjected to strategic environmental assessment techniques. In terms of governance, various institutions are responsible: the National Development Planning Commission at the national level, the Regional Coordinating Council at the regional level and the District Assemblies at the local level. The Land Use Planning and Management Programme was launched to enhance the capacity of the Town and Country Planning Department, which has succeeded in providing the staff with ICT and GIS capacities.

Planning system in practice

Sectoral coordination is lacking due to historic administrative legacy, which leads to conflicts during plan making between various agencies. The long term Land Administration Project 2003 was launched to remedy land use plan implementation and to foster transparent land allocation and management. A decentralised system should bring the system closer to land owners and other interested parties in development. The proposed system is expected to be self-financing through levies and charges. However the lack of completed decentralised plans and professional staff is inhibiting the progress. Planning education remains too limited and needs expansion. While institutional change is progressing, public participation remains poor as traditional exchanges are dominated by small groups.

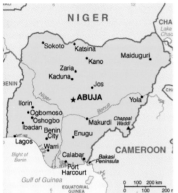

FAST FACTS

- **Total Area:** 923,768 km²
- **Total Population:** 174,507,539
- **Population Growth:** 2,5 %
- **Unemployment Rate:** 37%
- **GDP:** $478.526 billion
- **GDP per capita:** $2,827
- **GDP growth rate:** 13,62%

SETTLEMENTS STRUCTURE

- **Capital City:** Abuja
  1,857,000 pop

- **Largest City:** Lagos
  10,203,000 pop

- **Density:** 189 pop/km²

- **Urban Population:** 50,3%

INSTITUTIONAL STRUCTURE

Republic composed of 36 states and 1 federal capital territory.

Read on: www.nigeria.gov.ng; wrf.nige-riagovernance.org; www.climatechange.gov.ng

Administrative competence for planning
The Department of Urban and Regional Planning under the Ministry of Housing and Urban Development (MHUD) is responsible for the national urban development policy. The Ministry of Land, Survey and Country Planning is responsible for town and regional planning. The Urban Development Boards are responsible for implementation and enforcement of planning provisions. The State institutions usually extended their responsibilities for planning matters to the local government level.

Main planning legislation
The main legal bodies are the Town and Country Planning Law 1946 and the Planning Law 1992. Supportive laws are the Land Use Act 1978 and the National Urban Development Policy 1997. There are a fair number of states that still operate under the 1946 law, as the 1992 law is yet to be approved by most State Assemblies for implementation.

Planning and implementation instruments
The planning system is centralised. The government of the state gives authority for the preparation of urban development plans and, after they are accepted by the MHUD, the State Urban Development Board approves and implements the plan. The Federal government has urban planning departments in all major towns for land preparation and development on federal land. Regional development plans are prepared by the Ministry of Land and Survey with respect to the State Regional Plans and to the Ministry of Works and Housing statements.

Development control
Development control is in the hands of the Urban Development Board. The approval of any development permit is subject to the production of several requirements.

Sustainability and governance
The Federal Environmental Protection 1988 and the National Oil Pollution Regulatory Act are primary laws. The National Environmental Safety Regulatory Authority enforces national environmental standards. The executive and legislative powers share roles of policy, law making, implementation and oversight of physical development, and there is very little policy and law making at local government level. The use of ICTs in planning has started recently. Many planning institutions have adopted digital tools for planning production and for engaging the public.

Planning system in practice
Planning has a long history since colonial times and is totally embedded in bureaucratic structures, which makes the process complex and slow, notwithstanding corruption and lack of skilled personnel. Despite stringent planning controls a lot of informal development takes place. Informal development permits are issued, especially on urban fringes. Planning is not adjusted to fast urban growth. Developers proceed without permission, due to undue delays of the planning process. Decentralisation legislation is expected to remedy some of the bureaucratic hurdles of the planning process, especially at the local level of implementation.

SIERRA LEONE

FAST FACTS

- **Total Area:** 71,740 km²
- **Total Population:** 6,092,000
- **Population Growth:** 1,9 %
- **Unemployment Rate:** -
- **GDP:** $ 4,929 billion
- **GDP per capita:** $725.3
- **GDP growth rate:** 20.1%

SETTLEMENTS STRUCTURE

- **Capital City:** Freetown
  941,000 pop
- **Second City:** Bo
  149, 957 pop
- **Density:** 82,7 pop/km²
- **Urban Population:** 40%

INSTITUTIONAL STRUCTURE

Republic composed of 4 regions: Freetown and surroundings and 3 provinces composed of 12 districts divided into 149 chiefdoms.

Read on: www.mlcpe.gov.sl; www. statehouse.gov.sl; www.sierra-leone.org/ laws.html

Administrative competence for planning
The Ministry of Lands, Country Planning and Environment is responsible for the management of state owned land, planning and development, and approval and enforcement of the building codes. The Ministry of Local Government and Community Development implements the local decentralisation programme, assisting in the identification, planning, implementation and evaluation of the programmes for poverty reduction and economic revitalisation. At the traditional level, the Paramount Chiefs are responsible of the custody of the chiefdoms lands.

Main planning legislation
The Public Land Act 1896 is still in force, responsible for the regulation of the use of public lands. The Town and Country Planning Act 1946/2001 initially applied to the colonial territories, covers the entire territory. The Local Government Act 2004 is the legal framework for local councils. The Chieftaincy Act 2009 is about the responsibilities of the Paramount Chiefs.

Planning and implementation instruments
Municipalities are responsible for the creation and improvement of human settlements and the drawing up of their respective Development Plans. The local residents have to be consulted before the council can approve or revise the development plan.

Development control
Development control is the responsibility of the state, which regulates the land owners' rights. Land management is a key area, in which local traditions have crucial weight. The Paramount Chiefs hold the land in trust for the families of a particular chiefdom.

Sustainability and governance
To speak about sustainability in contexts of great insecurity and poverty is complex. The Agenda for Prosperity assumes sustainability as the second pillar of the Natural Resources Strategy and takes planning and sustainable management as strategic issues. Governance and the public sector reform compose the seventh pillar of the Agenda. Although the new technologies are burdened by poor implementation, the Agenda includes ICT's as the fourth pillar of International Competiveness. The limited access to the Internet confines an economic field with great potential for growth.

Planning system in practice
The development of urban areas has been inhibited by poor planning practice, the fast growth of settlements and activities, extensive sprawl and the inadequate provision of basic infrastructure. There are several factors at work: week and out dated legislative framework, poor technical capacity, a system of land tenure rooted in traditions and customary laws, lack of a land policy adapted to current needs, and lack of coordination and transparency of the planning bodies. Strategic planning is a suitable framework to implement in contexts of emergency and technical difficulties. It is essential to maintain international cooperation to strengthen the local structures.

SOUTHERN AFRICA
BOTSWANA

FAST FACTS

- **Total Area:** 581,736 km²
- **Total Population:** 2,024,787
- **Population Growth:** - 0.9 %
- **Unemployment Rate:** 17.9 %
- **GDP:** $14.8 billion
- **GDP per capita:** $ 7,136
- **GDP growth rate:** - 2.0 %

SETTLEMENTS STRUCTURE

- **Capital City:** Gaborone
  231,626 pop
- **Second City:** Francistown
  98,963 pop
- **Density:** 3.48 pop/km²
- **Urban Population:** 45.7%

INSTITUTIONAL STRUCTURE

Republic composed of 10 rural and 5 urban districts.

Read on: www.gov.bw; www.mewt.gov.bw

Administrative competence for planning

Planning is vested in the Minister of Lands and Housing; the Department of Town and Regional Planning; the Town and Country Planning Board and the Local Authorities, comprised of the Land Boards, District Administration and District and Urban Councils and Tribal Administration, composed of kgotla and the village/ward development committees.

Main planning legislation

The current legislation was launched decades ego: Roads and Building The Town and Country Planning Act, 1977, updated in 2013, is the primary piece of legislation used for purposes of physical land use planning at national, district and local level. The National Settlement Policy 1998 has divided the country into four planning regions.

Planning and implementation instruments

The future National Physical Development Plan will deal with the spatial aspects of the nation's social and economic development. At regional planning level the plans are Regional Master Plan and District Settlement Strategy and District Integrated Land Use Plan. Urban Settlement Development Plan and Village Development Plan are conceived for urban and rural settlements. Local planning deals with details of development of neighbourhoods, districts, wards and sites in urban and rural settlements.

Development control

For planning and building permission an application has to be lodged formally with the Local Planning Authority.

Sustainability and governance

The government aims to achieve "Sustainable Rapid Economic Growth" through economic diversification and a sustainable environment. The Environmental Economics and Natural Resources Accounting programme facilitates the integration of the environment into the development planning process. The Environmental Impact Assessment legislation was approved in 2011. The potential effects of climate change in an arid country led to the Environment, Energy and Climate Change portfolio, 2013. The government is embarked on a decentralisation process since independence. To ensure transparency and accountability at local level the Local Authority Public Accounts Committees were established. Botswana places great importance on the availability of good quality information to facilitate research and communication and to provide good quality education.

Planning system in practice

Following the combination of different foreign models, the major urban settlements in Botswana are quite well planned, development is taking place in an orderly manner and infrastructure deployment has not lagged behind development. The machinery for creating and transforming the country's townscape and its socio-economic and political structures into new physical forms is well established along the line of public and professional scrutiny. The major challenges remain in the implementation capacity of the administration in a still highly centralised government system.

LESOTHO

SOUTH AFRICA

•Leribe

•Teyateyaneng

Mokhotlong•

⊛MASERU

Thaba-Tseka•

•Mafeteng

Mohales
•Hoek   Qacha's Nek•

•Quthing   SOUTH AFRICA

```
0      30      60 km
0      30          60 r
```

FAST FACTS

- **Total Area:** 30,355 km²
- **Total Population:** 1,936,181
- **Population Growth:** 0.34%
- **Unemployment Rate:** 19.2%
- **GDP:** $3 2,448 billion
- **GDP per capita:** $ 1193
- **GDP growth rate:** 4%

SETTLEMENTS STRUCTURE

- **Capital City:** Maseru
   386,000 pop
- **Second City:** Leribe
   300,170 pop
- **Density:** 61 pop/km²
- **Urban Population:** 27.6 %

INSTITUTIONAL STRUCTURE

Constitutional monarchy composed
of 10 districts.

*Read on: www.gov.ls/local/;
www.environment.gov.ls*

Administrative competence for planning

The dualism of democratically elected representatives and chieftainship is ingrained in planning development. The Ministry of Local Government and Chieftainship oversees the performance of line ministries and service providers and monitors the implementation of the district plan. Decentralisation is formalised into District, Village and Ward Development Committees. District Development Coordinating Committees have the task to oversee the planning process and to approve district plans from the District Planning Units.

Main planning legislation

The Local Government Act amended in 2004 establishes the three-tiered government structure. The Land Act amended in 2010 makes provisions for land acquisition for public purposes. The Town and Regional Planning Act 1980 makes provision for the structure plans for urban areas; for providing land development permissions and for planning control enforcement. The Land Administration Authority Act 2010 integrates different departments into the Land Administration Authority.

Planning and implementation instruments

The National Strategic Development Plan 2012/13-2016/17 serves as an implementation strategy for the Vision 2020. The Directorate of Lands, Surveys and Physical Planning undertakes physical planning and development control. Structure plans are provided for urban areas.

Development control

Development control is administered through the Development Control Code of 1989. Chieftainship became the central institution in ensuring that development efforts in the villages, wards and districts were undertaken.

Sustainability and governance

Environmental sustainability issues are linked with poverty, health, food insecurity, environment, land degradation, energy and biodiversity issues. The National Environmental Policy incorporates these considerations at all levels of decision making. Governance is included in the Vision 2020, proposing decentralisation, popular participation, Local Government Act implementation and strengthening of chieftainship institutions as governance institutions. Lesotho's ICT vision aims to integrate these technologies throughout all sectors of the economy.

Planning system in practice

Decentralisation and popular participation of the civil society remains evident at various levels but participatory democracy needs to be nurtured and strengthened. The chieftainship´s leadership role remains strong. Land development and management are intertwined with politics and leadership. Planning practice is confronted with resource and capacity constraints, lack of coordination and limited correlation throughout plan formulation, implementation to monitoring and evaluation. The existing planning machinery from the village level up through ward and district levels to the central level needs appropriate resources to impact positively on the urban-rural spatial divide.

FAST FACTS

- **Total Area:** 2,825,234 km²
- **Total Population:** 2,280,716
- **Population Growth:** 0.67%
- **Unemployment Rate:** 28,1%
- **GDP:** $13.11 billion
- **GDP per capita:** $10,800
- **GDP growth rate:** 5,3 %

SETTLEMENTS STRUCTURE

- **Capital City:** Windhoek
  322,500 pop.
- **Second City:** Rundu
  61,900 pop
- **Density:** 0,81 pop/km²
- **Urban Population:** 47%

INSTITUTIONAL STRUCTURE

Republic composed of 14
administrative regions.

Read on:www.gov.na; www.met.gov.na

Administrative competence for planning

National economic planning rests with Regional Councils and the National Planning Commission (NPC), which devises national strategies and resource allocation through five year plans. In 2004 it undertook the Vision 2030. Town and regional planning rests with the Ministry of Regional and Local Government and Housing and Rural Development (MRLGHRD) and the regional and local councils. Regional Development Coordinating Committees oversee regional planning. Regions and local authorities have considerable autonomy, including tax raising powers.

Main planning legislation

The two major pieces are the amended Town Planning Ordinance 1954, and the amended Township and Division Ordinance 1963. Regional and local authorities may regulate aspects of the built environment according to the Regional Councils Act 1992 and the Local Authorities Act 1992. The approval of a new Urban and Regional Planning Bill is expected.

Planning and implementation instruments

Each region has a Regional Development Coordinating Committee. Town and regional planners prepare proposals for submission to the NPC, which monitors, implements and evaluates them. Town planning schemes are drawn up by local authorities and define the land use rights. Only local authorities have drafted town planning schemes. Except for a few cases Regional Councils have not yet taken this step.

Development control

Farmland subdivisions for urban activities are approved by the MRLGHRD while urban land subdivisions are controlled by the Township Boards. Township development is often initiated by local or regional authorities since many local authorities own substantial farmland areas. This is not applied in the northern regions, where the farmland holders have to be compensated according to (tribal) tradition.

Sustainability and governance

The Ministry of Environment and Tourism controls the use of the natural resources. A National Strategy on Adaptation and Mitigation to Climate Change was developed in 2010. The Environmental Management Act 2007 mandates the EIA implementation. The Vision 2030 emphasises good governance to reduce environmental degradation, poverty and economic stagnation. The Ministry of Information and Communication Technology produced the Strategic ICT Plan 2009 -2013.

Planning system in practice

Realistic development is ineffective in the existing planning system. Dual legislation has led to power duplication: the Namibia Planning Advisory Board and the Townships Board have conflicting advisory status. Streamlining is necessary in view of the lack of qualified human resources to fulfil the newly introduced compulsory planning functions. The integration of environmental matters into planning is lacking despite the political will to incorporate sustainability principles into the planning system.

SOUTH AFRICA

FAST FACTS

- **Total Area:** 1,219,912 km²
- **Total Population:** 53,982,000
- **Population Growth:** 0.5 %
- **Unemployment Rate:** 36.8%
- **GDP:** $ 341.2 billion
- **GDP per capita:** $ 7,140
- **GDP growth rate:** 2.5%

SETTLEMENTS STRUCTURE

- **Capital Cities:**
  Pretoria (leg): 1.991,000 pop
  Bloemfontein (jur): 496,000 pop
  Cape Town (adm): 3.624,000 pop
- **Largest City:**
  Johannesburg 9.176,000 pop

- **Density:** 44 pop/km²
- **Urban Population:** 62%

INSTITUTIONAL STRUCTURE

Republic composed of 9 provinces, inlcuding 8 metropolitan areas, 44 districts and 226 local municipalities.

Read on: www.gov.za; www.cogta.gov.za; www.dta.gov.za; www.environment.gov.za

Administrative competence for planning
The Department of Co-operative Government and Traditional Affairs and the Office of the State President are in charge of national policies on matters affecting development. Provinces define provincial policies, adapting national policies to provincial circumstances. District municipalities produce integrated development plans. Local municipalities are in charge of integrated development plans and land use management plans.

Main planning legislation
The Development Facilitating Act 1995, set out the following principles integrated, compact, liveable settlements without sprawl. The Municipa Systems Act 2000 introduced the integrated development plan as the instrument to be adopted by metropolitan, district and local municipalities The Spatial Planning and Land Use Management Act 2013 is the integratec planning law that sets out the planning systems in South Africa.

Planning and implementation instruments
The National Spatial Development Plan 2006, National Developmen Plan 2010 and National Infrastructure Plan 2012 are the main nationa instruments. The Integrated Development Plan (IDP) is the principa strategic planning instrument. Every new Council that comes into office has to prepare an IDP for five years. Plans are approved by the provincia authority.

Development control
Provincial authorities are responsible for the administration o existing plans. District and Local Municipalities are responsible for the administration of IDPs and Land Use Management Plans.

Sustainability and governance
The National Framework for Sustainable Development provides the long-term vision in sustainability. Local Agenda 21 has been adopted to be applied at municipal level. Sustainability has influenced the revision o planning legislation and the development of environmental legislation Planning sustainable cities and regions is a key element of the Guidelines for Competencies for Planners. The participatory processes of IDPs have increased the consultation culture. Online applications and access to information are becoming widely used, but a large portion of the population lives below the poverty line and does not have access to these resources

Planning system in practice
The new forms of planning introduced in 2002 have not been as successful as was hoped about spatial development and the impact can be assessed in some years' time. Nevertheless various improvements were reached: a uniform system of planning, emphasis on service delivery, increased comm   eness, and recognition that informality is an integral part of the development process and needs appropriate approaches to engage it. The main concern refers to the mismatch between settlement characteristics and planning instruments and the disjuncture between the strength of customary landholders and leaders and the weakness of the current institutional arrangements for planning delivery.

SWAZILAND

FAST FACTS

- **Total Area:** 17,364 km²
- **Total Population:** 1,403,362
- **Population Growth:** 1.17%
- **Unemployment Rate:** 40%
- **GDP:** $6,345 billion
- **GDP per capita:** $ 3,475
- **GDP growth rate:** -1.5%

SETTLEMENTS STRUCTURE

- **Capital City:** Mbabane
  94,874 pop

- **Largest City:** Manzini
  110,537 pop

- **Density:** 68 pop/km²

- **Urban Population:** 21.2%

INSTITUTIONAL STRUCTURE

Constitutional monarchy composed of 4 districts.

Read on: www.gov.sz

Administrative competence for planning

The Ministry for Housing and Urban Development (MHUD) is responsible for housing and urban development, human settlements, national policies and strategies. Town or City Councils are responsible for planning and development control. The chiefs are responsible for managing the Swazi Nation Land, the chiefdom is an equivalent of the local council in the urban areas .

Main planning legislation

The Urban Government Act 1969, amended in 2003, provides the basis for the establishment of local authorities. The Town Planning Act 1961 established the arrangements for establishing townships. Others are: Land Utilisation Act 1951, Human Settlement Act 1988 amended in 1992, Rating Act 1967 amended in 1997, and Peri-urban Management Policy 1997.

Planning and implementation instruments

The National Development Strategy (NDS) outlines the country's development goals for 25 years, starting in 1997. The Ministry of Economic Planning and Development (MEPD) establishes a physical framework for the economic development plans. The main urban planning instrument is the Town Planning Scheme, made up of the Structure Plan, Development Plan and Development Code.

Development control

The Physical Planning branch of the MHUD is responsible for overseeing planning activities. In cities development control is carried out by the local authority. In rural areas tribal customs rule development.

Sustainability and governance

Swaziland faces severe environmental challenges, which affects the levels of poverty, one of the objectives of the NDS and the Poverty Reduction Strategy. The Environment Management Act 2002 provides the overall framework, implemented by Environmental Audits and Assessment and Review Regulations. The main institutions are the Swaziland Environment Authority, the MEPD and the municipalities. The system of governance is characterised by an interaction between the traditional law and customs and western models of governance. The National Information and Communication Infrastructure Policy was launched in 2006 to promote efficient service delivery.

Planning system in practice

Urban development programmes have generated a number of initiatives aimed to socioeconomic growth and structural transformation, but land management, water and food insecurity remain daunting challenges. High incidence of poverty, HIV and the environmental fragility are constraints of development efforts. Development planning has been affected by elusive factors, such as the perceptions of the Swazi king, local philosophy, and the role of language, names, race, gender, age and status. To overcome these 'royal' factor, 'colour' factor and 'blood' factor hindrances, the country has undergone a socioeconomic evolution.

America

FAST FACTS

- **Total Area:** 51,100 km^2
- **Total Population:** 4.301.712
- **Population Growth:** 1.24%
- **Unemployment Rate:** 7,9%
- **GDP:** $ 45.1 billion
- **GDP per capita:** $ 12,900
- **GDP growth rate:** 3,5%

SETTLEMENTS STRUCTURE

- **Capital City:** San Jose

  309.672 pop. 1.160,000 metro area

- **Second City:** Cartago

  132.057 pop

- **Density:** 84 pop/km2
- **Urban Population:** 75,9%

INSTITUTIONAL STRUCTURE

Republic composed of 7 provinces, 81 provinces and 377 districts.

Read on: www.invu.go.cr; www.mideplan. go.cr; www.mopt.go.cr

Administrative competence for planning
There are several institutions: National Institute of Housing and Urbanism (INVU), Ministry of Planning and Economic Policy (MIDEPLAN), National Council of Urban Planning (CNPU), National Environmental Technical Secretariat and Ministry of Public Work and Transportation.

Main planning legislation
There is an ample legal base: National Planning Law; Urban Planning Law; Native Reserve Law; Statutory Law of Environment Wild Life; Conservation Law; Land and Colonisation Law; Law of Biodiversity, Conservation and Use of Agricultural Land Law and Municipal Code.

Planning and implementation instruments
The National Urban Development Plan (PNDU) 2000 is the framework of spatial urban development and it is produced by the INVU with the support of the MIDEPLAN. The PNDU defines the Central Inter-oceanic Region as the principal planning unit, with the highest hierarchy within the national urban system, including the Greater Metropolitan Area (GAM). Municipal plans are normally prepared by the INVU due to the limited technical and economic capacity of local governments.

Development control
In spite of urban plans, the lack of capacity of local authorities to control urban growth allows land invasions and the formation of informal settlements.

Sustainability and governance
Costa Rica is known as a leader in placing natural capital at the centre of development. This is in part due to the success of its Biodiversity Law 1998. The country has stated a "green growth strategy" and a number of decrees have been introduced. Costa Rica is a highly centralised country, where the weakness of the local governments contribute to reinforce the central government's role. The participation of community, private sector and minority groups is very low. A 2010 report indicates that 53% of the population uses the Internet and more than one million people access the internet from home but an effective infrastructure for this purpose needs to be built.

Planning system in practice
The existing planning system presents overlaps, conflicts, duplication and vacuums and it is still unknown by a large part of the population, and even the administration. The INVU has been losing capacity due to a lack of equipment and personnel. The municipalities with some exceptions do not have the resources to produce plans and as a result they are assisted by private consultants which, due to the low economic benefit and the short time available, produce low technical quality projects with little participation. The implementation is slow, mainly due to the incapacity of the decision makers to conceptualise high-priority projects, the politicization of urban issues, the lack of agreements among partners and corruption. Some efforts have been made but it is necessary to promote an urban and planning culture to improve both participation processes and spatial planning practice.

EL SALVADOR

FAST FACTS

- **Total Area:** 21,040 km²
- **Total Population:** 6,460,271
- **Population Growth:** 0,25%
- **Unemployment Rate:** 5,5 %
- **GDP:** $ 50.94 billion
- **GDP per capita:** $ 8,000
- **GDP growth rate:** 2%

SETTLEMENTS STRUCTURE

- **Capital City:** San Salvador

  1,729,032 pop metro area
- **Second City:** Santa Ana

  269,386 pop
- **Density:** 307 pop/km2
- **Urban Population:** 62%

INSTITUTIONAL STRUCTURE

Republic composed of 14 departmentos (provinces) and 262 municipalities.

Read on: www.vivienda.gob.sv; www.marn.gob.sv; www.mop.gob.sv

Administrative competence for planning

The Vice-Ministry of Housing and Urban Development and the Ministry of Environment are the main entities with planning competences at national level. Local governments are responsible for planning their territories.

Main planning legislation

Development and Territorial Planning Law (LODT) 2011, Special Law on Land Subdivision for Housing Use 2012, Regulations for the Development and Territorial Planning Law Implementation 2015, Urbanism and Construction Law amended 2012, Municipal Code amended 2015, Development and Territorial Planning of the San Salvador Metropolitan Area (AMSS) Law 1993.

Planning and implementation instruments

National Development and Territorial Plan, regional plans, municipal codes and special plans for historical districts.

Development control

Local government ordinances regulate land use, public spaces and specific economic activities and environmental issues.

Sustainability and governance

The Ministry of Environment and Natural Resources was created in 1997 and the National Environmental Law was approved in 1998. The National Environment Strategy was approved in 2012 and the National Environmental Strategy and its Action Plan is expected. The National Plan for Climate Change was passed in 2015. Several steps have been taken to facilitate administrative decentralisation. Operating manuals have been drafted within the Project for Strengthening Local Governments. The Law on Access to Public Information was passed in 2011. The Directorate of Innovation and Information Technology of the Presidency of the Republic was created in 2013, in order to provide technology services to the central departments.

Planning system in practice

The importance of physical planning in public proposals is not at present, questioned. The new administration (2009-2014) has introduced important changes while maintaining the previously achieved progress. The creation of the Sub-Secretary for Decentralisation and Territorial Development, the consolidation of the Planning and Development Secretariat at the Presidential level and the approval of the LODT in 2011, set up the transference of powers to the provincial and local administrations. Although the law came into force in 2012, its implementation is still in its infancy. So far, the 14 provinces have the development plans promoted by the PNODT, including the AMSS. In addition, many municipalities have their municipal plans, which allow them to exercise land use regulations and to grant urbanisation and building permits. Nevertheless, in spite of these efforts, it is still necessary to move towards a greater use of the planning tools adopted in recent years. But despite the efforts launched during the last few years to promote and implement the administrative decentralisation process, it is still developing and poses a big challenge regarding the inter-institutional coordination.

GUATEMALA

Read on: www.segeplan.gob.gt; www.marn.gob.gt

Administrative competence for planning
Each municipality is an autonomous institution in charge of territorial planning in its jurisdiction. As there is no regional government, the governors of the departments have to coordinate regional policies that will be reported directly to the President.

Main planning legislation
The main general laws are the Political Constitution, the Municipal Code, the Councils of Urban and Rural Development Law, the Civil Code, the Urban Subdivision Law and the Preliminary Urban Planning Law.

Planning and implementation instruments
The Municipal Code regulates the coordination of policies among municipalities giving the possibility to create 'municipality unions' to devise and implement common public policies, such as public transportation, drinking water, waste disposal, water treatment and environmental policies. Guatemala City approved the Territorial System Plan (POT) in 2008. Other main cities regulate themselves by the mentioned national laws.

Development control
Land use, building and land subdivision must get special licences and approvals from the municipality. The lack of observation of any regulation may be sanctioned with pecuniary penalties, or even with the cancellation of the project.

Sustainability and governance
Urban sprawl is significant in Guatemala City. By 2020 it is expected that 24% of the population will live in the city while 76% will live in the surrounding suburbs. The environmental problems cannot be tackled by the local administrations since they operate using several laws that are not updated or known by the people. The Environmental Protection Law 1986 promoted the creation of the Ministry of Environment and Natural Resources. The Protected Areas National Commission, the Forests National Institute, several NGO´s and specialised offices of the Attorney General, the Congress of the Republic and the National Police are in charge of controlling environmental issues. The main efforts made in terms of ICT´s are related to the provision of new technologies in streets, parks, public transportation, and other public services to improve urban security.

Planning system in practice
Main shortcomings: responsibilities are completely a municipal matter. The legislation is general and vague and the regulations are usually not hierarchical, which gives rise to misunderstandings and contradictions as well as confusion among institutions, people and investors. There is a lack of specific rules to draw up and implement plans. Poverty, lack of housing, infrastructure and public facilities, migration to the main cities, environmental problems and corruption are the main problems for municipalities in dealing with planning. More integrated planning regulations developed with the participation of the inhabitants should prepare the ground for a more sustainable use of land and natural resources, better living conditions and a better balance between urban and rural development.

HONDURAS

FAST FACTS

- **Total Area:** 112,492 km²
- **Total Population:** 8,535,692
- **Population Growth:** 2%
- **Unemployment Rate:** 3,9%
- **GDP:** $ 18.552 billion
- **GDP per capita:** $2,169
- **GDP growth rate:** 2,6%

SETTLEMENTS STRUCTURE

- **Capital City:** Tegucigalpa Central District 1,100,000 pop.
- **Second City:** San Pedro Sula 676.959 pop
- **Density:** 76 pop/km²
- **Urban Population:** 46%

INSTITUTIONAL STRUCTURE

Republic composed of 18 provinces (departmentos), 298 municipalities, 3,731 villages and 30,591 hamlets.

Read on: http://copeco.gob.hn; www. serna.gob.hn; http://amhon.hn

Administrative competence for planning
Central government is responsible for national infrastructures and protection of environment and building heritage. The Ministry of Planning and External Cooperation have launched the Country Vision and National Plan 2012-2038 to structure the long-term planning instruments but they are not operational yet. Municipalities are vested to drawn up local planning instruments.

Main planning legislation
Municipalities Law 1990, General Environmental Law 1993, Cultural Heritage Protection Law 1997, Land Use Law 2003, Property Law 2004, National System of Risk Management Law 2009, Building Code 2010.

Planning and implementation instruments
At municipal level the instruments are: Regulatory Plans, Urban Development Plans and Tax Plans. The central level cooperates producing the Strategic Plan of Municipal Development and Municipal Development Plan oriented to Territorial Planning. Since hurricane Mitch, applying risk prevention in municipal development plans is compulsory.

Development control
There are no national policies regarding planning control. Very few municipalities have statutory planning instruments. Municipalities have no capacity to control the use of land. There are few instruments to control the building process: EIA, buildings standards and security measures. The municipalities with historic centres have a special plan for the protected areas.

Sustainability and governance
The historic centre plans and the urban plans drawn up for the medium cities affected by the maquila industry have some potential for urban planning with elements of sustainability. Since hurricane Mitch, risk management has become a transversal axis for planning. International cooperation to tackle the Honduras Central District problems is supporting sustainable cities proposals. The environmental agenda is still weak no matter whether the country is threatened by climate change and natural hazards. The main impact of ICT's has been to provide general information of some cities, but the challenge is to expand this service to other cities and municipalities.

Planning system in practice
Although the country does not have a regional urban development strategy the existing urban structure would have an enormous potential if it were accompanied by a land management strategy. Uncontrolled urbanisation aggravates the damage caused by natural threats and increases the investments needed to offset the damages. The institutional crisis and the lack of urban planning in the two major cities of the country must be urgently addressed. It is necessary to provide appropriate and flexible instruments to accommodate differences and needs of management at regional and urban levels. There is also an urgency for design and implementation of policies and instruments of urban planning at different scales of city and metropolitan planning.

NICARAGUA

FAST FACTS

- **Total Area:** 112,494 km²
- **Total Population:** 6,071,045
- **Population Growth:** 1,02%
- **Unemployment Rate:** 7,4%
- **GDP:** $ 30.05 billion
- **GDP per capita:** 4,800 $
- **GDP growth rate:** 4,7 %

SETTLEMENTS STRUCTURE

- **Capital City:** Managua
  1,042,012 pop
- **Second City:** León
  210.615 pop
- **Density:** 54 pop/km²
- **Urban Population:** 58,5%

INSTITUTIONAL STRUCTURE

Republic composed by 15 departments and two autonomous regions.

Read on: www.ineter.gob.ni; www.mti.gob. ni; www.marena.gob.ni

Administrative competence for planning
The state, the autonomous regions and the municipalities have competences regarding planning.

Main planning legislation
The main instrument is the Standards, Guidelines and Criteria for Territorial Planning Decree. Others are the Environmental and Natural Resources General Law 1996, the Land Management General Policy 2002 and the Municipal Law 2013. The Land Use and Development General Law 2009 and the Urban Planning General Law 2006 are still in the legislative pipeline.

Planning and implementation instruments
Municipal governments are responsible for the preparation and implementation of the Municipal Territorial Planning Plans and the urban development schemes. Managua approved its last General Municipal Development Plan in 2000.

Development control
Land use is a municipal competence. The construction permit is the mechanism which supervises the projects and allows the detection of illegal constructions.

Sustainability and governance
The Standards, Guidelines and Criteria for Territorial Planning Decree sets out the general criteria for preserving the territorial environmental conditions. Planning and normative instruments have a special focus on environmental sustainability. The municipal authorities have the duty to carry out special programmes i.e. reforestation, erosion control, aquifers protection. Although municipal governments have to provide channels for public participation, citizens have little room for intervening since land-use planning and land development are not instituted. The Municipal government is the main custodian of land property, ecological values and urban maintenance. Other actors are the central government, developers, corporations, private companies and individuals. The e-government is progressing.

Planning system in practice
Despite the existence of urban and regional planning legislation, it does not clarify the role of the municipalities. The plans produced are poorly handled due to the limited resources, the implementation is partial due to the lack of capacity, the benefits are little known by the public, so they are not requested. It is essential for the country to approve the General Urban Planning Law and the Land Use and Development General Law, which are in the National Assembly pipeline since 2006 and 2009. This would facilitate the adjustment of current problems: awareness and education about the sustainable use of land to the public and private sectors and to the most vulnerable sectors of society; the strengthening of the institutions, the legal regime and the administrative framework to ensure the effectiveness of the rules and regulations to promote territorial development in the country and the effective coordination among the various administrative levels.

BARBADOS

FAST FACTS

- **Total Area:** 431 km²
- **Total Population:** 277,821
- **Population Growth:** 0.33%
- **Unemployment Rate:** 11.5%
- **GDP:** $4.277 billion
- **GDP per capita:** $16,200
- **GDP growth rate:** -0.6%

SETTLEMENTS STRUCTURE

- **Capital City:** Bridgetown
  98,511 pop
- **Second City:** Speightstown
  3,634 pop
- **Density:** 645 pop/km2
- **Urban Population:** 31,6%

INSTITUTIONAL STRUCTURE

Parliamentary democracy within the Commonwealth composed of 11 parishes.

Read on: www.townplanning.gov.bb; www. gov.bb

Administrative competence for planning

The Town and Country Development Planning Office is in charge of national planning. The Minister for Planning and/or the chief planner have control over whether and where development will be permitted under the Development Order 1972.

Main planning legislation

Town and Country Planning Act 1968 (TCPA), Town and Country Planning Development Order 1972 and Environmental Management and Land Use Planning 1998.

Planning and implementation instruments

The first National Physical Development Plan (PDP) 1970 was revised or amended several times; a new one is expected in 2015. The National Strategic Plan 2005 – 2025 sets the national development agenda over a twenty year period. The Medium Term Development Strategy was adopted in 2009. The regional land use plan for one of the most rapidly growing regions is expected to be completed by the end of 2014.

Development control

The TCPA prescribes that no development shall be undertaken upon any land without the permission of the Chief Town Planner to give regard to the PDP. Building regulations are not yet a part of the planning system but there is a Draft Building Standards Act currently under consideration.

Sustainability and governance

The Environmental Management and Land Use Planning 1998 produced several inputs: Physical Development Plan 2003, Environmental Management Plan, Draft Environmental Management Act, Barbados Sustainable Development Policy 2004, etc. In 2012 the Government prepared a Green Economy Scoping Study. A National Sustainable Energy Framework has been formulated. The main stakeholders in physical planning process are a wide range of formal and informal organisations along with the public. ICT's are quite heavily used in the conception of plans. The systems have not yet been developed for the transfer of digital information in the consultation processes among the many agencies.

Planning system in practice

The planning system as a mechanism to guide development is constrained by the fact that the development planning process continues to lag significantly behind the actual development process. The proactive role of planning needs to be triggered by a planning system that is driven by the development plan process and there is an urgent need to have the system re-organised to incorporate this strategic and integrative role into the development process. There is a need for greater transparency in the planning process, and for increasing the opportunities of public participation. Appeals procedures are very restricted and participation in plan making non-existent. There remains a great gap between planning and development and a need to attribute greater importance to the protection of nature, pollution control and the inclusion of environmental assessment in the planning process.

DOMINICAN REPUBLIC

FAST FACTS

- **Total Area:** 48,670.82 km²
- **Total Population:** 10,010,590
- **Population Growth:** 1.25%
- **Unemployment Rate:** 14%
- **GDP:** $ 138.3 billion
- **GDP per capita:** 12,800 $
- **GDP growth rate:** 4 %

SETTLEMENTS STRUCTURE

- **Capital City:** Great Santo Domingo
  3,125,000 pop
- **Second City:** Santiago de los
  Caballeros 584,828 pop
- **Density:** 206 pop/km2
- **Urban Population:** 75%

INSTITUTIONAL STRUCTURE

Republic composed of 31 provinces, a National District, 155 municipalities and 228 municipal districts.

Read on: http://economia.gob.do/mepyd; http://www.ambiente.gob.do

Administrative competence for planning
The National System of Economic and Social Planning and Administration 2000 institutionalized planning decentralisation, integrating regional and municipal bodies in this process.

Main planning legislation
Spatial planning has a comprehensive legal framework providing sectoral laws, regulations and control mechanisms. The National Development Strategy 2010-2030 (NDS) guides the general policies. The future Regional Law will create the Operational Planning Regions. The Law 176-07 on Municipal District and Municipalities 2007 regulates planning and environmental management through various instruments.

Planning and implementation instruments
Although no National Planning Plan exists, some mechanisms of regulation for the Tourism Sector, key cities and watersheds have been adopted. The Urban Planning Offices are responsible for producing and implementing municipal development plans, as well as controlling the use of land and the construction activities in the urban and rural areas of their territory.

Development control
Despite the extensive legal framework on planning and land use control, the lack of resources at the local level has weakened the capacity provided for these purposes.

Sustainability and governance
Following the international commitments on sustainability, the country has created the Ministry of Environment and the National System of Protected Area, whose implementation depends on the political will, citizen engagement, economic incentives and the existence of appropriate instruments. In line with the Declaration of Santo Domingo for the Americas Sustainable Development (2010), 15 priority areas were selected to improve the existing situation. Regarding the use of ICT's, the national average of the Public Access Centres is two for every 5357 people. Some communities have gained significant empowerment through this mechanism.

Planning system in practice
Although various instruments exist to promote a decentralised planning process, the results have been isolated and failed to mobilise their implementation. The centralised planning model remains in spite of the existing regional and sub-regional development centres, dedicated to administrative actions rather than effective interventions. Development control is a pending issue that requires structural changes. Although national development planning emphasises the protection and conservation of natural resources, the economic leading role in the development process is maintained. The priority actions that tend to be tackled are, among others, the review and update of the NDS and the multi-annual investment plan; the use of new procedures to implement land use planning, environmental management, and the strengthening of the human capacities at regional and local levels.

HAITI

FAST FACTS

- **Total Area:** 27750 km²
- **Total Population:** 10,250,000
- **Population Growth:** 2,5%
- **Unemployment Rate:** 33 %
- **GDP:** $ 7.843 billion
- **GDP per capita:** $ 785
- **GDP growth rate:** 2.9 %

SETTLEMENTS STRUCTURE

- **Capital City:** Port-au-Prince
  2,470,762 pop
- **Second City:** Cap Haïtien
  261,864 pop
- **Density:** 370 pop/km²
- **Urban Population:** 52%

INSTITUTIONAL STRUCTURE

The Republic of Haiti is organized into 10 departments, 42 districts, 140 municipalities and 570 communal sections.

Administrative competence for planning

Central level skills are shared between several ministries: Planning and External Cooperation (MPCE), Public Works, Transport and Communications, Agriculture, Natural Resources and Rural Development; Interior and Local Authorities, Environment, and Economy and Finance. The Inter-ministerial Committee on Spatial Planning (CIAT) established in 2009 coordinates the activities of these ministries. This framework is still under construction. At department and district levels, the delegations and vice-delegations represent the central government in the departments and districts respectively. At local level, mayors, supported by the ministry and/or NGO's, set up communal development plans and urban projects.

Main planning legislation

Laws and regulations are scattered and not easily identifiable. There is a lack of a framework law defining the basic principles of urban planning and land use, and the operating instruments.

Planning and implementation instruments

After the January 12th earthquake CIAT published in 2010 a territorial planning strategy for the national territory "Haiti Tomorrow". At regional level, plans are aimed to achieve the national strategy. At urban level, standards have been established to be followed in the urban planning field. At neighbourhood level the procedures have been defined to be followed by rehabilitation projects. Some municipalities had an urban plan, but none were followed up or updated.

Development control

Controls are very low in the current situation. The land use changes are little monitored and poorly controlled. The strategy used to implement the plans was to join all the stakeholders in the plan.

Sustainability and governance

Sustainable development is included in all territorial planning but not in an integral perspective. Spatial planning is a small business sector since the construction sector is dominated by self-construction. The country´s shortage favours the development of monopolistic or quasi-monopolistic situations and the risks of corruption. Efforts are made to encourage better governance. Mobile telephony and Internet is spread across the country, used to disseminate all kind of information but the high level of illiterates reduces people´s full participation.

Planning system in practice

The fragility of the democracy, government and bureaucracy makes the implementation of any planning system difficult, despite the efforts exerted by public authorities. The strong dependence on international assistance implies an extremely weak administration and a great difficulty to control processes and actions. The CIAT has made significant progress, such as a legislative and regulatory project to clarify laws applying to land, urban and environmental planning, a programme on land security, strategic and political plan and technical reinforcement.

JAMAICA ⋈

FAST FACTS

- **Total Area:** 10,991 km²
- **Total Population:** 2,697,983
- **Population Growth:** 0,69%
- **Unemployment Rate:** 14,9%
- **GDP:** $24.28 billion
- **GDP per capita:** $8,700
- **GDP growth rate:** 1.1 %

SETTLEMENTS STRUCTURE

- **Capital City:** Kingston
  584,833 pop metro area
- **Second City:** Portmore
  182,153 pop
- **Density:** 245 pop/km²
- **Urban Population:** 54 %

INSTITUTIONAL STRUCTURE

Constitutional parliamentary democracy and a Commonwealth realm composed of 14 parishes.

Read on: www.mwh.gov.jm; www.nepa. gov.jm; http://localauthorities.gov.jm

Administrative competence for planning

Spatial planning is administered by the Local Planning Authorities, the Town and Country Planning Authority and the National Environment and Planning Agency.

Main planning legislation

Town and Country Planning Act 1957, Local Improvements Act 1914, Towns and Communities Act amended 1997, Municipalities Act 2003, Natural Resources Conservation Authority Act 1991.

Planning and implementation instruments

The Central Government is preparing a new National Spatial Plan linked to the National Development Plan Vision 2030. Regional Plans and most of the Local Plans have been prepared by national level entities. Local planning authorities are in the process of preparing Local Sustainable Development Plans. Development Orders are legal documents used by the planning authorities to guide spatial planning for the area described as "Order Area".

Development control

Licenses and development permits are undertaken by the Local Planning Authorities and the Town and Country Planning Authority.

Sustainability and governance

In support of the Agenda 21 the Government started a process of local government which resulted in the preparation of Parish Profiles in a participatory manner as a precursor to the Parish Sustainable Development Plans. Parish Development Committees were established to allow public participation. The Government had embarked in the Land Administration and Management Programme, seeking an integrated and bottom up/participatory approach. Due to the potential impacts of climate change the Department of Climate Change under the Ministry of Water Land Environment and Climate Change was established in 2013.

Planning system in practice

Since the Constitution adopted at independence in 1962, the establishment of the central agencies has led to the fragmentation of spatial planning and a weakening of the local government in the matter. During the latter decades of the 20th century and due to the IMF's austerity programmes, many of the local level functions and responsibilities were removed. Many efforts were made by the central government to improve the local level involvement: Local Government Reform Programme, not fully implemented; Parish Development Committees; Public Sector Reform/Modernisation; and the Programme Development Assistance Centre included in the National Environment and the Planning Agency, whose expectations have not been materialised. There has been an ongoing effort to amend the Town and Country Planning Act 1957 to the preparation of Development Plans instead of Development Orders and the provision of a legal basis for their preparation, which it currently does not have. There has been mention of giving legal backing/status to the National Spatial Plan which is expected to establish the framework for the national spatial development.

FAST FACTS

- **Total Area:** 5,126 km²
- **Total Population:** 1,300,000
- **Population Growth:** 0.4%
- **Unemployment Rate:** 3.7%
- **GDP:** $ 157,417.80
- **GDP per capita:** 18,000$
- **GDP growth rate:** 2.3%

SETTLEMENTS STRUCTURE

- **Capital City:** Port-of-Spain
  50,300 pop
- **Largest City:** Chaguanas
  51,300 pop
- **Density:** 280 pop/km²
- **Urban Population:** 14%

INSTITUTIONAL STRUCTURE

Republic composed of 9 regions, 3 boroughs, the cities of Port of Spain and San Fernando and Tobago ward.

Read on: www.planning.gov.tt; www.ema. co.tt

Administrative competence for planning

The Town and Country Planning Division (TCPD) is in charge of the preparation and approval of development plans at the national, regional and local levels.

Main planning legislation

The Planning and Facilitation of Development Act was approved in 2014. Related legislations are the Environmental Management Act, the Regional Corporation Act, the Municipal Act and the Regulations on roads, water supply and disposal, drainage and fire prevention.

Planning and implementation instruments

The National Physical Development Plan (NPDP) is the top planning level based on an integrated and comprehensive approach. Regional development plans and local plans are prepared by the national Town and Country Planning Division. In 2010, to advance the decentralisation process; fourteen development plans were prepared for local authorities but they have not yet received statutory approval.

Development control

It is administered by the Town and Country Planning Division.

Sustainability and governance

The country adopted the principles of Agenda 21, included in all NPDP's. The National Protected Areas Policy was established in 2011 and the National Climate Change Policy 2011 proposes the inclusion of climate change vulnerability and impacts and adaptation options in the NPD. The public administration transparency in the development process is secured by engaging all stakeholders, including the Environmental Management Authority and NGOS through public consultations. However the centralised system of decision-making and the fragmented administration make coordination difficult. Local governments have limited capacity to make decisions. The lack of appropriate mechanisms reduces community involvement. ICT´s has been successfully used in the conception and dissemination of plans.

Planning system in practice

It is expected that the recently approved Planning and Facilitation of Development Act will address previous administrative deficiencies, in particular, the devolution of planning to the local authorities, the improvement of public participation, social equity, efficiency and transparency. Past administrative constraints have undermined the value of planning. In the absence of development plans decisions were made on applications submitted to the TCPD. The power to grant or refuse permissions has created conflicts. In parallel, a number of state agencies were created with both direct authority and indirect influence to make arrangements for development. The sectoral projects imperatives and the political interference force decisions that contradict spatial development plans. Meaningful public participation has grown in recent times. Communities and professional organisations representing concerns of the built and natural environment have become more empowered. The advocacy role of planners in conflict resolution is being recognised more than ever before.

CANADA

FAST FACTS

- **Total Area:** 9,984,670 km²
- **Total Population:** 34,834,841
- **Population Growth:** 0,76 %
- **Unemployment Rate:** 6,9 %
- **GDP:** $1.518 trillion
- **GDP per capita:** $ 43100
- **GDP growth rate:** 1.6%

SETTLEMENTS STRUCTURE

- **Capital City:** Ottawa
  883,391 pop. 1,282,500
  metro area
- **Largest City:** Toronto
  2,615,060 pop. 5.5 million
  metro area
- **Density:** 3.79 pop/km²
- **Urban Population:** 81%

INSTITUTIONAL STRUCTURE

Constitutional monarchy with a parliamentary democracy, confederation composed of 10 provinces and 3 territories.

Read on: www.ec.gc.ca; www.nrc-cnrc. gc.ca; www.historicplaces.ca

Administrative competence for planning

Planning is delegated to regional or municipal governments, under provincial government supervision. Local governments have no constitutional rights depending on the policies of the province in which they are situated. Each part of the country operates under a different system of planning although there are many similarities.

Main planning legislation

Provincial planning legislation consists of a Municipal Act and a Planning Act. Most provinces issue policy directives to which local governments must adhere.

Planning and implementation instruments

Each municipal government has a municipal plan known as the General Plan, Strategic Plan, Master Plan or Official Plan. Other initiatives are related to regional and metropolitan planning and spatial planning by indigenous communities, embedded in the comprehensive community planning process.

Development control

Local authorities are responsible for development control according to a zoning law and other land use controls devised by them. Planning permission is automatic if the proposal is conform to the local plan.

Sustainability and governance

The Federal Sustainable Development Act 2008 is the legal framework of the Federal Sustainable Development Strategy 2013-2016. The Canadian Environmental Assessment Act 2012 focuses on major projects and their environmental effects. Municipalities have limited constitutional and jurisdictional power. In turn, they have a comparative advantage at using extensive linkages with organised interests at the local level: modern governance relies on consulting and harnessing the expertise and resources of the private and voluntary sectors. Public participation is widespread. There are several types of indigenous governance, ranging from full authority to no authority at all. Land code option is a growing trend currently in place for the 35 First Nations communities. The use of ICT's is widespread, at par with other developed nations.

Planning system in practice

Planning for declining regions, shrinking cities, uneven growth or smart growth (intensification in downtowns and inner cities or retrofitting buildings) remains a challenge for planning in Canada. There are sharp contrasts between concentrated urban growth and dispersed decline and ways to manage decline. The diversity, interconnectedness and complexity of most large urban regions forward-looking strategies that promote safe, liveable, culturally sustainable, eco-friendly, food-secure, healthy, walkable and safe neighbourhoods. Partnerships with the private sector, businesses and people connect communities and enhance result oriented planning. Transportation, minimising urban sprawl (particularly in large supra-city regions), eco-planning as well as planning for youth and aging population are issues planners have to take cognisance of for the next generation.

FAST FACTS

- **Total Area:** 1,964,375 km²
- **Total Population:** 119,700,000
- **Population Growth:** 1.18%
- **Unemployment Rate:** 4,7%
- **GDP:** $2.143 trillion
- **GDP per capita:** $10,481
- **GDP growth rate:** 2.4 %

SETTLEMENTS STRUCTURE

- **Capital City:** Mexico City
    19,013,000 metro. area
- **Second City:** Guadalajara
    4.434.878 area metro
- **Density:** 61 pop/km²
- **Urban Population:** 68 %

INSTITUTIONAL STRUCTURE

Federal republic composed of 31 states
with 2645 municipalities and a Federal
District with 16 delegations.

*Read on: www.semarnat.gob.mx; www.
sedatu.gob.mx*

Administrative competence for planning
Federal, state and municipal governments share planning responsibilities.
The last constitutional reforms bring new agencies to deal with territorial
matters at national level: the Agrarian, Territorial and Urban Development
Agency (SEDATU) and the Environment and Natural Resources Agency
(SEMARNAT).

Main planning legislation
The political Constitution lays down conditions for the planning system.
Relevant legislation is the General Law for Human Settlements and in the
Organic Law of Public Federal Administration.

Planning and implementation instruments
The National Development Plan sets up the national strategies. The
National Programme for Urban Development and Territorial Organisation
produces strategies for the settlements system while protecting the
environment. The State Programmes for Urban Development focus on of
each state. The Municipal Programmes for Urban Development and the
Programmes of Urban Development for Federal District Delegations and
Urban Development Programmes for Urban Centres and Partial Urban
Development Programmes deal with the city planning at local level
depending on their conditions.

Development control
Municipalities are responsible for development control of their own plans
which they also approve. They also issue building permits.

Sustainability and governance
The main concern refers to the climate change and the emissions
reduction, although the country only contributes 1.4% of the total of
nations. The main green laws are: Climate Change General Law 2012,
National Strategy for Climate Change 2013, Use of Renewable Energies
Special Programme 2013, and the Presidential Energy Bill (gas and oil)
approved in 2013, accompanied by its secondary legislation in 2014. It is
expected to reduce 30% of emissions in 2020 and 50% in 2050. Since the
1990s, professionals use ICT´s and they are fully used in the national and
state agencies, but at municipal level it is only about 70%. An important
effort should be made to overcome this situation.

Planning system in practice
It is expected that the recent national Reforms will facilitate territorial
planning since there is a line of work from national to state and municipal
levels that compels to promote it. Most of the municipalities are capable of
implementing their spatial planning since there is a homogenous procedure
for the implementation of plans and programmes. It is of particular interest
to promote medium size cities by State direct interventions. Nevertheless,
at times the planning methodology, based on general strategies, leaves
out specific local aspects. The spatial organisation strategies are not
projected for the long term and are affected by the unclear definition of the
sectoral programmes at any level. The existence of two different agencies
involved in territorial planning (SEDATU and SEMARNAT) could hinder the
process.

USA

FAST FACTS

- **Total Area:** 9,826,675 km²
- **Total Population:** 318,093,000
- **Population Growth:** 0.7%
- **Unemployment Rate:** 7,5%
- **GDP:** $16,799 trillion
- **GDP per capita:** $ 53,101
- **GDP growth rate:** 2.2%

SETTLEMENTS STRUCTURE

- **Capital City:** Washington D.C.
  646,449 pop
- **Largest City:** New York City
  8,337,000 pop
- **Density:** 34 pop/km²
- **Urban Population:** 81%

INSTITUTIONAL STRUCTURE

Federal republic composed of 50 states,
1 district and 5 territories.

Read on: www.blm.gov; www.hud.gov;
www.epa.gov

Administrative competence for planning

Federally owned property is planned and regulated by federal agencies. Each state implements its planning strategies by state agencies or by city and county governments. Local government is directly responsible for land use and development planning.

Main planning legislation

Federal legislation determines what physical changes are subjected to planning, implemented by the states or regional and local agencies. The 50 states have passed an array of planning and environmental laws.

Planning and implementation instruments

Cities and counties have four primary tools: master plan, zoning subdivision controls and capital improvements programming for infrastructure development.

Development control

Cities and counties can adopt certain specific planning regulations. Federal, state, and local government agencies have authority over specific types of projects and activities. Planning and environmental legislation can be adopted by federal and state legislative bodies.

Sustainability and governance

The U.S. has numerous national regulations to avoid, reduce or mitigate environmental impacts. It has ratified the United Nations Framework Convention on Climate Change in 1992, signed the Kyoto Protocol in 1998, but did not ratify it. The United States Green Building Council has created the LEED programme which provides criteria for sustainable development. The White House Office of Energy and Climate Change Policy was established as an advisory committee to the President, and the current administration has enacted a series of programmes and policies to develop renewable energy. The Environmental Protection Agency is the primary governmental organisation for sustainability programs. Two other agencies are the Department of Energy and the Federal Emergency Management Agency. In addition there are numerous NGO that actively participate in citizen affairs. ITC's are prevalent in government, academia and business.

Planning system in practice

The USA planning system is subjected to strong property and land use rights which may clash with public concern for environmental protection and resource management. Development is mainly initiated and conducted by the private sector and legislation is meant to support these initiatives not hamper them. There is a great diversity of planning philosophies and practices at state and local levels. New urbanism was initiated by the planning profession to achieve better urban conditions countrywide, by means of liveable communities and compact cities near transportation nodes. Several states have adopted individual sustainability programmes and policies which far exceed national efforts. And, as with land use and development planning, local government has taken a leadership role in implementing numerous sustainability measures, especially in metropolitan cities.

FAST FACTS

- **Total Area:** 2,791,810 km²
- **Total Population:** 40,091,359
- **Population Growth:** 0,95%
- **Unemployment Rate:** 18,3 %
- **GDP:** $ 771 billion
- **GDP per capita:** $ 18,600
- **GDP growth rate:** 3.5 %

SETTLEMENTS STRUCTURE

- **Capital City:** Buenos Aires
    11.460.575 metro area
- **Second City:** Córdoba
    1.368.601 pop metro area
- **Density:** 14 pop/km²
- **Urban Population:** 92,5%

INSTITUTIONAL STRUCTURE

Federal republic composed of 23 provinces, 503 departments and 1 Federal District.

Read on: www.minplan.gov.ar; www. ambiente.gov.ar

Administrative competence for planning
Central government is in charge of issues of national interest. Planning powers are delegated to the provinces and municipalities.

Main planning legislation
There is no national planning system. In 2011 the Ministry of Federal Planning, Public Investment and National Government Services produced the document "Argentina 2016: Policies and Strategies for the Development and Territorial Organisation" where a Territorial Development National Policy and a Territorial Strategic Plans were proposed, none of them were implemented. There are several environmental national laws affecting planning.

Planning and implementation instruments
Only two provinces have land use system regulations. In the remaining provinces, regulations come from cadastral by-laws and from the areas excluded from urban development due to natural risks. Municipal plans are composed of planning and building codes for urban and rural territories.

Development control
Municipal plans are mandatory and any activity requires an authorisation according to local ordinances. Sectoral administrations are requested to give consent before municipal approval.

Sustainability and governance
The legislation passed has not guaranteed the sustainable management of natural resources, since private interest gets hold of such resources in different ways: glaciers, native forests, land, and water, among others. The implementation of the Agenda 21 has been poor and has had little impact on the government´s decision-making. In terms of governance, Argentina has returned to the full exercise of democracy since 1983. The Constitution was reformed in 1994 to secure the rights of citizens, political practices and access to information. Although steps were made to improve accountability and political stability and absence of violence, the shortfalls refers to state effectiveness, regulatory quality, rule of law and, above all, control over corruption. Most local governments have webpages with basic information about their areas. The largest ones have achieved positive results regarding queries, claims, tax payments, publication of local laws, etc.

Planning system in practice
Planning exists only in political, social and professional discourses and the market forces are shaping the cities. These situations are related to the inefficiency and inequity of the system. Instead of being pro-active, the existing plans adopt existing tends. It is distressing that Argentina still does not have an integral planning legislation or taken advantage of the Territorial Strategic Plan proposed in 2013. Some positive steps are the progressive development of the urban planning and local development process, the approval of the Environmental General Act, the National Transport Plan and the activity of the Ministry of Federal Planning, Public Investment and National Government Services.

FAST FACTS

- **Total Area:** 1,098,581 km²
- **Total Population:** 10,027,262
- **Population Growth:** 1,7 %
- **Unemployment Rate:** 2,7%
- **GDP:** $ 30,601billion
- **GDP per capita:** $ 5,500
- **GDP growth rate:** 6,8%

SETTLEMENTS STRUCTURE

- **Capital City:** La Paz
    1,680,520 pop metro area
- **Second City:** Santa Cruz
    1,443,925 pop
- **Density:** 10 pop/km²
- **Urban Population:** 67%

INSTITUTIONAL STRUCTURE

Republic divided into 9 provinces (departamentos).

Read on: www.planificacion.gov.bo; www. mmaya.gob.bo

Administrative competence for planning
In the framework of the Political Constitution 2009, the Autonomies and Decentralisation Framework Law (LMAD) was passed in 2010 which stated the creation of the State Integral Planning System Law (SPIE), still not approved. The allocation of resources and the decisions of development policies are performed by the National Planning System (SISPLAN)

Main planning legislation
Governmental Administration and Control 1990, Popular Participation Act 1994, Administrative Decentralisation Act 1995 and Municipalities Act 1997.

Planning and implementation instruments
The National Development Plan sets out the government's economic and social proposal. The Bicentennial Patriotic Agenda, a development programme for Bolivia, was approved in 2014. Planning instruments are: Executive Plan and Regulatory Plan for urban issues and Spatial Organisation Plan for regional issues. Municipal Development Plans should be based on citizens´ participation.

Development control
Municipalities authorise planning changes and municipal amnesty to legalise illegal plot division or buildings. Local organisations, such us the Local Grassroots Organisation are important agents for the promotion of neighbourhood upgrading.

Sustainability and governance
The serious environmental threats affecting urban and rural areas have led to the approval of the Rights of the Mother Earth Law 2010 and the Agreements Law 2014 to regulate the activities of the Plurinational Mother Earth Authority. The social and political situation is extremely complex, a product of an extremely fragmented civil society, social exclusion, poverty, inequality and institutional weakness. The government has developed a new inclusive state apparatus, based on municipal, departmental, regional, and indigenous-peasant autonomies. ITC's would allow civic information and socialising the codes of modernity.

Planning system in practice
SISPLAN has consolidated the national, departmental and municipal scales as a reference for planning, but the planning model is more theoretical than practical since the linkages between the different planning instruments have not been resolved. Although public participation is encouraged, the results show that it arises from a particular situation rather than being structural. Communication between planners and public has been deficient and was not able to fulfil the expectations raised by the new planning system. The system is beyond its capacity to lead with problems of illegality, land misuse and disorganised urbanisation. The various plans are still incoherent, devised for short term objectives, focusing on the analytical phase without including policies or concrete proposals. The lack of implementation instruments allows unauthorised and illegal settlements. It may be too early to assess the full effects of SISPLAN.

BRAZIL

FAST FACTS

- **Total Area:** 8,514,876 km²
- **Total Population:** 198,700,000
- **Population Growth:** 0.77%
- **Unemployment Rate:** 5.4%
- **GDP:** $2.39 trillion
- **GDP per capita:** $ 11,320
- **GDP growth rate:** 2.3%

SETTLEMENTS STRUCTURE

- **Capital City:** Brasilia.
  2,562,963 pop
- **Largest City:** São Paulo
  10,659,386 pop 19,900,000
  pop metro area
- **Density:** 34 pop/km²
- **Urban Population:** 85%

INSTITUTIONAL STRUCTURE

Federal Republic composed of 26 States and one Federal District, and 5,564 municipalities.t, and 5,564 municipalities.

Read on: www.cidades.gov.br; www. mi.gov.br www.mma.gov.br

Administrative competence for planning
At federal level, urban affairs are the responsibility of the Ministry of Cities, created in 2003. The Ministry of National Integration is responsible for national and regional development policies, regional development plans, programmes and strategies. At state level, the State Departments for Urban Planning or Development together with the municipalities is responsible for local public policies. Municipalities regulate and promote urban development in their jurisdiction.

Main planning legislation
Federal Law 10257 2001 known as the "Statute of the City" establishes directives for urban policy in the country. Other provisions are the Federal Law of Urban Land Subdivision 1979, the Federal Constitution 1988, the Resolutions of the National Council for the Environment and the Civil Code 2002.

Planning and implementation instruments
City planning is compulsory for municipalities over 20,000 inhabitants through different instruments: master plans, designation of built up areas, land subdivision and zoning laws, and building regulations. Cultural heritage and environment preservation are joint responsibilities of all planning levels.

Development control
A Building Code is approved by each Municipality.

Sustainability and governance
Brazil has an excellent legislative apparatus with respect to environmental protection. The Ministry of the Environment has taken important actions in fighting deforestation. Concerning Agenda 21, after a strong impulse determined by the Rio Summit in 1992 the subject has been gradually abandoned. The Commission for Policy and Sustainable Development and for the Brazilian Agenda 21 prepared the Brazilian Agenda 21 in 2002, however little has been achieved to implement it. Few cities have a local Agenda 21. Major real estate companies have developed large projects under legal determination and subject to public hearings, but the different aspects of the negotiations between the government and the private entities are not always very clear to the population. There is a great governmental effort to expand the population's access to the Internet and the use of ICTs has been increasing in the public administration. Approximately 250 cities are transforming themselves into Digital Cities.

Planning system in practice
The "Statute of the City" established new legal instruments, amplified the role of the municipality in controlling urban land use and ensure community participation, but it has weakened supra-local levels like the States, and consequently the Metropolitan Areas. However, many municipalities do not internalise the idea of the plan as a management tool, while community participation is limited. Local building and urban standards, frequently based on international norms, are beyond the economic capacity of many people, thus giving rise to widespread informal developments, especially on the outskirts of large cities.

SOUTH AMERICA
CHILE

FAST FACTS

- **Total Area:** 756,945 km²
- **Total Population:** 16,341,929
- **Population Growth:** 1%
- **Unemployment Rate:** 6,7%
- **GDP:** $ 277 billion
- **GDP per capita:** $ 19,887
- **GDP growth rate:** 4.1%

SETTLEMENTS STRUCTURE

- **Capital City:** Santiago
     6.061.185 pop
- **Second City:** Valparaiso-Viña del Mar
     734.406 pop
- **Density:** 8.7 pop/km²
- **Urban Population:** 89%

INSTITUTIONAL STRUCTURE

Republic composed of 15 regions, subdivided in provinces and communes.

Read on: www.minvu.cl; http://portal.mma. gob.cl; www.mop.cl

Administrative competence for planning

The Ministry of Housing and Urban Development (MINVU) is in charge of urban planning at national level and the review, approval and modification of the planning instruments at all levels. The MINVU Regional Secretariats elaborate regional and inter-communal plans and oversee the planning processes at the local level, particularly in urban areas.

Main planning legislation

Law on Urban Planning and Construction 1975, Urbanism and Construction General Ordinance 1992 and Technical Standards to be applied in projects elaboration.

Planning and implementation instruments

There is no binding instrument of national planning but in 2013 a National Urban Development Policy was approved. At regional level, the MINVU Regional Secretariats are in charge of Regional Urban Development Plans, Inter-communal Plans and Metropolitan Plans. Communal urban planning is performed through the Municipal Land Use Plan.

Development control

The Municipal Land Use Plan sets the rules for land use changes, subdivision of land or building. If the municipality does not have this instrument, the rules of higher territorial plans are applied.

Sustainability and governance

The Environment Law 1994 establishes the instruments for environmental evaluation and management. Territorial planning has changed from a centralised model to a horizontal one based on the relations between the governmental agencies and the participation of the key stakeholders in urban development. However, in the absence of an institutional framework linking territorial planning citizen participation movements have emerged with the aim to modify and/or stop large plans and projects The Transparency and Access to Public Information Law 2008 obliges the state administration to make the existing territorial plans available in their websites. The MINVU Urban Observatory web site contains all the plans produced in the country. The wealthier municipalities have implemented a similar service.

Planning system in practice

The plan to update the planning tools implemented by the MINVU has allowed the drawing up or the upgrading of regional plans and municipa plans, demonstrating the technical and financial dependence on these administrations regarding central government. The existence of multiple legal exceptions obviating the regulations of the municipal plans reduced their capacity to organise urban development. Examples of these are the construction of social housing outside the urban perimeter, or the increase of floor area and building height. However, there is widespread consensus in the country about the need to strengthen planning implementation and enforcement. This challenge demands the updating of the General Law or Urban Planning and Construction in order to strengthen the powers of the regional and local administrations.

COLOMBIA

FAST FACTS

- **Total Area:** 1.141.748 km²
- **Total Population:** 47,387,109
- **Population Growth:** 1,18 %
- **Unemployment Rate:** 9.2%
- **GDP:** $ 642.7 billion
- **GDP per capita:** $13,500
- **GDP growth rate:** 5%

SETTLEMENTS STRUCTURE

- **Capital City:** Bogota
  7.467.804 pop
- **Second City:** Medellin
  2,184,000 pop
- **Density:** 4,1 pop/km²
- **Urban Population:** 76%

INSTITUTIONAL STRUCTURE

Republic composed of 32 departments, 10 special districts and 1,100 municipalities.

Read on: www.dnp.gov.co; www.minambiente.gov.co; www.minvivienda.gov.co

Administrative competence for planning

The National Planning Department (DNP) is responsible for monitoring the implementation of the national policies. The departments coordinate the relationships between national and territorial entities and provide guidance for territorial development. Municipalities and special districts are responsible for land use planning and the promotion of citizen participation.

Main planning legislation

There is an array of legal bodies concerning planning matters, but the main ones are the Law on Territorial Planning 1997 and the Law on Mechanisms of Transference of Construction and Development Rights 1998.

Planning and implementation instruments

At national level, the four-year Indicative Plans are based on the National Development Plan proposals. At municipal level there are three types of plans depending on the size of their population: Land Use Plan for municipalities up to 100,000 inhabitants; Basic Land Use Plan, between 30,000 and 100,000 inhabitants, and Basic Land Use Scheme for less than 30,000 inhabitants.

Development control

The urban regulations of the use, settlement and exploitation of building land are the following: structural regulations, to fulfil the objectives of the spatial development plan; general regulations concerning land use and intensity of use, and complementary regulations to outline actions and proceedings for short term development.

Sustainability and governance

The Law 99-1993 stated the creation of the Ministry of Environment and the National Environmental System, which defines the roles of the different administrations and the conditions for public participation. The internal armed conflict induced the migration of 5 million people, a situation that forced the national government to organise new political institutions and planning mechanisms. The Victims and Land Restitution Act 2012 and the National System for Comprehensive Attention and Reparation of Victims (SNARIV) are in charge of the related matters. The challenge of people´s relocation demand different roles and responsibilities, particularly at municipality level, for which it is necessary to clarify processes and procedures.

Planning system in practice

The territorial decentralisation model has been able to create the basic conditions for the territorial entities to provide goods and services and to reduce the levels of poverty, but their implementation capacity is limited due to appropriation of the administrations by political groups linked to legal or illegal interests. Since the criteria for development planning differ from land use and environmental preservation, the overlapping of administrative functions is used by local authorities to implement arbitrary instruments regulating land use and licensing environmental or community activities. Attention should focus on the management deficiencies arising from patronage or corrupt practices.

ECUADOR

FAST FACTS

- **Total Area:** 256.370 km²
- **Total Population:** 15,761,731
- **Population Growth:** 1,35 %
- **Unemployment Rate:** 5 %
- **GDP:** $88.186 billion
- **GDP per capita:** $11,200
- **GDP growth rate:** 4%

SETTLEMENTS STRUCTURE

- **Capital City:** Quito
  2,505,344 pop

- **Largest City:** Guayaquil
  2. 560,505 pop

- **Density:** 61pop/km²
- **Urban Population:** 64%

INSTITUTIONAL STRUCTURE

Republic composed of 4 regions, 24 provinces, 3 districts, 221 cantons and 1,500 parishes.

Read on: www.planificacion.gob.ec; www. gestionderiesgos.gob.ec.

Administrative competence for planning
National spatial planning is in charge of the National Secretary of Planning and Development (SENPLADES). Provinces, cantons and parishes have the responsibility to produce and implement their own physical plans.

Main planning legislation
The main statutes are the Ecuador Constitution 2008 which sets up that the Decentralised Autonomous Governments (GAD) should plan their development and formulate the respective territorial plans, articulated with national, regional, cantonal and parish planning. Other legislations are the Organic Law on Territorial Organisation and the Code of Planning and Public Finances.

Planning and implementation instruments
The National Plan for Good Living 2009-2013 establishes the sectoral policies for territorial planning according to the national strategy. Each GAD will produce and implement the Spatial Development Plan (POT) based on the instruments and institutions of the National Decentralised Participatory Planning System.

Development control
Municipal and metropolitan POT's will provide regulation, control and penalties regarding land use. The Ministry of Housing and Urban Development, the Chamber of Building of Quito and the Executive Committee of the NEC (Ecuadorian Building Normative) produce the official parameters for the construction.

Sustainability and governance
The Constitution defines a sustainable development model. Each GAD will implement environmental management policies following the national guidelines. There is a National System for Prevention, Risks Management and Natural Disasters. Yasuni National Park is the main reservoir of biodiversity on the planet, home of two indigenous communities. The Constitution established citizen participation as a way to strengthen the representative and participatory democracy. The city of knowledge Yachay is the first planned city in Ecuador, which looks at biotechnology and ICT's as the main drivers of national economic development.

Planning system in practice
The process of decentralisation is seeking the drawing up of the development plans including active citizens' participation using the mechanisms stipulated in the Constitution. The Autonomous Decentralised Governments implement their plans according to the guidelines provided by the upper tiers of government, which allow greater efficiency in the implementation and control processes. The main objective of the country is to coordinate plans and programmes, while identifying the potential of each region. The state has a permanent connection with the GAD's, in order to promote Ecuador not only as a territorially planned country, but as an economically strong country in relation to the rest of the Latin-American countries.

GUYANA

FAST FACTS

- **Total Area:** 214,969 km²
- **Total Population:** 747,884
- **Population Growth:** -0,04%
- **Unemployment Rate:** 11,1%
- **GDP:** $5.498 billion
- **GDP per capita:** $ 6,900
- **GDP growth rate:** 3,3%

SETTLEMENTS STRUCTURE

- **Capital City:** Georgetown
    118,363 pop
- **Second City:** Linden
    29,232 pop
- **Density:** 3,5 pop/km²
- **Urban Population:** 26,4%

INSTITUTIONAL STRUCTURE

Republic composed of 10 administrative regions.

Read on: www.chpa.gov.gy; www.lands. gov.gy

Administrative competence for planning

Central Housing and Planning Authority (CHPA) under the Ministry of Housing, is in charge of development control, urban development and planning. Guyana Lands and Surveys Commission (GLSC) performs national and regional land use planning. Local bodies have limited planning competences.

Main planning legislation

The Town and Country Planning Act 1946 provides the statutory basis for the preparation and adoption of town planning schemes, and for zoning.

Planning and implementation instruments

There is no zoning enabling legislation nor well defined comprehensive zoning ordinances tied to the building permit and enforcement process. Approved town plans do not exist for most of the urban areas, and regional plans are only now being developed. The main planning instruments are development control standards to guide the issuing and review of building permits.

Development control

The CHPA oversees development control matters which are otherwise shared between the central and the local level. Residential buildings with less than three stories in urban areas are controlled by the municipalities alone. For areas which have an approved plan building applications can be assessed for compliance with the plan.

Sustainability and governance

A Sustainable Development Bureau has been established under the Office of the President, in charge of leading the national effort to identify sustainable goals and targets. The Energy Agency promotes the development of renewable energy. The Environmental Protection Agency implements environmental policy and promotes environmental management. The Forestry Commission regulates forestry. There are a number of bodies that engender inclusive governance. To ensure coordination in the land and natural resources and environment sectors, a cross-sectoral committee has been established to resolve and avoid conflicts. The National Touchaus Council comprising the Captains of Amerindian Villages. ICT's capacity is increasingly being established and applied in city and regional land use planning.

Planning system in practice

The GLSC has prepared land use plans for each of the regions of the country. CHPA has prepared several town plans, including extensive public consultations. Two critical aspects can be identified: the concurrent jurisdiction of different institutions for regional planning and the lack of enabling legislation for regional planning, thus although plans are being drawn up and approved their implementation is not backed up by enforcement capability. Also the local level is lacking technical and professional competence to carry out its planning responsibilities adequately and for that reason the central authorities are carrying out local planning with some local consultation.

PARAGUAY

FAST FACTS

- **Total Area:** 406,752 km²
- **Total Population:** 6,672,633
- **Population Growth:** 1,2%
- **Unemployment Rate:** 11,2 %
- **GDP:** $ 30.56 billion
- **GDP per capita:** 6,800 $
- **GDP growth rate:** 12 %

SETTLEMENTS STRUCTURE

- **Capital City:** Asunción
  512,919 pop
- **Second City:** Ciudad del Este
  312.652 pop
- **Density:** 17 pop/km²
- **Urban Population:** 60%

INSTITUTIONAL STRUCTURE

Republic composed of 17 provinces (departamentos) and 245 municipalities including the capital district.

Read on: www.stp.gov.py; www.seam. gov.py

Administrative competence for planning

Two State Secretariats are involved in national territorial planning: the Technical Economic and Social Development Planning Secretariat, whose role is to devise indicative national plans, and the Environment Secretariat, in charge of applying environmental regulations. The provincial governments are responsible for formulating plans in accordance with the national plan. Municipalities are drawing up urban plans.

Main planning legislation

There is no a specific legislation about physical planning but there is an ample set of sectoral plans affecting the territory, mainly related to environmental issues. The Organic Municipal Law 2010 defines the role of the local governments, including territorial planning.

Planning and implementation instruments

The National Development Plan 2008-2013 designed the strategic guidelines for the country. The provinces produce plans, programmes and development projects. Municipalities have to draft two types of plans: Sustainable Development Plans and Urban and Territorial Development Plans.

Development control

Controls are performed through municipal ordinances, building codes and building standards, although very few municipalities have these instruments.

Sustainability and governance

The National Environmental Policy assumes that spatial planning is one of the basic tools for the country´s sustainable development. The Secretariat of Environment establishes and implements measures to protect the environment. The lack of transparency related to the activities of the agents of the public administration and the private sector is a constant criticism. The use of ICTs in the production and dissemination of plans, and in the public participation in planning is still in its initial stages.

Planning system in practice

Paraguay does not have a land use law and the related legislation is dispersed. The absence of social, economic and environmental policies to direct the urban growth has led to an uncontrolled rural migration which has given place to large illegal settlements in the fringe areas of the main cities. Cities follow the traditional management model, characterised by the lack of prevision and the invisibility of environmental problems. Regarding territorial planning, the interest of the national government over territorial opportunities has been traditionally focused on the land capacity for agricultural purposes, equating this vision to the territorial planning concept. The return to democracy in the late 1990s did not include physical planning in the national agenda but an interest of solving territorial misbalance started by 2000. The non-existence of a comprehensive and clear legal framework prevents the implementation of planning proposals, nevertheless few urban development plans have been drawn up as pilot projects.

PERU

Administrative competence for planning
The Directorate of Urbanism of the Ministry of Housing, Construction and Sanitation is in charge of urban planning at national level. Regional governments are vested to develop regional land development plans while municipal land use planning can be developed by both, provincial and district municipalities.

Main planning legislation
The most important urban planning legislation is stated in the Organic Law of Municipalities 2003. Several laws exist at national level, including the Environment Law 2005.

Planning and implementation instruments
Al national level there is the National Strategic Development Plan towards 2021. Regional governments prepare and approve regional development plans in agreement with the municipalities and civil society. Provincial governments produce territorial and metropolitan plans.

Development control
The formal urbanisation process falls under the municipal ordinances and two codes: Law of Subdivisions and Building Construction 2007 and National Regulation for Building Construction amended 2014.

Sustainability and governance
Sustainable development and environmental management have become a state policy. Several proposals were approved: National Climate Change Strategy 2003, National System of Environmental Management 2005, Environmental Law 2005, Ministry of Environment 2008, National Environmental Policy 2009, Environmental Action National Plan 2011-2021, Environmental Action National Agenda 2013-2014. The 2015-2016 Agenda is in progress. Formally, urban and territorial planning processes endorse the principles of decentralisation, administrative coordination, public and private partnership and citizen participation. However, the national legal framework for territorial governance is only partially applied. There is very little impact of ICT's on the planning process although efforts were made by creating the National Office for Electronic Government and Information Technology and the Digital Agenda in 2011.

Planning system in practice
The existing legislation is complex and planning instruments are not adequate to solve urban problems. Physical planning has been largely neglected since the national planning priorities have a strong economic bias. The strong dependence of local governments on national level decision-making and the low level of coordination among the different public instances favours client list relationships, centralism and corruption. Urban development plans are prepared according to a "blueprint" format, far from the local reality. Monitoring and evaluation are not common practices. Planning activities depend on several different authorities, which generates lack of authority and confusion. The magnitude of the informal urban processes is a clear confirmation of the negligible influence of the plans to guide and regulate urban growth.

SURINAME

Read on: www.gov.sr

Administrative competence for planning

The responsibility for physical planning lies with the central government. The National Planning Office is responsible for national and regional planning while the Ministry of Public Works is responsible for spatial plans for settlements.

Main planning legislation

Planning Act 1973 gives the provisions for national and regional planning. Urban Planning Act 1972 gives the provisions for urban destination, development and cultivation of land.

Planning and implementation instruments

National and regional plans, Structure and zoning plans and Allotment/ parceling of urban land

Development control

The control mechanisms for larger integral spatial plans are not in place. Suriname still approaches spatial planning in a more fragmented way, due to focusing on the small scale. Main control mechanisms are allotment and building regulations.

Sustainability and governance

There are several national laws for the protection of natural areas. The Nature Preservation Law was approved in 1954. Suriname has signed Agenda 21 and is party to several conventions and agreements. Sustainability of the spatial plans has to be laid down in a maintenance plan. Such a plan does not yet exist and will be developed within the scope of the zoning plans. Stakeholder groups comprised of the government, private sector, NGO's and civil society participate in the design of land use plans through consultations and workshops. These consultations contribute to the acceptation of the plans, as well as to corrective measures. During the implementation phase, stakeholders assist monitoring and are evaluating each phase of the project through participation in activities such as training and awareness programmes. In the implementation phase stakeholders assist monitoring and evaluation of each phase of the project. Availability of local content and services on-line is limited and government websites are mostly informational.

Planning system in practice

There are no official spatial plans at the larger, integral scale. Therefore there is no legal document which can be used for guiding and managing spatial developments. The present planning mechanisms are not in balance and spatial planning in practice is reflected in the allotment process, which is the scope with which Suriname approaches spatial planning. Policy makers have not recognised the importance of planning. Spatial planning is uncontrolled and the lack of zoning plans makes it possible to have urban development (or any other spatial development) at almost any location. Currently, the government is working towards having spatial plans established. Preparations for structure plans and zoning plans are in process, despite initiatives to upgrade spatial planning and the need for improvement is substantive.

URUGUAY

FAST FACTS

- **Total Area:** 177,879 km²
- **Total Population:** 3,286,314
- **Population Growth:** 0,19%
- **Unemployment Rate:** 6%
- **GDP:** $70,25 billion
- **GDP per capita:** 20.500$
- **GDP growth rate:** 3,5%

SETTLEMENTS STRUCTURE

- **Capital City:** Montevideo
  1.742.850 pop metro. area
- **Second City:** Salto
  104.028 pop
- **Density:** 19 pop/km²
- **Urban Population:** 96 %

INSTITUTIONAL STRUCTURE

Republic composed of 19 provinces (departamentos) and municipalities.

Read on: www.mvotma.gub.uy; www. mtop.gub.uy

Administrative competence for planning

At a national level, the National Directorate of Panning (DINOT) of the Ministry of Housing, Planning and Environment (MVOTMA) is in charge of national and regional plans. The departments have competences to produce and approve master plans. The sectoral national institutions draw up their own plans without much coordination and consultation of the national planning directorate.

Main planning legislation

The Law 18308 on Territorial Planning and Sustainable Development 2009 sets up the National and Departmental Planning System. The Urban Centres Law 1946 still remains as the main urban regulation text.

Planning and implementation instruments

DINOT has to elaborate the National Directives. Regions are in charge of producing Regional Strategies. Departmental planning instruments are Directives, Ordinances and Local Plans.

Development control

The public sector agencies have the competence to authorise land subdivision projects and building permissions according to the national law and local ordinances. It is frequent that law and ordinances exceptions are authorised under stakeholder pressures.

Sustainability and governance

There is a social concern about environmental sustainability. The country signed the most important U.N. environmental conventions and incorporates environmental protection as a political objective. But the environmental care exists only in the political discourse since the priority is to favour economic investment. The economic growth process, the spatial expansions of cities and the changes of land use are mainly unplanned processes, and are led by big national and international capital. The MVOTMA web page publishes the synthesis of the private proposals and its own analysis and recommendations. The use of ICT's allows people to know about permissions and government decisions.

Planning system in practice

Spatial planning practice has not been used systematically as a tool of territorial administration. Only few cities and Departments have drawn up their plans and only few obtained legal approval. Participation practices are used but they have little chance to change the adopted proposals. The substitution of the traditional cattle rising activities in favour of agriculture and mining production for export have produced rural poverty, migrations and slums increments on urban fringes. Environmental impacts affect the whole territory even though some environment protection actions have been taken. However, the environmental authority is pressured by different stakeholders to get the requested authorisations. There is a need of a new legal framework to provide planning tools and procedures, to increase the institutional coordination and to empower local actors.

VENEZUELA

FAST FACTS

- **Total Area:** 912,050 km²
- **Total Population:** 30.206.307
- **Population Growth:** 1.7%
- **Unemployment Rate:** 7,1%
- **GDP:** $ 438,28 billion
- **GDP per capita:** $ 6,401
- **GDP growth rate:** - 0.5 %

SETTLEMENTS STRUCTURE

- **Capital City:** Caracas

  5.380.668 pop

- **Largest City:** Maracaibo

  2.106.723 pop

- **Density:** 34 pop/km²
- **Urban Population:** 94%

INSTITUTIONAL STRUCTURE

Federal republic composed of 24 states, 335 municipalities and 1,084 parishes.

Read on: www.mppp.gob.ve, www. minamb.gob.ve; www.mvh.gob.ve

Administrative competence for planning

The Ministries of the Popular Power for Planning and Development, for Communes and Social Movements, for Eco-socialism and Water, for Housing and Habitat, among others, establish public policies from the national to the communal level. These policies conform the obligatory legal framework and guidelines to be addressed in the formulation of plans at national, regional-state, local-municipal and communal levels.

Main planning legislation

Between 2008 and 2012 a set of legislations replaced the previous ones to give way to the "XXI Century Socialism". The main one is the Territorial Planning and Management Organic Law 2008 and several acts aimed to empower community councils: Communal Councils Organic Law 2009, Popular and Public Planning Organic Law 2010 and Community Management Law 2012.

Planning and implementation instruments

Each administrative level has the competences of drafting plans: Sectorial Planning National Plan, Regional Development Plan, State Development Plan and Municipal Development Plan.

Development control

Any activity with spatial impacts should request and obtain a Constancy of Conformity of Use from the authorities in charge of the territorial plans. For spontaneous urbanisations the territorial legislation proposes Urban Progressive Developments aimed to improve and legalise these areas. All plans have to be submitted to public consultation.

Sustainability and governance

The 1999 Constitution stipulates that the state shall develop a planning policy to meet the demands of sustainable development with active citizen participation. The Environmental Organic Law updated in 2006 sets the rules and guiding principles for environmental management. The 1999 Constitution established multilevel territorial governance but in practice the model is not applied due to the antagonism existing in the political sphere. The country has a poor performance in terms of transparency and freedom of the press. E-government has brought government services closer to the citizens and the majority of municipalities have websites to perform e-government.

Planning system in practice

The new legislation seeks to solve city and planning difficulties, but many of the problems remain and new ones are arising from the new laws. The radical changes in the urban planning and management system towards the creation of the communal state generate a confrontation of powers which deepens spatial and socio-political segregation and the fragmentation of existing social cohesion. The disconnection between plan formulation and management and between spatial and development plans has reduced the capacity of local governments. The lack of governance and rule of law hamper the existence of a long term national planning vision. The creation of autonomous community councils, legally and financially dependent on the central government, has diluted the role of the local authorities.

Asia & Pacific

BANGLADESH

FAST FACTS

- **Total Area:** 147,570 km²
- **Total Population:** 149,700,000
- **Population Growth:** 1.37%
- **Unemployment Rate:** 5%
- **GDP:** $ 534.6 billion
- **GDP per capita:** $848
- **GDP growth rate:** 6.32%

SETTLEMENTS STRUCTURE

- **Capital City:** Dhaka
  5,378,023 pop
  10,356,500 (metro. area)
- **Second City:** Chittagong
  3,760,000 pop
- **Density:** 1,015 pop/km²
- **Urban Population:** 35.1%

INSTITUTIONAL STRUCTURE

Republic composed of 7 administrative divisions, 64 districts) and 482 sub-districts, divided into 4,451 unions and 87,316 villages.

Read on: www.plancomm.gov.bd; www.mohpw.gov.bd; http://bip.org.bd; www.buet.ac.bd

Administrative competence for planning

The Ministry of Planning prepares economic plans for the country. 2002 a new type of national plan was introduced: Poverty Reduction Strategy Papers. The Ministry of Housing and Public Works includes the Development Authorities for the metropolitan areas and the Urban Development Directorate, responsible for the physical plans of the remaining urban areas. The rural and urban local government systems are governed by the Ministry of Local Government, Rural Development and Cooperatives. Local authorities can formulate and implement local plans.

Main planning legislation

From 1950 to 1970 the legislation was centred on the expansion of major cities. The new legislation focuses on local planning activities: Local Government Ordinance 2008 for implementing local development plans assigned by the central government, and Local Government Ordinance 2009 to produce physical development plans at Division level.

Planning and implementation instruments

Due to the existing urban situation the instruments are concentrating on rehabilitation and upgrading, land readjustment for community redevelopment, provision of serviced land, regularisation of illegal settlements, etc. For new areas, land use zoning is used to control densities and to protect natural and living environments.

Development control

Land use, density control or infrastructure provision is controlled by the corresponding authority. The Bangladesh National Building Code 1993 details standards for building construction.

Sustainability and governance

The pursuit of sustainable development is a constitutional obligation. The Ministry of Environment and Forest is responsible for the corresponding legislation. There are several laws, i.e. Environment Pollution Control Ordinance 1977, Bangladesh Environmental Conservation Act 1995 and Environmental Conservation Rules 1997. Bangladesh has endorsed Agenda 21 and a National Conservation Strategy has been prepared, followed by a National Environment Management Action Plan. Authorities try to incorporate local participation in planning but the lack of stakeholders' knowledge may exclude them. The websites of 'development authorities' ease the dissemination of plans. There are no digital infrastructures regarding the built environment and mobility.

Planning system in practice

The present planning system is both complex and diverse due to the overlapping of planning powers between the central and the local governments. There is no national body for national physical planning and the metropolitan tier (region) is weak. There is a growing consciousness about urban planning in recent years due to visible problems of Dhaka and Chittagong. Some improvement has taken place and both planners and citizens are putting pressure on the government to strengthen planning into an integrated system at national level. the decentralisation process. It is expected that the new planning law will stipulate the functions of the planning council at the central level as well as offices of physical planning at the national and governorate levels. An appropriate planning education is needed to train future planners.

INDIA

FAST FACTS

- **Total Area:** 3,287,263 km²
- **Total Population:** 1,251,695,584
- **Population Growth:** 1.22%
- **Unemployment Rate:** 8,6%
- **GDP:** $ 7.376 trillion
- **GDP per capita:** $ 5,900
- **GDP growth rate:** 7.2%

SETTLEMENTS STRUCTURE

- **Capital City:** New Delhi
  24,953,000 pop
- **Second City:** Mumbai
  20,741,000 pop
- **Density:** 381 pop/km²
- **Urban Population:** 33%

INSTITUTIONAL STRUCTURE

Federal Republic composed of 29 states and 7 union territories.

Read on: http://india.gov.in; http://envfor. nic.in

Administrative competence for planning

Planning is hierarchic and remains centralised despite efforts to decentralise. The Ministry of Urban Affairs and Local Self Government is in charge of planning. The Indian Planning Commission is in charge of planning policies related to the national 5 year plans. NITI (National Institute for Transforming India) was set up in 2015 to foster infrastructure to power growth through connectivity. The States have planning powers at their level and regulate development control. Efforts are made to devolve planning powers to cities, districts and municipalities but implementation is uneven and their powers very limited.

Main planning legislation

The Town and Country Act 1969 with various amendments is the main national planning law. Town and Country Acts exist at State level guided by the Model Town and Country Planning Act, the National planning guidelines, the National Building Code and manuals and toolkits issued in compliance with the national planning framework. The Masterplan for Delhi was legislated centrally through the Delhi Development Act 1957. The centrally legislated Slum Improvement Act 1965 was first applied to Delhi.

Planning and implementation instruments

Planning laws and bodies empowered to make plans, adopt and evaluate them are the main planning instruments at union, state and city levels. The states are empowered to develop their own planning instruments and devolve them at district level following the 73rd & 74th constitutional reforms. The planning instruments are metropolitan, regional plans, master plans, zonal plans and local area plans. India is undergoing rapid urbanisation and the planning system is not able to control its many informal settlements which are emerging in urban as well as rural areas.

Development control

Development control procedures are incorporated in the state planning acts. They are very detailed, prescriptive, in a number of phases. The state commissioners are in charge of implementation and can recall permits in case of non compliance. Only licensed professionals can apply for planning consent and resubmit applications. Public participation is weak and mainly indirect.

Sustainability and governance

Managing the environment formed part of the 12th plan (2012-2017) advocating faster more inclusive sustainable growth. Yet, initiatives under Agenda 21 are left to NGOs and the private sector. Planning remains very bureaucratic and in the hands of administrations which open development to the market despite long standing explorations of devolution of powers and greater citizen empowerment.

Planning system in practice

The Indian planning system is not capable of mustering the rapid urbanisation process, nor of stemming mounting environmental degradation and lacks effective institutional capacity and technical tools for sustainable development. Urbanisation and rural urban migration remain major challenges, as are regional disparities, lack of infrastructure, poor water and air quality and waste disposal.

FAST FACTS

- **Total Area:** 2,724,900 km²
- **Total Population:** 16,909,800
- **Population Growth:** 1.14%
- **Unemployment Rate:** 5.1%
- **GDP:** $203,520
- **GDP per capita:** $12,118
- **GDP growth rate:** 38.99 %

SETTLEMENTS STRUCTURE

- **Capital City:** Astana
  778,200 pop
- **Second City:** Almaty
  1,475,400 pop
- **Density:** 6.2 pop/km²
- **Urban Population:** 55%

INSTITUTIONAL STRUCTURE

Republic composed of 14 regions (oblast), subdivided in sub-regional municipal districts, and 2 cities of national importance subdivided in city districts.

Read on: www.minplan.kz; www. minregion.gov.kz; www.egov.kz; www. nationalplan.kz; www.grado.kz

Administrative competence for planning
The central government passes laws and issues and supervises national sectoral policies. The Ministry of Economy and Budget Planning (MEBP) and the Ministry of Regional Development (MRD) are the main bodies in charge of territorial development. Regional and local governments are in charge of regional and local planning.

Main planning legislation
The main legislative bodies are, among others, the System of State Planning 2009, the Law on Government and Local Self-Government 2001, the Land Code 2003, the Environmental Code 2007 and the Architectural, Town Planning and Building Activities 2001.

Planning and implementation instruments
The main planning instrument is the Master Plan for the Organisation of the Territory of the Republic of Kazakhstan. The Interregional Master Plans for Territorial Development are carried out and controlled by the MRD with the approval of the MEBP. Master Plans for Settlements are drawn up by local authorities.

Development control
The appropriate level in charge of development control are mainly the municipalities, The Chief Architect and the Department of Architecture and Urban Planning implement control, but representatives of the regional level may also participate in the process of controlling public development. Private initiatives are possible, subject to approval in principle by relevant executive public bodies.

Sustainability and governance
The national government is aligned with international sustainable initiatives: Agenda 21, Millennium Summit 2000, World Summit on Sustainable Development 2002, UN Commission on Sustainable Development, Environment for Europe, Environmental Sustainability in Asia, and World Business Council for Sustainable Development. The country starts developing a sustainable energy sector and the International Expo 2017 will focus on the future of this issue. E-government is a priority at the highest political level and the elaboration of an e-government strategy emphasises the role of information and communication technology for better governance. The Analytical System of the Master Plan for the Organisation of the Republic of Kazakhstan was built up to serve as a decision-making support.

Planning system in practice
The planning system in Kazakhstan has been considerably improved during the last years: a switch towards 'long-term strategic planning'; the development of state institutions responsible for coordination of the territorial planning from nation to local level; the change from local level master planning towards a more comprehensive system of multi-level planning; and the improvement of the coordination among different administrative levels and civil society. However, planning practice is still embedded in the soviet planning culture and it is necessary to educate and retrain planners to face a new reality. the decentralisation process. It is expected that the new planning law will stipulate the functions of the planning council at the central level as well as offices of physical planning at the national and governorate levels. An appropriate planning education is needed to train future planners.

KYRGYZSTAN

FAST FACTS

- **Total Area:** 199,951 km²
- **Total Population:** 5,776,500
- **Population Growth:** 2%
- **Unemployment Rate:** 14.6%
- **GDP:** $ 6.47 billion
- **GDP per capita:** $ 2,400
- **GDP growth rate:** 3.85 %

SETTLEMENTS STRUCTURE

- **Capital City:** Bishkek
  854,000 pop
- **Second City:** Osh
  255,900 pop
- **Density:** 29 pop/km²
- **Urban Population:** 35.3%

INSTITUTIONAL STRUCTURE

Republic composed of 7 provinces divided into municipal districts and villages, and two independent cities of national importance.

Read on: http://www.stat.kg; www.for.kg/ news-210509-ru.html

Administrative competence for planning

The Parliament is responsible for national policies and development strategies. Strategic, economic, social, environmental and territorial planning is executed by the Cabinet of Ministers, composed of several bodies: 15 Ministries, 7 state agencies, 8 special state commissions, 2 inspections and 3 state funds. Regional planning is a provincial competence, including departments of ministries, governmental agencies and departments on urban planning and architecture. Local level planning is the competence of districts, including departments of ministries and governmental agencies, and villages. Civil society is also engaged in the planning system through the work of NGOs and local communities.

Main planning legislation

There are more than 150 laws, regulations and standards relevant to some degree to urban planning and development, the main ones being the Land Code 1999, the Law on Urban Planning and Architecture 1994, amended in 2014 and the Code on Urban Planning and Construction 2013.

Planning and implementation instruments

The planning system has been developed recently in the framework of the urban planning reform (2001-2005), a project sponsored by USAID (United States Agency for International Development). The Code on Urban Planning and Construction, 2013, defined the basis for drawing up national, regional and settlement master plans. Drafts have been produced for some regions and cities. A detailed analysis of existing practices has been carried out and suggestion made for practical steps in the development of the urban planning system.

Development control

The State Inspection on Ecological and Technical Safety ensures the implementation of the Standard Rules of Housing Development, Land Tenure and Improvement of Settlements (2009). 11 cities have developed these rules.

Sustainability and governance

The National Sustainable Development Strategy (2013 – 2017) is a strategic document aimed to build a democratic state, to achieve a sustainable development and to integrate the country in the global economy. Self-governance at the local and regional levels is the basic principle. To favour economic development there are favourable conditions for local and foreign investors, particularly in the tourism and transportation sector. Unfortunately, urban planning and construction have not been considered as priority targets.

Planning system in practice

Kyrgyzstan has the preconditions for a viable planning system since laws, rules, regulations and standards have been approved and some master plans were produced, but much more is still needed to do: allocation of resources to appropriate planning institutions, defence of ownership rights by transparent functional legislation, reduction of state control, fighting against corruption, etc.

MALDIVES

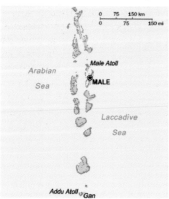

Administrative competence for planning

The Department of National Planning, Ministry of Finance and Treasury, is responsible for the National Development Plan and strategic spatial planning policies. The Ministry of Housing and Infrastructure is responsible for planning guidance for islands and cities. The Ministry of Tourism, Arts and Culture is responsible for the development of resort islands and tourist facilities. The Ministry of Environment and Energy is responsible for environment protection. The Local Government Authority, Ministry of Home Affairs, coordinates the activities of the Atoll and Island Councils.

Main planning legislation

There are no planning legislation, building legislation or building codes. The main laws are: Maldivian Land Act 2002, Environment Protection and Preservation Law 1993 and EIA Regulations amended 2011.

Planning and implementation instruments

There are few regional and local planning instruments and building controls. The Maldives National Building Act 2010 is in draft and only used as a reference, consequently, no monitoring or enforcement mechanisms are used. The government has prepared the development plan for 20 islands and the Strategic National Action Plan for Disaster Risk Reduction and Climate Change Adaptation (2010-2020).

Development control

There is no formal development control system. The Malé City Council issues building permits. The Housing Development Corporation controls developments on Hulhumalé Island. For other inhabited islands, developments are approved by the Ministry of Housing and Infrastructure. The Ministry of Tourism controls resort islands and tourist facilities. The Maldives National Building Code Handbook 2008 defines the building requirements.

Sustainability and governance

Sustainability is a key factor in the Maldives vital for survival under climate change. The National Adaptation Programme of Action and the Maldives Climate Change Policy Framework are comprehensive instruments to adapt to climate change. However
EIA Regulations are not binding. The Strategic National Action Plan for Disaster Risk Reduction is promoting decentralisation, governance, communities' empowerment, local development and risk sensitivity.

Planning system in practice

The Decentralisation Act 2010 has not led to the devolution of planning yet. People remain concentrated on a few islands despite the new development of Hulhumale island. The greater Malé area remains the focus of planning development and implementation while the process in other atoll islands is much slower. The strategic National Action Plan may help to foster sectoral cooperation giving priority to planning implementation. The quality of the current plans reflects the limited planning capacity, training, experience and baseline data. A more informal, flexible and organic approach to planning is needed instead of the currently practised formal planning legislation route.

PAKISTAN

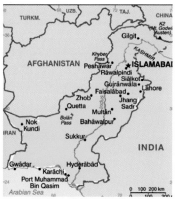

FAST FACTS

- **Total Area:** 796,095 km²
- **Total Population:** 207,830,424
- **Population Growth:** 2.69%
- **Unemployment Rate:** 19,68%
- **GDP:** $231 billion
- **GDP per capita:** $802.45
- **GDP growth rate:** 3.59%

SETTLEMENTS STRUCTURE

- **Capital City:** Islamabad
  1,264,448 pop
- **Largest City:** Karachi
  14,664,932 pop
- **Density:** 261 pop/km²
- **Urban Population:** 33%

INSTITUTIONAL STRUCTURE

Federal Republic composed of 4 provinces divided in districts and tehsils, a capital territory, federally administered tribal areas, Gilgit-Baltistan region and Azad Jammu & Kashmir self-governing territory.

Read on: www.pakistan.gov.pk; www. pc.gov.pk; environment.gov.pk

Administrative competence for planning

The state defines the development planning framework and the policies which are incorporated in the development and planning initiatives at regional and district levels. The tehsil authorities are responsible for the preparation, approval and implementation of spatial plans and the exercise of building and planning controls.

Main planning legislation

No entirely dedicated setup exists at the Federal Level to control and guide planning activities. The Devolution Plan of 2000 put into effect through the Local Government Ordinances of 2001 was passed individually by each province. The Punjab Local Government Ordinance came into effect in 2001, and was adopted later on, with some alterations in the Sindh and KPK regions.

Planning and implementation instruments

The state prepares and implements policies such as National Housing Policy 2013, Environmental Conservation Strategy 2009, Five Year Development Plans, etc. At provincial level the instruments are diverse. At district level, they are master planning and development plans and at tehsil level, land use classification, re-classification and redevelopment plan, action area plan, housing schemes layout plan, land subdivision rules, etc.

Development control

District, tehsil and union councils plan the development through zoning and building regulations, but the enforcement is weak, which results in many infringements.

Sustainability and governance

Environmental protection awareness has increased over the years. Pakistan Environmental Protection Agency Act 1997, EIA, Initial Environmental Examination, National Conservation Strategy 2001, Environmental Management Reports and Plans are compulsory for existing and new developments. National Conservation Strategies bind all levels of governance. Although the Local Government Ordinance 2001 enhances public participation it is still at infancy stage.

Planning system in practice

Cities and small towns are growing fast and the overall situation presents housing shortage, slums and squatter settlements, inefficient public transport networks, encroachments, inadequate social facilities and infrastructures. The absence of consolidated Town Planning Ordinances affects planning activities at all governmental levels. The devolution of power to districts and tehsils has promoted numerous planning initiatives but steps toward implementation require considerations. Several factors are affecting planning practice: ignorant attitudes of professionals as well as the public, political pressures, long bureaucratic procedures, technically ill-qualified officials or non-technical officials running government offices, lack of funds to carry out projects resulting in red tape and low quality professional services from the private sector. However, disaster risk reduction is expected from development and land use plans at district and tehsil levels, as well as more active community participation.

CENTRAL ASIA
SRI LANKA

FAST FACTS

- **Total Area:** 62,705 km²
- **Total Population:** 20,653,000
- **Population Growth:** 1%
- **Unemployment Rate:** 4.9%
- **GDP:** $71.57 billion
- **GDP per capita:** $2,399
- **GDP growth rate:** 8%

SETTLEMENTS STRUCTURE

- **Capital City:** Colombo
  642,163 pop
- **Second City:** Kandy
  110,049 pop
- **Density:** 329 pop/km²
- **Urban Population:** 18.3%

INSTITUTIONAL STRUCTURE

Republic composed of 9 provinces and 25 districts.

Read on: www.pubad.gov.lk; www.nppd. gov.lk; www.urbanmin.gov.lk

Administrative competence for planning

Three levels are responsible for the planning system: provincial, district and local. There are several national planning agencies: the Urban Development Authority, responsible of urban plans; the National Physical Planning Department, responsible for national and regional planning, and the Board of Investment, responsible for the Export Processing Zones plans. The National Development Policy Framework, launched in 2010, sets the country´s future vision and its role in South Asia.

Main planning legislation

The basic physical planning legal framework is based on British rules. The main law is the Town and Country Planning Ordinance 1946, amended in 2000 as the Town and Country Planning Act Nº 49. Other legal bodies are the Urban Development Authority Law 1978, which established the Urban Development Authority and the Planning and Building Guidelines and Regulations for the urban areas, the Board of Investment Law, the National Environmental Act 1980, the National Housing Development Authority Act 1979, the Coast Conservation Act 1981, the Sri Lanka Land Reclamation and Development Corporation 1968, amended in 2006, and the Sri Lanka Disaster Management Act 2005.

Planning and implementation instruments

The National Physical Planning Department produced the National Physical Planning Policy and Plan, approved in 2007. The Urban Development Authority promotes economic, social and physical development of the declared development areas and provides assistance to local authorities. The Board of Investment plans and designs the Export Processing Zones.

Development control

The hierarchy of the plans provides the framework for controlling development and the use of land.

Sustainability and governance

The main outcome of the National Physical Planning policy was the delimitation of fragile areas. The Coastal Fragile Area is providing a natural buffer zone to protect people from adverse natural effects, such as coastal erosion, tsunamis and increased sea level resulting from global warming.

Planning system in practice

Local autonomy for carrying out planning and development activities is limited due to the lack of resources and qualified technicians. This is giving rise to growing dependency of local planning authorities on the national planning agencies. The interest of the state is to impel national and regional development in priority areas: the Colombo Metropolitan Region and Northern and Eastern regions affected by terrorist activities. This has reinforced existing regional disparities. It is expected that the Department of National Physical Planning will be able to reduce disparities through the preparation, implementation and approval of provincial physical plans.

UZBEKISTAN

FAST FACTS

- **Total Area:** 447,400 km²
- **Total Population:** 30,488,600
- **Population Growth:** 65%
- **Unemployment Rate:** 5,2%
- **GDP:** $ 62,6 billion
- **GDP per capita::** $3,272
- **GDP growth rate:** 65,71

SETTLEMENTS STRUCTURE

- **Capital City:** Tashkent
  2,352, 900 pop
- **Second City:** Samarkand
  509,000 pop
- **Density:** 68 pop/km²
- **Urban Population:** 51%

INSTITUTIONAL STRUCTURE

Republic composed of 12 regions (viloyat), divided into municipal districts, and the Autonomous Republic of Karakalpakstan.

Read on: http://www.gov.uz/ru; www. davarx.uz; www.uznature.uz

Administrative competence for planning

Town-planning projects at various levels have to pass complex town-planning examinations according to the orders established by the State Committee for Architecture and Construction, under the Cabinet of Ministers. The capital city, Tashkent, is an independent administrative and legal unit.

Main planning legislation

There is an array of legal bodies, the main ones being: SHNK 2.07.01-03 (planning and building for urban and rural settlements), SHNK 1.03.10-06 (instruction for the urban and rural planning documentation), and SHNK 1.03.06-13 (Rules on State examination).

Planning and implementation instruments

There are 12 types of project development: 5 for the national level, 2 for the regional level, 3 for the district level, as well as 5 for the local level.

Development control

Each administrative level has the capacity to control its territorial development.

Sustainability and governance

Uzbekistan adopted the National Strategy for Sustainable Development in 1997. Several laws, codes and guidance documents on environmental protection and rational use of natural resources were approved. The country ratified a number of international conventions. The State Committee for Nature Protection coordinates the execution of several international projects. Uzbekistan has a comprehensive programme for the development of the national information and communication system for the period 2013-2020. The introduction of "Electronic Government" is also expected soon.

Planning system in practice

Since the independence in 1991, the government has aimed at promoting self-government. However, the presence of the state permeates all governmental levels and maintains lower levels subordinated hierarchically, thus blurring their responsibilities. The lack of a comprehensive urbanisation policy has led to a "concentration model", concentrating the economic activities and the population in cities and major towns. The urban population growth rate is several times larger than the rate of job creation. Planning and implementation depend on municipal budgets, which depend on their economic achievements. At the beginning of 2012, 88 small and medium-sized cities were included in the rural administrative apparatus, without any urban planning responsibility. Chronic shortages of local budgets lead to an accelerated wear of the local infrastructure. The following tasks are put forward: improve the territorial development policy and the institutional arrangements for managing urban settlements; develop new urban development standards; integrate housing and urban utilities reconstruction on the basis of plans for a period of 20-30 years; prioritise urban infrastructure in line with the pace of the urbanisation process; regulate rural migration to large cities and, above all, produce comprehensive programmes of a strategic nature.

CAMBODIA

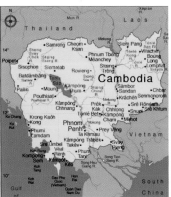

FAST FACTS

- **Total Area:** 181,035 km²
- **Total Population:** 14,677,000
- **Population Growth:** 1.3%
- **Unemployment Rate:** 2.7%
- **GDP:** 15,191 mill
- **GDP per capita::** $1,036
- **GDP growth rate:** 7.6%

SETTLEMENTS STRUCTURE

- **Capital City:** Phnom Penh
  1,501,725 pop
- **Second City:** Siem Reap
  230,000 pop
- **Density:** 80 pop/km²
- **Urban Population:** 30%

INSTITUTIONAL STRUCTURE

Constitutional monarchy composed of 24 provinces and 1 municipality, subdivided into districts and

Read on: www.mlmupc.gov.kh; www.mop. gov.kh; www.csacambodia.org

Administrative competence for planning

The Ministries of Land Management, Urban Planning and Construction (MLMUPC), Public Works and Transport, Economy and Finance, and Environment are represented in the National Committee for Land Management and Urban Planning where all major decisions on planning are taken. The institutional framework and the technical capacities are still limited, especially at provincial and local level.

Main planning legislation

The emerging legal framework is a mix of policies, laws, circulars and regulations, among others the Rectangular Strategy and National Strategic Development 2014-2018, the National Policy on Spatial Planning (NPSP) 2011, the Organic Law 2008, Law on Land Management and Urban Planning 2013, in draft, and Land Policy 2009.

Planning and implementation instruments

The MLMUPC are covering the demand for urban development plans, albeit constrained by the lack of an adequate planning format. Except for the Battambang master plan, all municipal plans are elaborated by the national government. Not many have been produced and most of those are not yet approved. The NPSP has proposed a hierarchy of plans: regional/global supra national level i.e. ASEAN and Greater Mekong Sub-region; national strategic development plans, provincial spatial plans, district land-use master plans, capital/municipal land-use master plans and land-use plans and commune land-use plan.

Development control

Sub-decree No. 86 on Construction Permits 1997 remains the legal document which is being used to control urban development (land use) and provide construction permits.

Sustainability and governance

Cambodia has adopted the UN agenda for sustainable national development. The Development Cooperation and Partnership Strategy 2014-2018 is aimed to promote sustainable development in support of the Rectangular Strategy and the National Strategic Development Plan. The National Programme for Sub-National Democratic Development 2010-2019 sets up the principles of democratic participation in management systems. The Ministries of Interior, Economy and Finance, and Planning and the State Secretariat for Civil Service are working on the issue with uneven results.

Planning system in practice

While a relatively complete legal and administrative system for urban planning and environmental management has been put into place, its application and enforcement is much less developed. Traditionally, planning work is carried out at the national level with international assistance. The capacity of sub-national agencies for drafting and implementing plans is very limited. It is expected that the National Urban Development Strategy is going to promote innovative local development plans with improved public participation. A land valuation and taxation is necessary so that the general public can share in the enormous private profits derived from rapid urban growth.

CHINA

FAST FACTS

- **Total Area:** 9,596,960 km²
- **Total Population:** 1,360 million
- **Population Growth:** 0.49%
- **Unemployment Rate:** 4.05%
- **GDP:** $9,17 trillion
- **GDP per capita:** $6,760
- **GDP growth rate:** 7.67%

SETTLEMENTS STRUCTURE

- **Capital City:**Beijing
   21,150,000 million pop
- **Largest City:** Shanghai
   24,150,000 pop
- **Density:** 141.6 pop/km²
- **Urban Population:** 41%

INSTITUTIONAL STRUCTURE

Socialist republic composed by 22 provinces plus Taiwan as a claimed province, 5 autonomous regions, 4 municipalities directly under central government and 2 special administrative regions.

Read on: www.stats.gov.cn/english; www. mlr.gov.cn/mlrenglish; http://english.mep. gov.cn

Administrative competence for planning

The Ministries of Land and Natural Resources, Housing and Urban-Rural Development and Environmental Protection are in charge respectively of natural resources management, planning and construction in rural and urban areas, as well as environmental policy. Land use issues are the responsibility of the Ministry of Land and Resources. Large cities deal directly with the central government. Cities have powers to enact local laws related to city planning and related matters.

Main planning legislation

Law on Urban and Rural Planning 2008, Urban Real Estate Management Property Law 2007, City Planning Law 1989, Environmental Protection Law 1989, Land Administration Law 2004, in process of amendment, and Urban Real Estate Administration Law 2009.

Planning and implementation instruments

Every province, prefecture, city and county should have their plans, approved by the next higher level authority. The practice is to produce 15 year plans, with annual revisions to co-ordinate national policies. City plans take account of the provisions of the national plans and the local Five Year Plans. Plans are produced according to demands and their structure may vary substantially. Projects can modify planning determinations.

Development control

Any proposal requires official certification from registered Design Institutes previous to governmental authorisations. Enforcement of the law is extremely efficient. Land use right is granted by the state for a certain number of years in return for a fee.

Sustainability and governance

The Chinese Agenda 21 was approved in 1994, followed by several environmental laws, resources management laws, regulations, and environmental standards. The document The China's Policies and Actions on Climate Change was issued in 2014. There is a seriously concern about the future availability of energy, water and environmental resources. The 12th Year Plan sketches planning strategies and programmes regarding sustainable development. Any urban plans should be available to the public on the government's website.

Planning system in practice

The government is attempting to reduce the complexity and rigidity of the existing planning system. The switch from a socialist to some form of market economy has reduced the efficiency of the traditional master plan. Competition among cities has an impact on demands for regeneration especially of areas with decreasing competitive advantages. In most cities large areas of housing blocks built to solve basics needs are co-existing with areas designed to demonstrate opulence, a situation which generates cross cultural misunderstandings, akin to the question of the protection of historical buildings, which are often considered as a symbol of past poverty. The environmental impact of increased economic success is an unresolved matter; the government is making efforts to address all these issues in spite of intense urbanisation pressures.

HONG KONG

Administrative competence for planning

Planning issues are under the jurisdiction of the Secretaries of Development, Transport and Housing, Food and Health and Environment There exist several authorities engaging in land use planning and management, but planning competence is entrusted in the Town Planning Board or the Director of Planning, or both. The planning system and the function of each department remain similar to the British colonial administration.

Main planning legislation

The Town Planning Ordinance 1939, revised in 2005, and the Country Parks Ordinance 1976 are still operative. The Town Planning Board deals with planning matters, except those under the Country and Marine Parks Authority (40% of the territory). Without a legal definition of town planning regulations, the Board has discretionary powers. Ordinances exist on building, conveyancing, property and housing.

Planning and implementation instruments

All land is owned by the government and offered for leasing at auctions so there is a direct control over its use and development. How to acquire building land remains a hot topic of discussion. The Territorial Development Strategy provides the framework for land use, transport and environment The Hong Kong 2030: Planning Vision and Strategy 2007 details future spatial integration. The Planning Department is in charge of town plans, the five Sub-Regional Development Strategy Plans and the Hong Kong Planning Standards Guidelines. The Urban Renewal Authority takes care of urban renewal projects. District Plans provide guidance for local development.

Development control

There are two statutory plans for land use and development control: Outline Zoning Plans which regulate development control, and Development Permission Area Plans for rural areas. The Development Scheme Plans of the Urban Renewal Authority control activities in these areas and building permits.

Sustainability and governance

The Study of Sustainable Development in Hong Kong for the 21st Century (1997- 2000) states that sustainable development is a government policy. A Council for Sustainable Development was established in 2003 Local communities are getting more aware of the need of planning for sustainability. The Town Planning Ordinance includes arrangements for public consultation but this is not implemented due to emerging but as yet immature local politics. The Statutory Planning Portal provides access to planning information.

Planning system in practice

The complicated set of land use mechanisms implies delays but prevents corruption. The Town Planning Ordinance amendments seek to rationalise bureaucracy but could jeopardise the well established land control mechanism. Private developers negotiate development control and land use changes with the administration. A certain degree of flexibility is the key factor to maintain laissez-faire implementation. Environmental corrective actions are not solving the pollution problems of the highly congested urban pattern of Hong Kong.

INDONESIA

Administrative competence for planning
Planning is undertaken at national, provincial, regional, district/ city levels. The National Development Planning Board and the National Spatial Planning Coordinating Agency are in charge of planning and spatial development policy under the deputy of Regional Authority and Regional Development, and the 5 year plans. With decentralisation the Province Planning Boards and Regency and Town Planning Boards are responsible for integrated regional and local planning. The Ministry of Works coordinates spatial and development planning and the Ministry of Finance is responsible for a fiscal balance between government and regions.

Main planning legislation
After decentralisation the Law 26/2007 on spatial planning provides the framework for long, medium and annual plans at national, metropolitan, regional, regency and district levels. Law 17/2003 strengthens local government budget systems. Laws 23/1997 and 31/2009 regulate environmental management.

Planning and implementation instruments
The National Spatial Plan and the national strategic regional spatial plan are the spatial framework policies under which detailed provincial, regency/city plans are drawn up, as well as regional development plans integrating several sectors and metropolitan spatial plans. The national infrastructure investment plan is a tool for resource allocation, while mid-term development plans are bottom up instruments.

Development control
Development control is legislated by laws 32/2004 and 26/2007 which allocate competence to local government. Location, land use change, and building permits are issued against payment. Land development violations are not sanctioned. In particular, peri-urban development remains uncontrolled, where developers acquire land with land ownership certificates, subdivide and let it. The provision of zoning regulations is not supported by zoning inspections to enhance development control.

Sustainability and governance
The notion of sustainability was introduced in Law 4/1982 as principles of environmental management which deal with environmental protection and conservation areas. In 2010 a national action plan was adopted to reduce green house gases RAN-GRK but implementation remains challenging. Indonesia subscribed to international agreements on climate change and CO_2 reduction and introduced environmental impact analyses. Yet, there is little integration between planning and environmental policy formulation.

Planning system in practice
Spatial planning does not seem to be able to contain rapid urbanisation to the detriment of natural resources, especially as development control is weak. Although national spatial plans and five year plans persist, regionalisation has taken place since the reform era, which brought about uneven development strategies and seems to lack coordination between regions. The national infrastructure plan is supposed to assist equitable economic development but implementation is left to the private sector.

FAST FACTS

- **Total Area:** 1,890,754 km^2
- **Total Population:** 255.993,674
- **Population Growth:** 0,92 %
- **Unemployment Rate:** 6,1%
- **GDP:** $ 888.6 billion
- **GDP per capita:** $10,600
- **GDP growth rate:** 5%

SETTLEMENTS STRUCTURE

- **Capital City:** Jakarta
  10,176,000 pop
- **Second City:** Surabaya
  2.834,000 pop
- **Density:** 135 pop/km^2
- **Urban Population:** 54%

INSTITUTIONAL STRUCTURE

Republic composed of 30 provinces, 348 regencies, 92 municipalities, 4,994 districts and 70,921 sub-districts.

Read on: http://www.indonesia.go.id/en/ministries/

JAPAN

Administrative competence for planning

The Ministry of Land, Infrastructure and Transport is responsible for national, regional and urban spatial planning, the Ministry of Agriculture, Forestry and Fisheries for rural development and the Ministry of Environment for national parks and nature conservation.

Main planning legislation

National Spatial Planning Act 2005, National Land Use Planning Act 1974, City Planning Act 1968 and Basic Act on Food, Agriculture and Rural Development 2005.

Planning and implementation instruments

Several instruments are applied at national, regional, prefectural and local levels: Spatial development plans, Land use plans, Basic plan on food, agriculture and rural areas, City planning areas, Master plan for city planning, Land use zones and other zoning systems areas, Urban facilities and urban development projects and District plans.

Development control

Control of development is achieved by the prefectures (or large cities) through development permission and building confirmation/permit.

Sustainability and governance

The 2012 Low Carbon City Promotion Act requires local governments to develop Low-Carbon Development Plans and to facilitate actions to integrate urban functions, to promote the use of public transportation, to enhance efficient energy use, to preserve and promote urban green areas. Japan is promoting a "compact and networked" urban structure to address its population decline and ageing challenges. The Urban Renaissance Act, revised in 2014, aims to maintain population density, to promote the use of public transportation and to guide the location of urban services to designated urban areas. Decentralisation and empowering municipal governments is a sustained trend of Japan's local autonomy system. Mergers of smaller municipalities have also been promoted since the end of 1990.

Planning system in practice

By 2040, Japan's population is expected to return roughly to the level of 1970, which implies that most Japanese cities are going to be less dense. In such urban areas with lower urban density, maintaining sufficient density to sustain the level of public service and the quality of urban life would be critical. Spatial planning for women, children and the elderly is also a key issue: planning is expected to play a key role in fostering an urban environment friendly for women with small children, particularly in major cities, and comprehensive elderly-care services and rental housing, with care services for those who stay at home, as alternatives to hospitalisation or long-term care facilities. Governance and fragmentation of city planning areas is another planning concern since the political administrative fragmentation may affect the economic growth of metropolitan cities. This situation could arise if municipal fragmentation, together with insufficient co-operation, leads to sub-optimal provision of transport infrastructure.

MALAYSIA

FAST FACTS

- **Total Area:** 330,290 km²
- **Total Population:** 28,300,000
- **Population Growth:** 1.3 %
- **Unemployment Rate:** 3.3%
- **GDP:** $336.9 billion
- **GDP per capita:** $24,500
- **GDP growth rate:** 5.6%

SETTLEMENTS STRUCTURE

- **Capital City:** Kuala Lumpur
  1,670,000 pop
- **Second City:** Subang Jaya
  1,553,589 pop
- **Density:** 86 pop/km²
- **Urban Population:** 71%

INSTITUTIONAL STRUCTURE

Constitutional monarchy composed of 13 state governments and 3 federal territories.

Read on:www.malaysia.gov.my; www. kpkt.gov.my

Administrative competence for planning
The main Vision 2020 provides focus for the national development. The Ministry of Housing and Local Government (MHLG) is answerable to the Parliament regarding services and strategies of town planning. The State government has exclusive powers over local authorities. State authorities are responsible for organising the local government and municipal services and assume the position of "central government" to the local authority. The local authority is the principal government agency which exercises control at the local level.

Main planning legislation
Town and Country Planning Act 172, 1976.

Planning and implementation instruments
The National Physical Plan is produced every five years by responding to the Malaysia Plan, the country's five years Development Plan, as well as to other national policies such as the Industrial Master Plan, Vision 2020, and Agricultural Plan. The Structure Plan is produced every five years regarding the development and use of land in the state. The Draft Local Plan can be prepared by a local planning authority before or during preparation of draft structure plans. Special Area Plans are for a specific area.

Development control
Planning permission is required before constructing any development.

Sustainability and governance
Malaysia was a pioneer in establishing a framework for environmental governance in the 1970s but its response to the post-1992 sustainable development agenda has been patchy and haphazard. This poor response delayed the more difficult task of concretising the institutionalisation of environmental policy. The MHLG supported green urbanism through its policies and guidelines since the mid 1990s and awards the best performing local authorities for their implementation of green neighbourhood initiatives.

Planning system in practice
Since independence, Malaysia's economic and social development strategies have been formulated within the framework of a succession of national five-year development plans. These plans are based on a pro-business growth approach. The market-oriented policies mean that the private sector is the country's engine of growth, while the public sector plays the facilitating role. Although the planning machinery and process seem to be rigid, in reality the process is flexible and pragmatic. This is due to the fact that planning is done at all planning horizons and levels and presents opportunities for revisions and incorporation of new strategies as well as to responding to new problems and opportunities as they arise. It enables development planning to respond to new challenges expeditiously. Therefore, in undertaking development planning, planners need to be pragmatic, flexible, pro-active and responsive.

MYANMAR

FAST FACTS

- **Total Area:** 653,290 km²
- **Total Population:** 51.486.253
- **Population Growth:** 1.03%
- **Unemployment Rate:** 4%
- **GDP:** $ 56.8 billion
- **GDP per capita:** $ 1,113
- **GDP growth rate:** 8.3%

SETTLEMENTS STRUCTURE

- **Capital City:** Nay Pyi Taw
  1,160,000 pop (Nay Pyi Taw
  Union Territory)
- **Largest City:** Yangon
  2,980,000 pop
- **Density:** 76 pop/km²
- **Urban Population:** 29.6%

INSTITUTIONAL STRUCTURE

Republic of the Union of Myanmar composed of 7 states, 7 regions, and 1 union territory: Nay Pyi Taw.

Read on: http://www.themimu.info; http:// unhabitat.org/myanmar

Administrative competence for planning

Key government functions are positioned at the township level, where a dual system operates: Yangon, Mandalay and Nay Pyi Taw cities have elected City Development Committees (CDC), with which to assume a wide range of powers including planning and urban management. Functions in other cities and townships fall under the local office of the General Administration Division (GAD), under the Ministry of Home Affairs.

Main planning legislation

The main Laws are the Constitution 2011, the City of Yangon Development Law 1990 and the Farmland Law 2012. There exists a highly comprehensive legislative system inherited from the colonial period but its areas of application are not clear at the moment. The Upper Burma Land and Revenue Regulation and the Lower Burma Towns and Regulation Act are the primary laws for municipal management and planning. The Union government is finalising a draft National Town Planning Law, which looks likely to go before Parliament in 2015.

Planning and implementation instruments

Until recently there has been an absence of formal urban planning. Only Yangon established a planning department in 2011 and prepared a master-plan, a transport master-plan and a draft land use and development control plans. The GAD is working to develop plans for around fifty secondary cities by 2016. Plans are concerned with strategic land use zoning. Detailed street layout, infrastructure, zoning are used when a planned town extension is proposed.

Development control

Outside of the main cities, the Ministry of Home Affairs oversees urban development issues. Compliance with land use regulations is a challenge for the planning system, where local level government does not have the capacity of monitoring and enforcement.

Sustainability and governance

None of the relevant legislation falls under sustainability. Environmental protection is a huge concern for major infrastructure projects, particularly dams and mines. Issues like Agenda 21 do get a look in but they are not a priority. The governance structure is still quite weak and emerging. The development of ICT is almost non-existent. The lack of data makes planning significantly difficult.

Planning system in practice

The Government is attempting to establish a formal planning system and regular planning processes. Main constraints are: lack of trained planners, severely limited resources within Ministries, limited knowledge of urban development and management and poor coordination between national and local bodies. The deficit in urban infrastructure, services and housing in major cities has led to slums proliferation. The lack of appropriate development controls enables the international capital to build developments across the city. Unfortunately the interest in urban planning has been low at all levels.

PHILIPPINES

FAST FACTS

- **Total Area:** 300,000 km^2
- **Total Population:** 107,700,000
- **Population Growth:** 1.81%
- **Unemployment Rate:** 7%
- **GDP:** $ 298.9 billion
- **GDP per capita:** $ 3,300
- **GDP growth rate:** 7.2%

SETTLEMENTS STRUCTURE

- **Capital City:** Manila
  21,200,000 pop (metro area)
- **Second City:** Quezon city
  2,761,720 pop
- **Density:** 359 pop/km^2
- **Urban Population:** 44.5%

INSTITUTIONAL STRUCTURE

Republic composed of 3 island groups subdivided into 17 regions, 81 provinces, 131 cities 1,494 municipalities and 41,995 barangays.

Read on: www.gov.ph; www.nscb.gov.ph; www.mmda.gov.ph; www.hudcc.gov.ph

Administrative competence for planning

The Housing and Urban Development Coordinating Council is in charge of planning issues. The National Land Use Committee is commissioned to prepare and revise the integrated National Physical Framework Plan. The Regional and Provincial Land Use Committees connect national and local levels. Local government units are required to have a comprehensive multi-sectoral development plan.

Main planning legislation

For over twenty years, there have been discussions about a new National Land Use Act to provide greater legislative weight about land use. The latest Act iteration has not yet been approved. The implementation of this Act would be overseen by a new National Land Use Policy Council.

Planning and implementation instruments

The Land Use Policy Guidelines are the core of the National Framework for Physical Planning. The Regional Physical Framework Plan is a 30 years plan that guides public and private sector decisions. The Provincial Physical Framework Plan links the regional plan with the municipal and city Comprehensive Land Use Plan plans. The Metropolitan Manila Development Authority and the Metropolitan Cebu Development Council are in charge of the capital, and the region and main centre of the island province of Cebu respectively.

Development control

The Housing and Land Use Regulatory Board handles development control policies and compliance. There is a Regional Officer in each region. The main development controls are the Zoning Ordinances derived from the Comprehensive Land Use Plans.

Sustainability and governance

The Philippine Agenda 21 is overseen by the Philippine Council for Sustainable Development. The main legislation is the Climate Change Act 2009 and the National Disaster Risk Reduction and Management Act 2009. Considerable work has been done to include these goals into the land use plans. The investment in ICT data and mapping provides the basis for future planning, especially in areas of natural disasters and climate change. The Local Government Code 1991 provides enough power to local administrations to fulfil their functions, but basic transparency, accountability and monitoring of local budgets and plan implementation is lacking.

Planning system in practice

The planning system is well established but becomes unstuck in its implementation. Rigid plans based on unrealistic trends and the lack of monitoring and sanctioning mechanisms cannot cater for the dynamics of the real world needs. Polarisation is widening between the many shanty towns and the gated communities. There are no government public housing projects offering accommodation to rent since there is a cultural belief that there is no demand for renting amongst the poor. Land-use zoning has not differentiated between income groups.

SINGAPORE

FAST FACTS

- **Total Area:** 718,3 km²
- **Total Population:** 5,469,724
- **Population Growth:** 1.3%
- **Unemployment Rate:** 1.8%
- **GDP:** $307,1 billion
- **GDP per capita:** $81,300
- **GDP growth rate:** 3%

SETTLEMENTS STRUCTURE

- **Capital City:** Singapore
  5,517,000 pop
- **Second City:** -
- **Density:** 6,875 pop/km²
- **Urban Population:** 100%

INSTITUTIONAL STRUCTURE

Republic composed of 5 regions.

Read on: www.singstat.gov.sg; www.plan-ning.org.sg; http://app.mnd.gov.sg

Administrative competence for planning

The government is responsible for the definition and implementation of the Concept Plans, key reference plans to guide land use changes, updated via 5 Yearly Minor Reviews, and 10 or 20 Yearly Major Reviews.

Main planning legislation

The Compulsory Land Acquisition Act enables the government to appropriate private land for development of public projects. The Land Compensation Legislation enables government to curb land speculation basing the land value on current or past value whichever is the lower. Hoarding land to wait for rise in value is thus risky and unattractive. The Resettlement Compensation Rates are fixing the rates in minute details, at favourable market values.

Planning and implementation instruments

At the national level, the Master Plan 1985 is still in force. The Concept Plans (1971, 1991 and 2001) express the long term national vision. The Development Guide Plan is the planning framework for districts of between 10 and 15 km2 where new settlements are planned. The private sector can make its own plans under specified conditions to accommodate the activities of a fast growing economy.

Development control

Among the specific instruments devised as planning conditions is the Development Charge, which us set at 50% of the increase in land price, between existing and amended planning parameters, payable by landowners or developers when applying for planning approvals. Documents required to calculate development charges are the 1958 Master Plan, the current DGP, and the half yearly published property valuation report.

Sustainability and governance

Sustainable principles in planning were translated into operational mechanisms: environmental improvement by producing plans and enforcing building rules and regulations; social stability providing homeownership for all, and economic growth aided by the resettlement from slums and squatter colonies to public housing. Land use change is considered a government right, so increased value of land is to be shared between government and landowners. High level of government credibility has assisted land appropriation for public purposes and the realisation of government programmes with strong citizen support.

Planning system in practice

Importance is attached to the identification and safeguarding of sites for future iconic projects to enable Singapore to remain firmly in the top league of global cities. There is a need to build with even more flexibility by reserving more large tracts of land for unexpected important uses, such as regional centres as secondary CBDs or bigger parks, while rigorously protecting land designated for housing areas from encroachment of low-rise apartment blocks. People see land as opportunities for profit making, therefore more prescriptive planning with best practices is a priority.

SOUTH KOREA

FAST FACTS

- **Total Area:** 100,188 km²
- **Total Population:** 50,004,000
- **Population Growth:** 0.43%
- **Unemployment Rate:** 3.2%
- **GDP:** $1,130 trillion
- **GDP per capita:** $22,670
- **GDP growth rate:** 2%

SETTLEMENTS STRUCTURE

- **Capital City:** Seoul
  9,976,000 pop
- **Second City:** Busan
  3,445,000 pop
- **Density:** 500 pop/km²
- **Urban Population:** 93%

INSTITUTIONAL STRUCTURE

Republic composed of 9 provinces, classified in five types: Provinces, a Special Autonomous Province, the Special City of Seoul, Metropolitan Cities and a Special Autonomous City.

Read on: www.upis.go.kr: www.kopss. go.kr; http://stat.seoul.go.kr/siss; http:// klis.seoul.go.kr/sis/main.do

Administrative competence for planning

The Ministry of Land, Infrastructure and Transport is responsible for national territorial planning, provides guidelines, standards and criteria for territorial planning and is in charge of the 20 years Comprehensive National Territorial Plan. It approves Province Comprehensive Plans, most regional plans and, eventually, Metropolitan City Plans. Provinces are responsible for the Province Comprehensive Plan. Metropolitan Cities, Cities and Counties prepare the City/County Master Plan.

Main planning legislation

The Framework Act on National Territory 2002 defines the planning system. The Planning and Use of National Territory Act 2009 divides the national territory into four zoning areas and provides regulations for Metropolitan and City/County Planning. Several special acts promote the construction of Multi-functional Administration City, Innovation Cities and Enterprise Cities.

Planning and implementation instruments

The Comprehensive National Territorial Plan is the framework for the Provincial Comprehensive Plans. Municipal spatial policies are included in the master plans of metropolitan cities, cities and counties.

Development control

The urban plans prepared by the municipal authorities set out a range of measures to regulate the use of land.

Sustainability and governance

The Presidential Commission on Sustainable Development 2000 aimed to implement the Agenda 21 strategies and gave birth to several initiatives: National Plan for Sustainable Development and the Sustainable Development Act 2007, National Comprehensive Environmental Plan 2006-2015, National Strategy for Green Growth 2008, Green New Deal Policy 2009-20150, Low-Carbon Green Growth Framework Act 2010, etc. In spite of this normative framework, there was a process under way of progressively weakening the legal and administrative support. In general, the planning process has become more democratic including opportunities for public participation. The increase of ICTs has improved planning governance.

Planning system in practice

During the 1960s and 1970s, the national government launched policies for industrialisation and urbanisation without any long-term vision. Ad hoc development acts allowed the construction of new cities and urban districts in a short period of time, particularly in the Capital Region. The coexistence of two ministries in charge of environmental and territorial policies reduces planning implementation. Although the democratic government system was restored in the 1990s and the powers of planning and development have gradually been transferred to local governments, the Capital Region still concentrates the best conditions. The centralist policy has shifted to mobilise growth and innovation to regions. The 4th National Comprehensive Territorial Plan has established seven megaregional economic zones as self-determining growth engines. What is needed is a reform of the legal and institutional systems for more collaborative planning governance.

TAIWAN

- **Total Area:** 36,009 km²
- **Total Population:** 23,240,639
- **Population Growth:** 0.21%
- **Unemployment Rate:** 4.2%
- **GDP:** $ 484,700 million
- **GDP per capita:** $ 20,900
- **GDP growth rate:** 2.2%

SETTLEMENTS STRUCTURE

- **Capital City:** Taipei City
    2,686,516 pop
- **Second City:** Kaohsiung City
    2,779,877 pop
- **Density:** 645 pop/km²
- **Urban Population:** 80.3%

INSTITUTIONAL STRUCTURE

Multiparty democracy composed of 6 special municipalities, 11 counties and 3 metropolitan cities.

Read on: www.ndc.gov.tw; www.cpami.gov. tw; www.tiup.org.tw/metro

Administrative competence for planning

The National Development Council initiated the Strategic Plan for National Spatial Development in 2010. The Construction and Planning Agency, Ministry of the Interior, is responsible for national and regional planning and supervision of urban planning, urban regeneration, new town development and building administration. Six special municipalities, metropolitan cities and counties are the local authorities responsible for city and rural planning.

Main planning legislation

Until the proposed National Land Planning Law will be approved, the main legislations are the Regional Planning Act and the Urban Planning Law.

Planning and implementation instruments

The National Comprehensive Development Plan 2014 is the highest statutory spatial plan. Special municipalities, metropolitan cities and counties should have their own Local Comprehensive Development Plan.

Development control

Although no unauthorised changes shall be made to any urban plan, in practice building permits are often granted on the basis of individual reasoning. Enforcement of development control in rural areas can be made through the discretion-base permission system. Building occupation and change of use should be permitted by the local government, but in practice illegal buildings are a major planning and political issue.

Sustainability and governance

The National Council for Sustainable Development was established in 1997. Specific legislation was approved, among them the Basic Environment Act 2002, the Sustainable Development Action Plan 2004 and the Adaptation Strategy to Climate Change 2012. The limited public involvement during the planning process had no capacity to face the existing pro-growth coalition. The Community Planner system 2000 was promoting the awareness of the emerging civil society on environmental and social justice issues. ICTs have been applied to several planning issues.

Planning system in practice

The planning legislation aims for a plan-led system to guide physical development, but the plans are used primarily to facilitate development instead of guiding it. Coordination among spatial planning and sectoral long-term development plans has not been achieved yet. Post-industrial Taiwan faces several challenges: urban restructuring, democracy and urban governance, community empowerment, environmental sustainability and cultural conservation. The planning system needs to adopt a vision-oriented planning approach with more qualitative thinking towards environmental sustainability, economic competitiveness and social equity. Furthermore, cross-boundary governance and dispute resolution capability need to be improved in order to cope with the newly restructured situation of six special municipalities.

THAILAND

FAST FACTS

- **Total Area:** 513,120 km²
- **Total Population:** 67,000,000
- **Population Growth:** 0.4%
- **Unemployment Rate:** 1%
- **GDP:** $380.5 billion
- **GDP per capita:** $5,340
- **GDP growth rate:** 3-4%

SETTLEMENTS STRUCTURE

- **Capital City:** Bangkok
  6,900,000 pop
  11,600,000 pop metro area
- **Second City:** Chiang Mai
  170,000 pop
  500,000 metro area
- **Density:** 130 pop/km²
- **Urban Population:** 40%

INSTITUTIONAL STRUCTURE

Constitutional monarchy composed of 77 provinces divided into districts and sub-districts. The urban areas are organized in municipalities.

Read on: www.nesdb.go.th; www.dpt. go.th; www.codi.or.th

Administrative competence for planning

The frequent changes in the country´s legal foundations explain the changing competences for urban and regional planning. Legislative competence lies with the national level while plan implementation is shared by local government and a large number of public agencies. The National Economic and Social Development Board is responsible for the national five year plans and general policy formulation. The drafting of plans all over the country is in the hands of the national Department of Public Works and Town and Country Planning.

Main planning legislation

The Town Planning Act 1975 (a new urban planning law is under consideration to cope with the growing complexity of urban planning and management) and the Building Control Act 1979, Building Control Act 1997, Land Readjustment Act 2004, Condominium Act 2008, Environment Act 1992. Municipalities are allowed to issue Municipal Bylaws to refine the contents of their plans and projects but they are not often issued.

Planning and implementation instruments

At national level, the national five year plans. At local level there are two types of statutory plans: general/comprehensive plan for the entire municipality or a specially designated area, and specific plan for selected areas within the area covered by the general plan, which has not been applied in practice.

Development control

The main enforcing planning instruments are the national laws and the municipality bylaws, of which there are many in Bangkok.

Sustainability and governance

Public environmental consciousness has grown beyond expectations. The Local Agenda 21 was heavily promoted and to some extent, successfully implemented. The emphasis has shifted from plan making to a broader management of change through good governance. There is a well-developed institutional landscape of public and private players, effective linkages to international organisations in both sustainable development and governance. Thailand is one of the most successful countries in introducing and using ICT everywhere throughout the country, and in all conceivable applications, including spatial planning.

Planning system in practice

During the past fifty years Thailand has made very considerable progress in many respects related to urban planning and management. Although there is no spatial planning system as such, the changes in urban, regional, and national planning levels show that the country has shaped its own original style of planning to meet the principal conditions facilitating equitable, proactive, and environmentally conscious planning. But the legislation has gaps that need to be filled and the legal framework offers possibilities that are not applied. Successful practices refers to mass transit interventions in Bangkok, historical centres conservation, legislation for condominium projects, and initiatives regarding environmental resources protection, micro climate improvement and public space and water bodies cleanliness.

VIETNAM

FAST FACTS

- **Total Area:** 330,972 km²
- **Total Population:** 89,708,900
- **Population Growth:** 1%
- **Unemployment Rate:** 6%
- **GDP:** $100 billion
- **GDP per capita:** $1,700
- **GDP growth rate:** 5.6%

SETTLEMENTS STRUCTURE

- **Capital City:** Ha Noi
  6,936,900 pop
- **Second City:** Ho Shi Minh
  7,818,200 pop
- **Density:** 271 pop/km²
- **Urban Population:** 34%

INSTITUTIONAL STRUCTURE

Socialist republic composed of 58 provinces and 5 cities under direct central rule; 60 provincial cities, 46 towns, 47 urban districts and 550 rural districts; 634 townlets, 1,461 wards and 9,052 communes.

Read on: www.gso.gov.vn; moc.gov.vn/ web/guest/english

Administrative competence for planning
The national government makes and controls key planning such as framework plans, special city plans, regional planning or any plan between more than 2 provinces/cities, and new or special strategic town/ zone. Provinces and central cities make and control physical plans in line with national directives. These plans include provincial urban system plan, provincial capital city plan and zoning, new urban area/town. Some decentralised districts, mainly in large cities, have area/zone detail plans. Wards/communes provide local baseline data to a city or local planning authority to support deployment of approved development projects.

Main planning legislation
The Urban Planning Law 2009 governs all aspects related to urban planning: planning principle, types, authority, and funding source. Government Decree 42, 2009, specifies the city ranks system and details on formulation, appraisal and ratifying urban planning. All cities/towns must prepare a master plan according to national urban system planning.

Planning and implementation instruments
National strategic guidelines for spatial development are produced and implemented by the Ministries of Construction, Transport, Commerce and Industries and Planning and Investment. Regional planning is performed by the same ministries for specific geographic regions of some provinces/ cities. Master plan and detailed plans refer to specific urban units.

Development control
Three basic documents are required for a development project: Building Ownership and Land Use Certificate, Planning Certificate and Construction.

Sustainability and governance
Legislation improvements contributed to environmental sustainability. Planning-related regulations advocate planned versus sprawl development. SEA and EIA are applied in strategic planning and city planning respectively. Major progress observed is the pursuance of a legal basis, transparency and the use of market forces in the multi-sector urban development. Planning is less political and more subject to broad public consultation. Professional associations play an active role in this process. Despite ICT applications in urban planning and management, there are still very limited ICT applications in the public sector.

Planning system in practice
Awareness of the importance of urban planning has been increasing as it impacts on urban spatial changes, land value and urban welfare. Some aspects need to be tackled: separation of state planning controller/ owner from planning consulting work, to establish a planning consulting market for fair competition, higher quality and cost-effectiveness; planning effectiveness by focusing on urban problem solving; planning consistency between periods; flexibility to revise; enhancing capacity of planning institutions and planners; building of a national planning information system to facilitate implementation, access to all sectors and the public, monitoring, evaluation and revision.

IRAN

FAST FACTS

- **Total Area:** 648,000 km²
- **Total Population:** 78,000,000
- **Population Growth:** 1.22%
- **Unemployment Rate:** 10.3%
- **GDP:** $350 billion
- **GDP per capita:** $16,500
- **GDP growth rate:** 1.5%

SETTLEMENTS STRUCTURE

- **Capital City:** Tehran
    8,200,000 pop
- **Second City:** Isfahan
    1,908,609 pop
- **Density:** 120 pop/km²
- **Urban Population:** 68.5%

INSTITUTIONAL STRUCTURE

Theocratic republic composed of 31 provinces.

Read on: www.mrud.ir; http://www.nezam-mohandesi.ir

Administrative competence for planning

The Ministry of Roads and Urban Development - a new ministry created in 2011- is responsible for urban planning.

Main planning legislation

The main legal body is the Urban Land Act. The Engineering Law includes the National Building Code, to be applied in the construction industry, particularly in seismic areas.

Planning and implementation instruments

The Fifth Development Plan (2010 – 2015) includes policies with social, economic and cultural matters that have repercussions on cities and urban planning, such as lending character to the features of city and countryside, reconstructing and maintaining Iranian-Islamic buildings; observing advanced criteria for making buildings, saving and fortifying structures; completing and implementing an engineering-cultural plan and preparing a cultural connection for important plans.

Development control

A specific council approves any change in the master plan of each city. It consists of representatives of relevant ministries, major stakeholders, and urban specialists.

Sustainability and governance

Iran faces major challenges in almost all domains of sustainability relating to environmental, social and economic dimensions of development, as well as natural disaster risk. Sustainability indices for the cities are unsatisfactory or at most at an intermediate level. Recent evaluation research shows that social and institutional capacities are not sufficient to progress towards sustainable cities. The administrative system for urban development management is highly centralised and hierarchic which slows down the decision making process, causes delays and inefficiency. ICT is now playing an important role in the dissemination of plans and decisions among public administrations and professionals at both national and city levels. However, in smaller cities the use of ICT is behind the larger cities and especially the capital.

Planning system in practice

Iran is facing the consequences of a rapid urbanisation and the growing complexities of urban transformation. Crucial aspects are not resolved, such as the capacity of the existing infrastructure, the shortage of green spaces, the protection of the urban heritage and the safeguarding of the historical and cultural identity in the new urban developments, despite the special attention given to this issue in the recent country-wide development plans. Urban development programmes are still guided by comprehensive plans inherited from the first plan for Tehran in 1968. By mid-1990 there was an attempt to include a qualitative approach in planning, but many of these projects were not put into practice. The value of the historical city centres has been reduced to the quantitative value of land. This is only one of the challenges ahead for Iranian decision makers, local managers and urban planners and designers.

IRAQ

FAST FACTS

- **Total Area:** 437,072 km²
- **Total Population:** 35,100,000
- **Population Growth:** 2.9%
- **Unemployment Rate:** 8%
- **GDP:** $191.2 billion
- **GDP per capita:** $5,700
- **GDP growth rate:** 29.5%

SETTLEMENTS STRUCTURE

- **Capital City:** Baghdad
  6,500,000 pop
  7,300,000 governorate
- **Second City:** Mosul
  1,642,000 pop
- **Density:** 80 pop/km²
- **Urban Population:** 69%

INSTITUTIONAL STRUCTURE

Republic composed of 18 provinces (governorates).

Read on: www.mop.gov.iq;
www.egov.gov.iq; www.imariskan.gov.iq;
http://cosit.gov.iq

Administrative competence for planning

Planning is undertaken by several ministries: Planning and Development Cooperation, Municipalities and Public Work; Construction and Housing, and Finance. The Kurdistan Region has its own ministries responsible for planning. Baghdad Mayoralty is responsible for the city's planning. Municipalities implement the plans and regulate development.

Main planning legislation

Building Regulations 1935, Municipality Management Law 1964, Municipal Revenue Law 1963. A new planning law has been drafted. The National Development Plan 2010-2014 lays out the vision and planning objectives. A Federal Council for Physical Planning was planned to be established to take over planning responsibilities.

Planning and implementation instruments

Structural plans are prepared for governorates. Master plans and detailed plans are produced for municipalities. There is a master plan for every urban centre. In the Kurdistan Region: Municipality Management Law 1993 lays down the procedures for the preparation and approval of municipal plans. The Baghdad Planning Regulations for Buildings and Land Subdivision 1999 guide the capital city master plan.

Development control

The procedures are governed by the Municipal Management Law, Roads and Buildings Regulations and instructions issued by the Ministry of Municipalities. Plans are enforced through applications for subdivisions and development permits.

Sustainability and governance

The Law of Protection and Improvement of the Environment 2009 is intended to solve the existing environmental problems. The NDP 2010-2014 accentuates the need of sustainable planning procedures. Except for Baghdad, urban plans are prepared by the central ministry. Provincial Powers Law amended in 2013, decentralises governance. Although a national strategy for e-governance was approved in 2007, ICTs for urban planning and management are limited. Apart from the Kurdistan Region, the contribution of the private sector is still very limited. The administrative corruption in key institutions is one of the major challenges.

Planning system in practice

Several problems affect planning practice: strong decision-making and financial control at the central level; limited capacity to undertake major plans; traditional master plans inadequate to solve social and economic local needs, lack of effective public involvement to ease planning implementation; lack of coordination and transparency between central and local governments. Political instability and corruption undermine development and impede the decentralisation process. It is expected that the new planning law will stipulate the functions of the planning council at the central level, as well as offices of physical planning at the national and governorate levels. An appropriate planning education is needed to train future planners.

ISRAEL

FAST FACTS

- **Total Area:** 22,145 km²
- **Total Population:** 8,180,000
- **Population Growth:** 1.8%
- **Unemployment Rate:** 5.6%
- **GDP:** $184,9 billion
- **GDP per capita:** $ 37,529
- **GDP growth rate:** 1.3 %

SETTLEMENTS STRUCTURE

- **Capital City:** Jerusalem
  829,900 pop
- **Second City:** Tel-Aviv-Yaffo
  418,600 pop
- **Density:** 367 pop/km²
- **Urban Population:** 91.8%

INSTITUTIONAL STRUCTURE

Parliamentary democracy composed of 6 administrative districts.

Read on: www.moch.gov.il;
http://sviva.gov.il; www.law.co.il; www.
cbs.gov.il

Administrative competence for planning

The National Planning Board Cabinet prepares and approves national policies, public infrastructure, district plans approval and planning appeals. The District planning commissions prepare district schemes and approve the local schemes prepared by the Local planning commissions.

Main planning legislation

The Planning and Building Law 1965, modelled after the British Mandate Town Planning Act of 1936, with some 50 amendments. The Law for the Protection of the Coastal Environment 2004, controls activities along a strip of 300 m from the Mediterranean shore line.

Planning and implementation instruments

Local Outline Schemes and Detailed Plans produced by the Local Planning Board deals with building permits and planning. District Planning Boards are in charge of preparing District Outline Schemes following the proposed National Outline Schemes. The National Planning Board formulates planning and building policies, prepares national outline schemes and approves the district outline schemes.

Development control

By-laws define development control procedures and standards implemented by bodies designated by the Planning and Building Law. Licensing is a function of the local planning committees, except for special permits issued by the National Board for planning and building of national infrastructures.

Sustainability and governance

Urban neighbourhoods' redevelopment; preservation of open space and agricultural land and saving the coastline from over- development are the major sustainability concerns. The implementation of the legal and planning network is shared by the local authorities and the government so several organisations concerned with environmental preservation are "watchdogs" in the process of submitting "objections" to the planning bodies. Except for large infrastructure projects, the initiation of developments tends to be more in the private sector. The web sites of the ministries and local authorities enable the public to get information and conduct part of the planning process.

Planning system in practice

The planning system is considered too rigid, centralised and top down. Central planning powers were increased with the coastal protection law. Besides physical control, the system does not engage other kinds of planning issues. Most of the newer amendments to the Planning and Building Law aimed to get more flexibility by the deletion of bureaucratic steps and the delegation of power to the municipalities and councils. Municipal plans of the more urbanised areas of the country have become more concerned with the economic and legal impacts of planning on property rights and on the municipal economy and budgets. A reform in the licensing of building permits is scheduled to become law on January 1, 2016.

LEBANON

FAST FACTS

- **Total Area:** 10.452 km²
- **Total Population:** 5,882,562
- **Population Growth:** 0,86%
- **Unemployment Rate:** NA
- **GDP:** $ 63.2 billion
- **GDP per capita:** $ 14,845
- **GDP growth rate:** 2,3%

SETTLEMENTS STRUCTURE

- **Capital City:** Beirut
  1,916,100 pop
- **Largest City:** Tripoli
  229,398 pop
- **Density:** 563 pop/km²
- **Urban Population:** 88%

INSTITUTIONAL STRUCTURE

Republic composed of 6 governorates, 25 districts (caza) and 994 municipalities.

Read on: www.cdr.gov.lb; www.cas.gov.lb; http://moe.gov.lb

Administrative competence for planning

Planning is centralised and hierarchical under the control of the Ministry of Works with specialised Councils CDR (Council for development and reconstruction in charge of metropolitan plans), CSU (Council of planning with representatives of ministries and cities -ratification) and DGU (Directorate of Urbanism in charge of master plans). Municipal issues are centrally ratified. Provinces and districts have a mere consultative role, except in Beirut and Tripoli which have their own planning departments.

Main planning legislation

Code of Urbanism 1983 and Construction Law 1983 and 2004. The SDATL (National Spatial Planning Framework) 2009 is the guiding document for planning for settlement structure and national economic development, infrastructure provision large development projects, environmental protection, natural, water and historic resource management.

Planning and implementation instruments

SDATL determines the content of metropolitan, master, land use and zoning plans. The latter focus on regulating building density and land occupancy rates but they cover only a small part and only of built up areas. Land division forms part of master plans but needs to be approved centrally. Land registry is poor and planning statistics are lacking. Beirut and Tripoli have produced integrated plans for the reconstruction of certain districts.

Development control

Provincial and local administrations are in charge of implementing development control which is legislated in the master plans and zoning plans. It is a very complex process in six stages subject to central ratification and re-examination. Public participation is poor and rights of appeal are very limited.

Sustainability and governance

The Ministry of Environment created in 1993 devises environmental policies and undertakes sectoral studies on waste disposal, air, water and soil pollution, and environmental management, imposes Environmental Impact Analysis (EIA) and raises awareness. Environmental legislation includes the Code of the Environment, EIA, natural and historic monument protection. UNEP and EU cooperation have led to national environmental statistics and agenda 21 programmes. Governance is dominated by the private sector and lacks involvement of civic society. The planning system and proliferation of Ministries involved in planning are not apt to cope with informal settlements and environmentally damaging development.

Planning system in practice

Lebanon's centralised spatial planning is not capable of coping with the adverse impacts of continued turbulence in Lebanon, nor with rapid urbanisation partly due to immigration. The planning system needs reforming to provide greater empowerment of local levels and civic society and more integrated and comprehensive spatial planning to achieve more sustainable development, improvement of the environment, better protection of natural resources and conservation of the built and cultural heritage.

PALESTINE

FAST FACTS

- **Total Area:** 6,023 km²
- **Total Population:** 4,330,000
- **Population Growth:** 2,8 %
- **Unemployment Rate:** 31%
- **GDP:** $9,775
- **GDP per capita:** -
- **GDP growth rate:** -

SETTLEMENTS STRUCTURE

- **Capital City:** East Jerusalem
  415,942 pop
- **Second City:** Ramallah
  39,538 pop
- **Density:** 719 pop/km²
- **Urban Population:** 53%

INSTITUTIONAL STRUCTURE

State composed of two areas divided into 16 administrative divisions.

*Read on: www.molg.pna.ps/Default.
aspx?lang=2; www.mopad.pna.ps/en/;
www.nsp.pna.ps/en/index.php?p=home
ww.law.co.il; www.cbs.gov.il*

Administrative competence for planning

At the national level, competences lie with the Palestinian National Authority (PNA) since 1993 (DoP signature); Palestinian Legislative Council (PLC); Ministry of Finance (after incorporation of Ministry of Planning and Administrative Development) and Ministry of Local Government for regional and local planning, Higher Planning Council, District and Local Planning Committees. Planning is de facto centralised, although there exist governorates and Regional Rural Planning Committees for regional planning and municipalities for local planning.

Main planning legislation

Town Planning Orders 1921 and 1936 (from British Mandate) still structure current statutory physical planning; Law of Planning for Cities, Villages and Buildings N° 31, 1955 and N° 79, 1966; the Planning and Building Act is still in draft and the 1996 new by-laws for planning and building apply to regulate areas with approved plans and areas without plans respectively. They tend to conflict with pre-1996 planning legislation.

Planning and implementation instruments

The National Spatial Plan 1998 is not yet regulated by law and is a basic topographic plan. Regional Plans were regulated in Gaza in 2005 but not realised. City-region plans of 2015 (with UN Habitat) are amalgamating statutory physical and non statutory development plans to link urban and rural areas. Local plans are regulated and action oriented (in the West Bank). There are outline plans/masterplans (only 2/3rd produced), detailed plans (subject to regional plans) and land division plans (re Art 28), few produced, rare for inherited and common land. The West Bank is divided into three zones, with Israeli authorities assuming full control over one of them representing 61% of the West Bank, including planning related jurisdiction. In 2002 Israel annexed block settlements in East Jerusalem. Administrative legacy is due to both military and administrative regimes.

Development control

Development control and issuing of building permits is subjected to a de jure planning system managed by Israel's planning and military authorities. This was achieved by Israel amending relevant Palestinian laws and by-laws under the centralised planning system inherited from Jordanian rule times.

Sustainability and governance

donor driven agendas and is shaping development and planning, driven by UN-related organisations as well as civil society. PNA adopted environmental adaptation and protection measures and action plans to foster resilience against man made and natural disasters. EIA is part of planning practice for large construction projects and green architecture is adopted by developers. ICT has been used to set up a national spatial data infrastructure widely accessible to the public.

Planning system in practice

Planning has to remain responsive to the geo-political dynamics. Development and strategic planning is practised voluntarily locally awaiting greater competence of local planning committees.

QATAR

FAST FACTS

- **Total Area:** 11,627 km^2
- **Total Population:** 2,334,000
- **Population Growth:** 9.3 %
- **Unemployment Rate:** 0.3%
- **GDP:** $212 billion
- **GDP per capita:** $102,785
- **GDP growth rate:** 7.7%

SETTLEMENTS STRUCTURE

- **Capital City:** Doha City
  800,000 pop
- **Second City:** Al Khor City
  194,000 pop
- **Density:** 172 pop/km^2
- **Urban Population:** 98%

INSTITUTIONAL STRUCTURE

Emirate composed of 8 municipalities.

Read on: www.baladiya.gov.qa, www.qsa.gov.qa/eng/index.htm

Administrative competence for planning
The Ministry of Municipality and Urban Planning (MMUP) is responsible for urban planning and for managing each Municipality. The Ministries of Environment and of Transport deal with specific development aspects. Various agencies have own technical standards and all procedures regarding roads, water, energy and telecommunications facilities.

Main planning legislation
Qatar does not have a formal, integrated, comprehensive legislative framework. There are a number of stand-alone regulatory instruments such as Interim Zones and zoning regulations for parts of Doha City and Al Rayyan Municipality, regulatory master plans prepared for the urban parts of the Al Wakra and the Al Khor municipalities, and various building regulations that apply to urban development.

Planning and implementation instruments
The MMUP's Urban Planning Department decides over mega projects and projects of national/regional significance. It is responsible for preparing and implementing the national spatial strategy- the Qatar National Development Framework, 2014, following the Government National Vision 2030. The MMUP initiated the Qatar National Master Plan Project, aimed to produce an integrated package of plans, policies and regulations applicable to national, municipality, city and town jurisdictions to guide the physical development over the next twenty years. The main regulatory planning instruments will be the Municipal Spatial Development Plans (MSDP).

Development control
Urban development control is divided between the Urban Planning Department, which deals with planning approvals, and each Municipality, which issues building approvals.

Sustainability and governance
Key planning strategies introduced by the National Spatial Strategy 2032 and the Municipal Spatial Development Plans are: compact cities and urban consolidation, higher density, hierarchy of centres mixed use developments, transit orientation, place making, environmental management and coordinated implementation of plans and policies. The implementation of an electronic, on-line system for lodging and assessing development applications, and for accessing policy documents and data such as zone plans and zoning regulations, is part of the new planning framework being developed.

Planning system in practice
The very rapid and major level of economic and population growth which has occurred particularly in the last decade or so, has led the Government to introduce various policy and administrative responses under the Qatar National Vision 2030 to address the challenges and opportunities of growth. The MMUP's planning initiatives, such as the preparation of MSDPs and a Planning Act to establish a modern planning framework, are the major initiatives to improve physical planning outcomes and sustainability objectives.

SAUDI ARABIA

FAST FACTS

- **Total Area:** 1,923,750 km^2
- **Total Population:** 27,136,977
- **Population Growth:** 1.49%
- **Unemployment Rate:** 11.2%
- **GDP:** $777,9 billion
- **GDP per capita:** $52,800
- **GDP growth rate:** 3.6%

SETTLEMENTS STRUCTURE

- **Capital City:** Riyadh
  6,991,006 pop
- **Second City:** Jeddah
  3,988,000 pop
- **Density:** 14,11 pop/km^2
- **Urban Population:** 82.9%

INSTITUTIONAL STRUCTURE

Monarchy composed of 13 provinces, divided in 133 districts, 16 regional municipalities (amanats), 269 municipalities and 1442 centres.

Read on: www.mep.gov.sa;
www.momra.gov.sa; www.scta.gov.sa;
www.sa.undp.org/content/saudi_arabia/

Administrative competence for planning

The King and the Council of Ministers produce the laws and decrees which form the basis of the planning legislation.The Ministry of Economy and Planning prepares the 5-year Development Plans. The Ministry of Municipal and Rural Affairs (MOMRA) is responsible for spatial planning and infrastructure provision. Other related administrations are the Ministry of Agriculture and the Tourism Development Authority. Regional and local municipalities undertake the plan preparation in collaboration with the MOMRA, which controls and approves plans and allocates funds. The main amarats have their own development authorities and companies. The Amanats are now authorised to sanction sub division plans.

Main planning legislation

Formal planning has been existing since the 1930s selectively. MOMRA was created in 1975 adopting a formal town planning approach with physical emphasis. The Council of Ministers Decision 127/2000 approves the National Spatial Strategy to promote spatially balanced development. In 2005 there was a step toward decentralisation transforming the main cities into an Amanah with the capacity of supervising all municipalities within the province.

Planning and implementation instruments

The National Spatial Strategy 2000 promotes a spatially balanced development by means of regional strategies and plans. At regional level, the regional offices representing ministries carry out the implementation of projects. In 2005 all cities and village clusters obtained municipal councils with some responsibility for planning.

Development control

MOMRA is mainly responsible for the development of standards and regulations. Various government ministries also develop their own standards, which may be adopted by MOMRA. As the regulations and procedures are in the form of royal decrees, resolutions, directives and ministerial circulars, MOMRA has brought them together and updated them in the form of a Model Land Development Code.

Sustainability and governance

While the entire national space is now comprehensively studied and planned to promote balanced development in all regions, the principles of sustainability and governance are not part of planning practice yet. Although some improvements were made regarding these matters, such as energy saving, the production of geo-spatial survey information and services and the evaluation of the status of the urban sustainability in selected places, this dimension has not been fully developed.

Planning system in practice

The planning system is static without follow up, evaluation and adjustment to fast changing circumstances and to different regions and cities identities. Planning agencies concentrate on implementing rules and regulations rather than on promoting and directing planned development. There is a shortage of trained and experienced planners at all levels. There is a need for a planning act and an autonomous spatial planning commission.

SYRIA ★★

FAST FACTS

- **Total Area:** 185,180 km²
- **Total Population:** 21,890,000
- **Population Growth:** 0.7%
- **Unemployment Rate:** 14.9%
- **GDP:** $ 46540
- **GDP per capita:** $ 2126,1
- **GDP growth rate:** 1.6 %

SETTLEMENTS STRUCTURE

- **Capital City:** Damascus

    4,477,000 pop (metro area)
- **Largest City:** Aleppo

    4,744,000 pop (metro area)
- **Density:** 118,2 pop/km²
- **Urban Population:** 56.9

INSTITUTIONAL STRUCTURE

Republic composed of 14 governorates, divided into districts including sub-districts, cities, towns and villages.

Read on: www.egov.sy; http://mohud.gov.sy; www.moen.gov.sy; www.mla-sy.org

Administrative competence for planning

The national government sets up national level policies and formulates economic and development policies. The directorates in the governorates and the local administrations implement and supervise national level policies on the ground.

Main planning legislation

Legislative Decree 107, 2012 and Law on Local Administration 2011 establish the local government administration system at provincial, city and town levels. Law on Spatial Planning and Regional Development 2010 guide the social, economic, cultural and environmental policies. Decree 5, 1982, on Urban Planning and its amendments sets the content and tools of urban planning.

Planning and implementation instruments

At the national level 11th Five Year Plan (2011-2015) outlines planning goals. At regional level the tools are the National Framework for Regional Planning and the Regional Plan. The Governorate Spatial Development Plan is the 15 years long-term development instrument. The Master Plan regulates urban planning for a period of 20 years.

Development control

Development control stipulations are embodied in the regional plans, the general master plans and the detailed plans as well as in the various laws and regulations.

Sustainability and governance

Steps have been taken for implementing environmental sustainability: the Syrian Nation Environmental Action Plan 2001, the Environment Protection Law 2002, the National Framework Strategy for Sustainable Development 2007 and the creation of the Ministry of State for Environmental Affairs, the General Commission for Environmental Affairs and the General Environmental Directorates. But laws need to be articulated with regional and urban planning and other legislations. Private and NGOs stakeholders are involved in planning processes but they are not an integral part. Some pilot projects have emphasised the importance of public participation and the involvement of the public. GIS has become an integral part of the planning administration and the country is in the process of implementing e-government.

Planning system in practice

The establishment of regional planning in 2010 and the focus on sustainability are steps towards building a concise planning system. But still top-down procedures dominate and it is early to assess the result of these attempts considering the current Syrian conditions. There is a gap between the long-term national investment plans, the decentralisation objectives and the development visions at the local level. Master plans are not apt to develop local economic and social interests. The planning system, the planning activities and the planning institutions should get prepared for the reconstruction of the country. A more strategic, flexible, integrated and proactive planning is needed.

UNITED ARAB EMIRATES

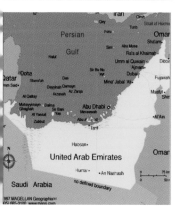

FAST FACTS

- **Total Area:** 83,600 km²
- **Total Population:** 9,346,129
- **Population Growth:** 2.71%
- **Unemployment Rate:** 4.20%
- **GDP:** $ 402 billion
- **GDP per capita:** $ 43,049
- **GDP growth rate:** 5.2%

SETTLEMENTS STRUCTURE

- **Capital City:** Dubai
  2,173,344 pop
- **Second City:** Abu Dhabi
  1,031,875 pop
- **Density:** 112 pop/km²
- **Urban Population:** 85.3%

INSTITUTIONAL STRUCTURE

Federation of 7 emirates.

Read on: www.upc.gov.ae; https://munici-palgateway.abudhabi.ae

Administrative competence for planning

With the exception of Abu Dhabi, all of the emirates' urban functions are managed by one local government covering the whole emirate. Since 2007 the Abu Dhabi Urban Planning Council (ADUPC) is responsible for all aspects of urban and regional planning within the emirate. The municipal planning departments remain but the scope of their urban planning function has been reduced.

Main planning legislation

Municipal planning organisations and the ADUPC are empowered to undertake urban planning and to control development by one or more emiri decrees (i.e. laws). However, these enabling acts do not detail procedures, rights and responsibilities.

Planning and implementation instruments

Each emirate has a high level spatial strategy, which is often referred to as a master plan. These higher level plans are implemented on a project by project basis. Structure plans refer to plans at a scale sufficient to identify areas to be preserved, locate major infrastructure or outline the urban structure. Master plans refer to plans at a sufficiently large scale and with sufficient detail to control the actual development of a project. Regulations, codes and policies vary in quality and detail between the various emirates, but are usually sufficient for their purposes.

Development control

Planning applications are managed by direct application to the municipal planning department, except in Abu Dhabi where there are informal arrangements between the ADUPC and the three municipalities depending on the size and characteristics of the licences.

Sustainability and governance

Within the Emirate of Abu Dhabi all private buildings must achieve an Estidama (i.e. sustainability) rating of one pearl and government buildings must at least rate two pearls. The UAE is effectively a first world country, but with some aspects of governance not quite as developed as the leaders of the first world. The whole of the UAE is highly literate in information technology, so websites, digital information, property transfers, etc. are usually fast and efficient.

Planning system in practice

Urban development was very important, particularly in Abu Dhabi and Dubai, which quickly grew to exceed one million inhabitants, with ports and airports that link them to the world economy. This was achieved, in part, by hiring urban planners from other parts of the world. Unfortunately, the lack of undergraduate urban planning and design courses at the main universities means that the graduate staffs are untrained in urban planning and design. In terms of planning process, there is no formal process or in-grained practice of converting the higher level plans into more detailed plans, such as structure plans for corridors or sectors and master plans for districts and communities.

AUSTRALIA

FAST FACTS

- **Total Area:** 7,692,024 km²
- **Total Population:** 23,032,700
- **Population Growth:** 1.8%
- **Unemployment Rate:** 5.8%
- **GDP:** 1.095 trillion
- **GDP per capita::** $46,400
- **GDP growth rate:** 2.3%

SETTLEMENTS STRUCTURE

- **Capital City:** Canberra
  374,912 pop
- **Largest City:** Sydney
  4,672,619 pop
- **Density:** 2.9 pop/km²
- **Urban Population:** 89.3%

INSTITUTIONAL STRUCTURE

Constitutional democracy and a Commonwealth realm based on a federation of 6 states and 2 territories..

Read on: www.planning.nsw.gov.au; www.abs.gov.au; www.udia.com.au; www. ag.gov.au

166

Administrative competence for planning

The Commonwealth Government has little role in planning except sporadic initiatives. The legal planning basis is enacted by each state's parliament overseen by government agencies. Local councils are in charge of preparing planning schemes following the states' policy frameworks.

Main planning legislation

Each state has a planning act and associated regulations in respect of land use and development. The acts enshrine obligations, rights and responsibilities for land use planning, oriented more towards physical and spatial control rather than social or economic matters.

Planning and implementation instruments

States planning provisions are delivered in varied ways depending on their legal frameworks. Regional planning is not widely developed but increasing efforts have been made in recent years in certain states towards it. Local agencies prepare and review local plans using state-prepared templates.

Development control

Plan implementation is almost exclusively effected at local government level. The development control system depends on a range of pre-prepared tests against which proposed land use and development are compared for appropriateness.

Sustainability and governance

A number of strategies encourage sustainable development, including endorsement of Agenda 21 principles and the National Strategy for Ecologically Sustainable Development. The national government uses its powers in order to influence land use and environmental outcomes. Large property companies, infrastructure and construction corporations and medium to small developers are important contributors to the development process. In case of clashes between local residents and developers local political activity is often strongly focussed on mediating changes, often combined with appeal or review processes in state level bodies. Online access to, and involvement in planning processes, such as plan making, development control and participation exercises are now commonplace in Australia.

Planning system in practice

Planning seems to be at the right level as it is not perceived to be controversial, however it favours urban sprawl. There is no coordination at federal level despite spatial impacts of national resource allocations. Conversely, the local level lacks implementation powers. Environmental issues, greater spatial polarity of wealth and service access are new planning challenges and their resolution would require better vertical and horizontal coordination. Neo-liberalism undermined sectoral coordination and the elimination of the regional planning level in a number of states weakened vertical coordination. Although significant energy is spent in resolving development control disputes, the ministerial intervention tends to stymie the development of fully coherent planning messages at higher-tier levels.

NEW ZEALAND

FAST FACTS

- **Total Area:** 268,680 km²
- **Total Population:** 4,242,048
- **Population Growth:** 1.2%
- **Unemployment Rate:** 6%
- **GDP:** US$ 175,000 million
- **GDP per capita:** $39,450
- **GDP growth rate:** 1.4%

SETTLEMENTS STRUCTURE

- **Capital City:** Wellington
  197,019 pop
- **Largest City:** Auckland
  1,438,446 pop
- **Density:** 15.8 pop/km²
- **Urban Population:** 86%

INSTITUTIONAL STRUCTURE

Parliamentary democracy and a
Commonwealth realm composed of 16
regions and 1 territory.

*Read on: www.mfe.govt.nz; www.doc.govt.
nz; www.dbh.govt.nz; www.lgnz.co.nz*

Administrative competence for planning

The Ministry for the Environment is responsible for preparing National Policy Statements and National Environmental Standards. The Minister of Conservation prepares the New Zealand Coastal Policy Statement and also approves regional coastal plans. Regional councils have to produce a Regional Policy Statement while city and district councils have to produce a District Plan.

Main planning legislation

There is no separate legislation for land use planning. The Resource Management Act 1991 provides an integrated framework for land use and environmental management. Separate legislation exists for the military, national parks and resource extraction. A Proposed National Policy Statement on Indigenous Biodiversity is in process, and preparatory work has been carried out for a further NPS on Urban Design.

Planning and implementation instruments

The planning system applies to land, water, air and the coastal environment beyond the littoral. The Coastal Policy Statement 2010 is the only national policy statement. Regional councils may prepare regional policy statements and non-statutory plans, annual plans and asset plans which form part of local authority planning instruments.

Development control

Permitted, controlled, restricted discretionary, discretionary non-complying activities are regulated and controlled. The assessment of environmental effects in the preparation and processing of development applications is a mandatory part of the resource consent and permitting process.

Sustainability and governance

The Resource Management Act is based on the concept of sustainable management. It forms part of bio-physical or environmental legislation but does not encompass social and economic matters suggested by the Rio 1992 Conference and Agenda 21. The Act sets out mandates for regional councils and local territorial authorities in matters of regional significance. Local councils are responsible for the integrated management of the effects of the use, development or protection of land, natural and physical resources.

Planning system in practice

The planning system is entirely focused on resource management and subordinates land use to environmental conservation principles. The 'rational adaptive' model of plan making required by the Resource Management Act has yet to be fully embraced in practice. Regional and local councils struggled to understand what was required for resource management plans. Central government has made several attempts at streamlining and simplifying the Act. Whilst much effort has gone into improving procedures, some environmental problems are proving difficult to address. In the future, the resource management system needs to focus more on implementation and the achievement of desired environmental outcomes rather than on the process.

PAPUA NEW GUINEA

FAST FACTS

- **Total Area:** 462,840 km²
- **Total Population:** 7,320,000
- **Population Growth:** 2.75%
- **Unemployment Rate:** 2.3%
- **GDP:** $ 2,834 billion
- **GDP per capita::** $1,758.52
- **GDP growth rate:** 4.58%

SETTLEMENTS STRUCTURE

- **Capital City:** Port Moresby
    364,145 pop
- **Second City:** Lae
    100,677 pop
- **Density:** 20 pop/km²
- **Urban Population:** 12.5%

INSTITUTIONAL STRUCTURE

Constitutional parliamentary democracy
and a Commonwealth realm composed
of 20 provinces, 1 autonomous region,
and 1 national capital district.

Read on: http://lands.gov.pg

Administrative competence for planning
The National Physical Planning Board (NPPB) - under the Ministry of Lands and Physical Planning - is in charge of matters of national and provincial interest. Provinces are empowered to have Physical Planning Boards but the NPPB can intervene at this level if needed. The National Capital District has a separate Physical Planning Board. Local Physical Planning Boards only exist within the National Capital District. Municipalities do not have own local planning authorities: they rely on their respective provincial planning boards.

Main planning legislation
The main planning legislation is the Physical Planning Act No. 32-1989, which establishes a comprehensive mechanism for physical planning at national and provincial levels of government and provides powers for planning and regulation of physical development. The Act binds the State and all land is subject to the Act in Papua New Guinea.

Planning and implementation instruments
Main instruments are provincial development plans, urban development plans, local development plans or subject development plans. The Department of Lands and Physical Planning oversees all matters regarding land registration and physical planning.

Development control
The Physical Planning Boards and the local authorities are in charge of control. This includes obtaining licenses and permits, completing required notifications and inspections.

Sustainability and governance
The Department of Lands and Physical Planning is responsible for integrating environmental planning into physical planning and development, and for conserving natural resources. Immediately after political independence in 1975, the state declared "Integral Human Development" as the fifth Directive Principle in its National Constitution. In the past two decades politics have largely been defined by attempts to reconcile differing views of development. It is believed that development must occur in ways which preserve resources for the future and which respect the multiplicity of social and cultural groups. The Department of The Papua New Guinea Scientific Society promotes the sciences, exchanges of scientific information, preserves scientific collections, and establishes museums while the University of Papua New Guinea and the Papua New Guinea University of Technology provide scientific and technical training.

Planning system in practice
Despite the fact that the country has a standard physical planning legislation, there is a wide gap between the planning standards and the actual quality of the environment in most of the urban areas, while the country relies heavily on donor assistance in the face of annual deficit budgets. These are considered serious issues because the country is naturally well-endowed.

SAMOA

FAST FACTS

- **Total Area:** 2,831 km²
- **Total Population:** 196,628
- **Population Growth:** 0.59%
- **Unemployment Rate:** 4.9%
- **GDP:** $ 705 million
- **GDP per capita:** $6,200
- **GDP growth rate:** 0.8

SETTLEMENTS STRUCTURE

- **Capital City:** Apia
  37,237 pop
- **Second City:** Salelologa
  6,062 pop
- **Density:** 64.7 pop/km²
- **Urban Population:** 20%

INSTITUTIONAL STRUCTURE

Independent state composed by 11 districts.

Read on: www.mnre.gov.ws/index.php/ divisions/puma; www.adb.org/countries/ samoa/main

Administrative competence for planning

The Planning and Urban Management Agency under the Ministry of Natural Resources and Environment, is responsible for preparing strategic urban planning tools, development consent, environmental impact control, and enforcement provisions.

Main planning legislation

The Planning and Urban Management Act 2004 sets the institutional arrangements, responsibilities and accountabilities for planning legislation and implementation. Other regulations are the Planning and Urban Management Regulations 2007 and the Planning and Urban Management Regulations 2008.

Planning and implementation instruments

The Agency may develop physical plans through a formal statutory process outlined in the Act, including town planning and zoning. It coordinates key infrastructure and land development programmes and projects at the national, regional, district, village and site specific levels. The Agency has a range of growth strategies such as the Strategy for the Development of Samoa 2012 -2016, the Coastal Infrastructure Management Strategy, the Coastal Infrastructure Management Plans and the Cultural and Natural Heritage Conservation Policy.

Development control

The environmental impacts of activities are primarily controlled by the Act through the requirement to apply for development consents. The Sustainable Development Section is the lead Section in Development Control and issuing of Development Consent.

Sustainability and governance

Sustainable Management Plans assist the Agency in carrying out rules controlling the use of resources in an area. The plan may be made at national, regional, district, village and site-specific levels. These plans have yet to be made but progressive steps are being undertaken such as ensuring the Coastal Infrastructure Management Plans as transitional plans or piloting this approach for the Vaitele area near Apia.

Planning system in practice

The Agency has improved the planning situation in several ways: launching regulations and policies to assist development control, increasing the amount of consent applications, responding to the amenity complaints, strengthening the procedures, maintaining the direction and involvement of planning, and increasing the awareness of these activities under the Act. On the other hand, there is significantly pressure in relation to: information dissemination, improvement of the compliance and monitoring programme, increase of resources to ensure improved operational efficiencies and effectiveness and fine tune enforcement activities. Improving the planning system will involve: refining the administration of the Act, streamlining and integrating legislative requirements for addressing planning and development matters, providing information to the private sector and local groups and providing information to planning practitioners.

Europe

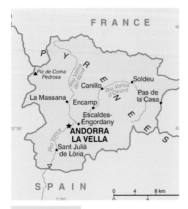

FAST FACTS

- **Total Area:** 467,63 km²
- **Total Population:** 76.098
- **Population Growth:** -
- **Unemployment Rate:** -
- **GDP:** $ 3.163 billion
- **GDP per capita:** 38.532 €
- **GDP growth rate:** -1.6%

SETTLEMENTS STRUCTURE

- **Capital City:** Andorra la Vella
  22.546 pop
- **Second City:** Escaldes-Engordany
  13.853 pop
- **Density:** 162,73 pop/km²
- **Urban Population:** 85.1%

INSTITUTIONAL STRUCTURE

Parliamentary co-principality composed of 7 parishes.

Read on: www.estadistica.ad/ www. cartografia.ad/geoportal/ www.mediam-bient.ad/

Administrative competence for planning

It is a two tier system. At the local level, the "comuns" (communes) have full planning powers over the parishes. The rest of planning competences – spatial planning, sectoral plans, planning guidelines, etc. – falls within the remit of the Government of Andorra. It is also worth explaining the particular political and administrative organisation of the country. Andorra is a parliamentary co-principality with two heads of state, namely the Bishop of Urgell and the President of the French Republic. The territory is structured into seven administrative divisions or parishes, within which the communes operate.

Main planning legislation

The General Law on Spatial Planning and Urban Development (2000) aims at regulating the planning system including land use, urban planning and construction throughout the country.

Planning and implementation instruments

Each tier has different instruments according to the scope of the intervention. While central government planning instruments, guidelines, projects of national interest and sectoral plans deal with the wider spatial planning issues – with special attention to the road network across the country - the planning instruments of the communes (master plans, partial plans and special plans) are focused on strategic urban planning matters and the development of the parishes.

Planning process and development control

Development in the parishes is determined and regulated by the Partial Plans and the Special Plans. These instruments operate in accordance with the Master Plans, which establish the general land structure for the parishes. Master Plans are subject to review every four years. Public participation in this process only happens when the new document has been drafted by the expert team working for the commune. The new Master Plan can be 'called-in' by the state if the Ministry of Spatial Planning believes that the commune has not represented the public interest accurately.

Sustainability and governance

The Regulation of the certification of energy efficiency in buildings Law (2012) is part of the energy model described in the Energy White Paper of Andorra. The law aims to establish a common evaluation method of energy efficiency in buildings and to regulate the construction of energy efficient buildings. The Centre for Sustainable Andorra, a facility of the Department of Environment of the Government of Andorra, acts as an open forum for those actors and stakeholders who deal with sustainability issues.

Planning system in practice

The main challenge that planning is facing in Andorra is the loss of scarce and precious natural resources due to ill-planned urban growth. Thus, it is urgent to calculate the carrying capacity of Andorra's territory to set appropriate limits to growth. In addition, the existing legislation concerning environmental and sustainability matters needs updating. Finally, it is necessary to integrate the principles of sustainable development into other sectorial laws, such as transportation and road building.

AUSTRIA

FAST FACTS

- **Total Area:** 83,855km²
- **Total Population:** 8,401,940
- **Population Growth:** 0.55%
- **Unemployment Rate:** 5.6%
- **GDP:** $436.1 billion
- **GDP per capita:** $45,400
- **GDP growth rate:** 0.3%

SETTLEMENTS STRUCTURE

- **Capital City:** Vienna
  1,741,000 pop
- **Second City:** Graz
  265,778 pop
- **Density:** 101 pop/km²
- **Urban Population:** 66%

INSTITUTIONAL STRUCTURE

Federal republic composed of 9 states and 2,357 municipalities.

Read on: www.oerok.gv.at/ www.raumpla-nung.steiermark.at/ www.uba.at/

Administrative competence for planning

This is a three tier system with competences for planning split between the national, the federal states and the municipal levels. Central government has competences over national sectoral policies, including planning. Federal states enact their own spatial planning laws, plans and projects and they are also responsible for planning at the regional level. As a result there are nine spatial planning laws in Austria. Municipalities have full competences over local planning and its development.

Main planning legislation

There are no legislative provisions for spatial planning at the national level. Each federal state enacts and implements its own spatial planning laws. ÖROK, the Austrian Conference on Spatial Planning is a federal organisation coordinating federal and regional planning interests. Municipalities can create associations at regional level (e.g. PGO, Vienna planning association east).

Planning and implementation instruments

There is a strategic instrument for overall spatial development in Austria. This is the Austrian Spatial Development Concept (ÖREK), last updated in 2011. In addition to ÖREK, there are spatial planning and sectoral programmes at the federal state level; regional spatial planning programmes; and local development schemes (ÖEK), zoning or land use plans (FWP) and detailed building plans (BBP) at the municipal level. European structural funds have brought in an additional layer to the planning system because of their emphasis on the regional level, which had no representation in the planning system until the country joined the EU.

Planning process and development control

Local authorities have full planning powers at municipal level. However, local development schemes must be in accordance with regional and state plans and programmes. Although local plans are approved by the Planning Advisory Board (Planungsbeirat) of the city, these must also be reviewed and approved by the corresponding state supervisory authority.

Sustainability and governance

Disaster prevention planning, especially in the fields of avalanches and floods, has gained more relevance recently, due to the worsening of weather conditions over the last years. At local level, cities are trying to tackle CO_2 emissions by changing mobility patterns and controlling the location of new development areas. Cross border cooperation with the surrounding countries has been a relevant planning issue since they joined the EU. INTERREG-programmes (EU funded) have been playing an important role in facilitating this cooperation.

Planning system in practice

The Austrian planning system is similar to other European countries in that the local level plays a leading role in land use planning. However, the increasing relevance of cross border regions, as well as the environmental challenges posed by the impacts of climate change and urban sprawl, demand greater coordination between the different tiers of the planning system and their decision making bodies.

BELGIUM

FAST FACTS

- **Total Area:** 30,528km²
- **Total Population:** 11,323,973
- **Population Growth:** 0.76 %
- **Unemployment Rate:**8.5%
- **GDP:** $ 527.8 billion
- **GDP per capita:** $ 41,700
- **GDP growth rate:** 1%

SETTLEMENTS STRUCTURE

- **Capital City:** Brussels

   2,029 million pop

- **Second City:** Antwerp

   990,000 pop

- **Density:** 370,94 pop/km²
- **Urban Population:** 97.9%

INSTITUTIONAL STRUCTURE

Constitutional monarchy composed of three independent regions: Wallonia, Flanders and Brussels.

Read on: www.ruimtelijkeordening.be/ www.dgo4.spw.wallonie.be/dgatlp/ http:// be.brussels/

Administrative competence for planning

The federal level has only indirect competence concerning spatial planning. Since the 1980 constitutional reform, the Flemish, the Walloon and the Brussels Capital Region are responsible and competent for their own spatial planning and environmental policy. Nevertheless, the Federal Government still has some responsibilities in environmental policy. It is competent for environmental strategies and implementation of EU directives. It also remains competent for certain fiscal matters, including related to land and property.

Main planning legislation

There are three different planning systems in Belgium. The legal basis for the Flemish planning system is the decree on spatial planning of 22 October 1996, 18 May 1999 and 27 March 2009, 4 April 2014. For the Walloon planning system it is the Decree of 27 November 1997, 1 October 2002 (CWATUP), adapted from the old Belgian system. The Brussels planning system is laid down in the Brussels 'Spatial Planning Code' (COBAT/OOPS).

Planning and implementation instruments

The main difference between the three systems, with regard to their instruments, has to do with the particular administrative structure of each region. The Flemish region encompasses instruments for the regional, the provincial and the municipal level; the Walloon region, for regional and municipal levels; and the Brussels Capital region, for regional and municipal levels. The three cases share a distinction between strategic instruments and operational ones. Maps and plans are key tools in both types and some of these plans have a legally binding status.

Planning process and development control

Development control happens at all levels of each planning system – e.g. at regional, provincial and municipal levels in the Flemish case. In all three cases, the content of infra levels must be in accordance with that of supra levels. In addition, the Flemish system applies the 'subsidiarity principle', to improve coordination and effectiveness of the planning process.

Sustainability and governance

Environmental issues are addressed by each region according to their own studies. Municipal planning instruments provide further guidance on environmental issues in the Walloon and Brussels cases. The lack of adequate platforms for consultation between the regions is a major challenge for the governance of the country and the regions themselves. The fact that the territories covered by the Communities (entities that deals with language-related and person-related matters) do not necessarily match with the territory of the regions, adds another layer of complexity to the governance of Belgium.

Planning system in practice

Cross-regional effects on spatial development have led to the constitution of an inter-regional 'information forum for spatial development' (2012). The lack of adequate levers (e.g. financial instruments) to back up regional policies is a major threat for the future viability of the three planning systems, due to the interdependency of their instruments at different levels.

BULGARIA

FAST FACTS

- **Total Area:** 111,001.90 km²
- **Total Population:** 7,245,677
- **Population Growth:** -5.6%
- **Unemployment Rate:** -12.9%
- **GDP:** $53.01 Billion
- **GDP per capita:** $3,316
- **GDP growth rate:** 0.9%

SETTLEMENTS STRUCTURE

- **Capital City:** Sofia

  1,291,591 pop
- **Second City:** Plovdiv

  338,153 pop
- **Density:** 65.28 pop/km²
- **Urban Population:** 72.90%

INSTITUTIONAL STRUCTURE

Republic composed of 28 provinces, 264 municipalities and 5,302 settlements.

Read on: www.government.bg/ www. mrrb.government.bg/

Administrative competence for planning

Competences for planning are split into four levels: national (Council of Ministers), regional (Regional Development Councils), provincial (Provincial Development Council) and municipal (Municipal Council). Regions were established in order to comply with European spatial planning requirements and they have become the focus of the current planning system in Bulgaria.

Main planning legislation

It is mainly determined by two laws: the Regional Development Act, SG 50/2008, SG 22/2014, which sets out the broad principles of regional and local planning for strategic (socio-economic) planning and spatial planning; and the Spatial Planning Act, SG 1/2001, SG 53/2014, which defines in detail the principles of spatial development at the level of the municipality (settlements, neighbourhoods, individual properties and the main building regulations).

Planning and implementation instruments

There are two types: Spatial Planning Documents (SPD) at national, regional, provincial and municipal levels, which are based on the strategic (socio-economic) planning and programming documents for the development of the regions; and General Development Plans (master plans) and Detailed Plans, which guide the overall development of municipalities in accordance with the content of the SPDs.

Development control

Development control happens at all levels of the planning system. The Minister of Regional Development retains the highest authority, overseeing strategic planning and programming at the national level. The Regional Development Council is responsible for regional planning. Governors are responsible for the provincial level and finally, the Mayor and the Municipal Council control the plans and strategies stipulated by RDA and SPA at the local level.

Sustainability and governance

The concept of 'sustainable development' underlies the development and implementation of spatial plans. In addition, environmental assessments must be carried out at the local level, prior to the approval of any General Development Plan or any Detailed Plan. Public participation of citizens and stakeholders happens at the municipal level (General Development Plan) through public hearings and on-line consultation. Representatives of the local municipalities, representatives of NGOs and interested groups can also engage with the plan making process at regional level through public hearings at the Regional Development Councils.

Planning system in practice

The main challenge is the lack of well-defined and properly allocated public property rights, due to the country's recent communist past and its transitions to a market driven society. The implications of this situation are manifold - for instance, the over-exploitation of valuable natural enclaves for tourism (e.g. Black Sea coast), during the positive market cycles. The limited public engagement in the planning process (just in the final stages and as a mere consultee) is another area for improvement.

CROATIA

FAST FACTS

- **Total Area:** 56,594 km²
- **Total Population:** 4,398,000
- **Population Growth:** -0.9%
- **Unemployment Rate:** 19.7%
- **GDP:** $57.16 billion
- **GDP per capita:** $20,900
- **GDP growth rate:** -0.4%

SETTLEMENTS STRUCTURE

- **Capital City:** Zagreb
    688,163 pop
- **Second City:** Split
    167,121 pop
- **Density:** : 75.7 pop/km²
- **Urban Population:** 57%

INSTITUTIONAL STRUCTURE

Republic composed of 21 counties, 429 municipalities and 6,755 settlements.

Read on: www.mgipu.hr/default. aspx?id=3967 www.nipp.hr/default. aspx?id=340

Administrative competence for planning

At the national level, it lies with the Ministry of Construction and Physical Planning and is performed by the Croatian Institute for Spatial Development. At the regional level, it lies with the County prefect and is performed by County/City planning professional authorities. At the local level, it lies with the Town or City Council and is performed by the planning authorities.

Main planning legislation

Spatial Planning and Construction Law (1994. 1998, 2007, 2013) and its associated regulations, ordinances and standards.

Planning and implementation instruments

At the national level, there are the following spatial planning instruments: the National Spatial Development Plan; the Spatial Plan of the Special Area (prescribed for all areas under national and international protection regimes); and the Urban Plan of national importance. At the regional level, there is the County Spatial Plan, the Spatial Plan of the City of Zagreb and the Urban Plan of county importance. Finally, there are the following instruments at the local level: the City and Municipality Spatial Plan; the General Urban Plan; and the Urban Development Plan.

Development control

Implementation and development control are the most neglected facets of the planning process in Croatia. In fact, "illegal construction" has been one of the long-standing and persistent problems in Croatia. Responsibilities for development control lie with the executive authorities at the local level. The control instruments are mainly the location/building permits.

Sustainability and governance

Competences for environment protection lie with the Ministry of Environmental and Nature protection. This could explain the weakness of the planning system in addressing environmental issues. Public participation is expected to be incorporated at all levels of the planning process. However, the general public is perceived by other actors as an unequal participant in planning discussions, insufficiently objective, or utterly incompetent. In order to improve this situation, web sites for the Capital Zagreb and few other cities are facilitating access to planning information more broadly.

Planning system in practice

Since gaining independence in the early 1990s, the planning system has tried to turn away from the old socialist methods of planning, towards more flexible forms of urban management and governance. The EU collaborated closely with the Croatian government on the drafting and implementation of the principles defined in the Spatial Planning Strategy (1997), which are consistent with the informal European document, ESDP. This has led to political reforms towards democratisation and privatisation of land and property. However, planning practice still faces the challenge of addressing new demands with an outdated set of tools; a lack of adequately trained personnel with necessary knowledge and expertise; long-lasting issues like illegal constructions; and the on-going recovery of the built environment from the impacts of the war.

CYPRUS

Note: The contents of this box refer only to the Republic of Cyprus and not to the Turkish administered territory on the North of the island, which has no international recognition as a country since its occupation in 1974.

FAST FACTS

- **Total Area:** 9,251km²
- **Total Population:** 1,126,664
- **Population Growth:** 2 – 2,5%
- **Unemployment Rate:** 15.3%
- **GDP:** $ 23,613 billion
- **GDP per capita:** $25,249
- **GDP growth rate:** - 4%

SETTLEMENTS STRUCTURE

- **Capital City:** Nicosia
  246,400 pop
- **Second City:** Limassol
  184,100 pop
- **Density:** 90.7 pop/km²
- **Urban Population:** 65%

INSTITUTIONAL STRUCTURE

Republic composed of 6 districts.

Read on: www.moi.gov.cy/moi/tph/tph. nsf www.moi.gov.cy/moi/urbanguard/ urbanguard.nsf

Administrative competence for planning

It largely lies in central government hands, with a minor role for local authorities. Spatial planning and urban policy is within the remit of the Ministry of Interior, through the Department of Town Planning and Housing and the Planning Board. Municipalities have competence over development control only.

Main planning legislation

The main goal of the Town and Country Planning Law (1972) was to encourage coordination of physical and infrastructure planning with economic and social development planning. The events of 1974 have prevented such integration, leaving a gap in the operation of the planning system.

Planning and implementation instruments

The law introduced a three tier hierarchy of Development Plans: Island Plan, never implemented due to the events of 1974; the Local Plan, for major urban areas, areas of exceptional importance or areas undergoing intensive development pressures; and Area Scheme, more detailed and specifically project-oriented. To sort out the planning gap at a national level, a Policy Statement for the Countryside was introduced in 1992.

Planning process and development control

The Department of Town Planning and Housing is the main organisation responsible for development control. However, local authorities have direct responsibility for building permits and licensing in the main urban areas. The lack of a strategic plan for the whole island coupled with pro-development Local Plans, have resulted in unhealthy land use competition between different areas of a same city.

Sustainability and governance

Planning in Cyprus is gradually embracing the sustainability agenda as part of the requirements to enter the EU, which took place in 2014. Public participation in the plan making process is merely consultative. ICT is still under-developed. All plans and all submissions are paper based. Publication of notices is via local newspapers.

Planning system in practice

The continuing Turkish military occupation of a substantial portion of the country is still a major structural challenge which affects all strategic planning decisions. The lack of an overarching vision for the island, coupled with highly protected property rights and growth-led planning instruments, have accelerated suburban expansions. This situation has caused the decline of urban centres, especially in the divided capital of Nicosia, due to loss of commercial and retail activities to shopping centres in the fringes. On the positive side, there is significant momentum (as of end of 2014) for the preparation of a cross-departmental Island Plan for the territory of the Republic of Cyprus. Regeneration is taking place in the UN controlled buffer zone which divides Nicosia.

CZECH REPUBLIC

FAST FACTS

- **Total Area:** 78,867km²
- **Total Population:** 10,537,818
- **Population Growth:** 0,16%
- **Unemployment Rate:** 7,9 %
- **GDP:** $ 195,7 million
- **GDP per capita:** $ 26,590
- **GDP growth rate:** 2,5 %

SETTLEMENTS STRUCTURE

- **Capital City:** Praha (Prague)
  1,2 million pop
- **Second City:** Brno
  400,000 pop
- **Density:** 133 pop/km²
- **Urban Population:** 76%

INSTITUTIONAL STRUCTURE

Republic composed of 14 regions and over 6,000 municipalities.

Read on: www.mmr.cz/en/Ministerstvo
www.mzp.cz/en/ministry

Administrative competence for planning
Competences are split into three levels: national, regional and local National and regional authorities have competence over spatial and strategic planning – e.g. national and regional infrastructure priorities while local authorities have competence over development planning..

Main planning legislation
Planning and Building Act (2006). Its main aspiration is to encourage a sustainable development of the territory.

Planning and implementation instruments
It is a three tier system in which the determinations of a lower tier must be in accordance with the determinations of an upper one. The Spatial Development Policy is produced in accordance to the 2006 Act and any other relevant sectoral law – e.g. environmental laws. This instrument represents the upper tier of the system. The Principles of Spatial Development specify development areas and axes, corridors for major infrastructure lines and identify major projects of public interest. These represent the middle tier of the system. Finally, the Local Territorial Plans and Zoning and Regulation Plans represent the lower tier of the planning system. The former determine the land uses and use densities for the municipality while the latter set out the specific regulations for the implementation of those uses.

Planning process and development control
Development control happens at the local level through the Building Office, which grants planning permissions and building permits to those proposals that conform to the statutory plans and regulations. However, it is common place that big developers and investors lobby to introduce changes to the planning regulations in order to make their proposals viable. Consequently, Local Plans are constantly being amended, which undermines the reliability of this planning instrument and raises serious doubts about the role of local authorities in controlling development.

Sustainability and governance
The principle of sustainable territorial development underlies the Czech Planning and Building Act (2006). However, the social and economic dimensions are more loosely monitored than the environmental one.
Participation in the plan making process is non-existing at the spatial planning level and very minimal at the development planning level. However, things have improved since 2006, when the law required all plans, data and relevant documents to be made publicly available on-line. The lack of appropriate ICT services thus represents a major threat to public participation.

Planning system in practice
The political change towards democracy and market economy in the 1990s has challenged the role of planning in the Czech society. Thus, private developers have become active players in the plan-making process while public bodies have become reactive players. This situation, coupled with an increasingly under-resourced public sector, challenges the idea of the 'public interest' in planning and should call for a revision of the institutional capacity of the planning bodies.

FAST FACTS

- **Total Area:** 43,000 km2
- **Total Population:** 5,600,000
- **Population Growth:** 0.23%
- **Unemployment Rate:** 7.5%
- **GDP:** $340.8 billion
- **GDP per capita:** $44,300
- **GDP growth rate:** 1%

SETTLEMENTS STRUCTURE

- **Capital City:** Copenhagen
  1,700,000 pop
- **Second City:** Aarhus
  326,676 pop
- **Density:** 130 pop/km²
- **Urban Population:** 87.7%

INSTITUTIONAL STRUCTURE

Constitutional monarchy composed of 5 regions and 98 municipalities.

Read on: eng.mim.dk/topics/planning-and-land-use/ naturstyrelsen.dk/planlae-gning/plansystemdk/

Administrative competence for planning

The core responsibility for spatial planning and land use functions lies at the local level, while at the national level the Nature Agency, at the Ministry of the Environment, acts as a facilitator of the planning system and monitors the planning tasks carried out by the municipalities.

Main planning legislation

The 2007 Planning Act, published by the Ministry of Environment.

Planning and implementation instruments

The National Planning Reports and the Overview of National Interests, published by the Ministry of the Environment, are the main national planning instruments. These outline the aims and requirements of the government with respect to municipal planning. In addition, National Directives are prepared and adopted by the Ministry of the Environment to set out legal provisions on specific issues of national interest (e.g. infrastructure corridors). The Municipal Plan is the main political instrument of the council for development control and serves as a strategy for social and economic development and environmental sustainability. These Plans must be in accordance with the determinations of the Overview of National Interest. Finally, Local Plans are the main instrument of implementation at the municipal level. These can be initiated by the local authority or by private developers.

Development control

It lies with the local authorities entirely. Development is allowed in urban and summer cottage zones. In rural zones, developments or any change of land use for other purposes than agriculture and forestry are prohibited or subject to a special permission from the municipal authority. The Building Act regulates the granting of building permits, which must be consistent with adopted planning regulations.

Sustainability and governance

Sustainability and environmental priorities are highly incorporated both within the planning system and the system of land use control. Many municipalities have shaped their municipal plans to the strategies for Local Agenda 21. More recently, the Planning Act has been amended in order to allow for climate change considerations to be included in local plans.

Public participation in the planning process happens prior to adoption and implementation of plans but not while these are being prepared. Since 2007, spatial plans have to be recorded in the national planning information system. In addition, the e-governance portal (digital platform) offers citizens the chance to provide direct feedback on proposed development plans during the statutory eight-week consultation period.

Planning system in practice

The spatial coordination previously provided by the county level has been significantly altered after its abolition and the rescaling of planning tasks and responsibilities to the local level primarily. The current economic context might put the new system to the test and reveal whether it can provide a coordinated answer to global challenges at a local level.

ESTONIA

FAST FACTS

- **Total Area:** 45,000km²
- **Total Population:** 1,313,271
- **Population Growth:** -0.2%
- **Unemployment Rate:** 7.4%
- **GDP:** $25.95 billion
- **GDP per capita:** $27,000
- **GDP growth rate:** 2.1%

SETTLEMENTS STRUCTURE

- **Capital City:** Tallinn
  436,576 pop
- **Second City:** Tartu
  97,005 pop
- **Density:** 29,2 pop/km²
- **Urban Population:** 68%

INSTITUTIONAL STRUCTURE

Republic composed of 15 counties and 215 municipalities.

Read on: www.siseministeerium.ee www. planeerijad.ee www.arhliit.ee

Administrative competence for planning

At the national level, the Ministry of Internal Affairs (MIA) has the competence for planning at national level whereas the Ministry of Economy and Communication has the competences over building activity. The County Governor has the competences for planning at the county level. Finally, municipalities have full competences over planning at local level.

Main planning legislation

The former Planning and Building Act (1995) was reviewed in the 2000s and replaced by the Planning Act (PLA) and the Building Act (BA) in 2003. Both of them were harmonised with EU legal principles, paying more attention to safety of buildings and planning, energy efficiency and sustainability.

Planning and implementation instruments

The National Spatial Plan (2012) provides guidelines for county plans and international planning co-operation as well as guidelines for the development of key spatial elements – e.g. infrastructure corridors. The (non-mandatory) County plans are prepared when deemed necessary – for the whole county, part of it or for sectorial purposes. At the local level, municipalities must have a Comprehensive plan, which can be privately initiated but must be carried out by the local authorities. Comprehensive Plans outline the main objectives of spatial and economic development as well as land uses for the municipality. Detailed plans set out the basis for building activities in smaller parts of a municipality. They can also be initiated by any individual but they could be carried out by the corresponding local authority or contracted out to a specialist – i.e. an architect or a planner. Every tier of the planning system should be in accordance with the upper ones.

Planning process and development control

Local authorities have full powers over development control.

Sustainability and governance

The Assessment and Environmental Management System Act (AEMSA) regulates the delivery of environmental assessment procedures in the plan making process. Plans for nature reserves and heritage preservation regulations are outside the remit of the MIA although they are also taken into account in the planning process. Citizen participation in the plan making process happens at the county and local level and only in the final stages – public consultation prior to approval. Queries raised by individuals following the public exhibition of the plan are answered and settled by the same corresponding supervisory body.

Planning system in practice

Property and land reforms are still dealing with the problems triggered by the expropriations that happened during the Russian occupation. Accordingly, protection of private property rights has become a key concern of the Estonian government. This fact challenges the planning system in practice since it contradicts the spirit of the PLA, based on the Scandinavian planning system that places the public interest above private ones. This conflict is best illustrated in those instances where the individual interests behind a Detailed plan have resulted in the amendment of the Comprehensive Plan.

FAST FACTS

- **Total Area:** 338,435km²
- **Total Population:** 5,500,000
- **Population Growth:** 0.45%
- **Unemployment Rate:** 8.5%
- **GDP:** $271.2 billion
- **GDP per capita:** $40,300
- **GDP growth rate:** 0.1%

SETTLEMENTS STRUCTURE

- **Capital City:** Helsinki
  616,000 pop
- **Second City:** Espoo
  260,000 pop
- **Density:** 18pop/km²
- **Urban Population:** 69%

INSTITUTIONAL STRUCTURE

Republic composed of 19 regions and 336 municipalities.

Read on: www.ym.fi/en-us www.localfin-land.fi/en/authorities/regional-councils/Pages/default.aspx

Administrative competence for planning

At the national level, competences lie with the Ministry of Environment (MoE), which is responsible for the legislation and national land use guidelines, the environmental protection and the management of land resources. At the regional level, the 19 Regional Councils lay down the regional development and regional land use planning objectives. Finally, the 336 municipalities have full competences of planning at the local level.

Main planning legislation

The Land Use and Building Act (LBA 2000) represents a revision of the previous Building Act (1958) that led to the rapid urbanisation of the country in the 1960s.

Planning and implementation instruments

The National land use guidelines cover key infrastructure networks as well as natural and built-up areas of national significance. National goals are then spatially expressed in Regional land use plans. The Local master plan lays down the objectives of land use in the municipality. The detailed plan lays out the organisation of land use and building within the municipality. In addition, municipal Building ordinances are set out in accordance to the National Building Code. Finally, a specific tool to support cooperation between the municipalities in the city regions and the state has been recently created (2012) – i.e. Letter of Intents (MAL).

Planning process and development control

Due to the self-governing character of the Finnish local government system, municipalities have full powers over the development control of planning. Building ordinances are municipalities' primary tool for controlling construction.

Sustainability and governance

The concept of 'sustainable development' underpins the whole planning system and the LBA specifically calls for sustainable planning and construction. Citizen participation in the plan making process is also encouraged in the LBA. For instance, procedures for participation and impact assessment must be set at the start of every new plan. Moreover, participation is open to all parties – any individual - with an interest in the plans. However, the direct participation of individuals has led to many appeals in which personal interests are overtaking the public interest.

Planning system in practice

Many planners regard the Finnish planning system as logical, systematic and enabling, allowing them to concentrate on creative work. The citizens generally experience the planners and planning system as reliable and fair. However, the economic recession of the 1990s brought about the creation of numerous public-private partnerships, which has led to the increasing relevance of private planning consultants and the transformation of many planning authorities into planning managers. In addition, the acceleration of the Finnish urban sprawl (fennosprawl) represents a major threat to Finland's 'sustainable development'. The weakness of the regional level in the strategic guidance of land-use planning and in regional resource programming might be at the root of the problem.

FRANCE ▮▮

FAST FACTS

- **Total Area:** 674,843km²
- **Total Population:** 63,320,000
- **Population Growth:** 0,5%
- **Unemployment Rate:** 9.8%
- **GDP:** $2.847 trillion
- **GDP per capita:** $40,400
- **GDP growth rate:** 0.4%

SETTLEMENTS STRUCTURE

- **Capital City:** Paris
  2,240,621 pop
- **Second City:** Marseille
  852,516 pop
- **Density:** 97,8 pop/km²
- **Urban Population:** 86%

INSTITUTIONAL STRUCTURE

Republic composed of 13 regions, 101 departments (5 overseas) and 36,681 communes.

*Read on: www.territoires.gouv.fr/ministere
www.developpement-durable.gouv.fr/*

Administrative competence for planning
At the national level, competences fall mainly within the remit of the Ministry of Housing, Equality, Territory and Rural Policies. Competences at the local level are shared between 13 (+5 ROM) regional administrations, 101 departments and 36,658 communes. Both of them are represented by the same elected councillors. These have direct competence for planning at local level.

Main planning legislation
The Spatial Planning and Development Act (1995) and the Spatial Planning and Sustainable Development Act (1999) form the general framework. The Planning Code sets out the rules of all the planning steps. In addition, the Solidarity for Urban Renewal law (2000) and the Town Planning and Housing law (2003) incorporate the concept of sustainable development into the planning system.

Planning and implementation instruments
The national government develops national sector plans and Public Service Plans (SSC) as national guidelines. The regions devise Regional Spatial Planning and Development Schemes (SRADT; SRADDT) as locally oriented medium-term plans. The Spatial Planning Directives (DTA; DTADD) set forth the state's basic policies concerning a specific territory, are also locally-oriented plans that relate to both regional spatial improvement and municipal-level urban planning. At the local level, the Territorial Coherence Scheme (SCOT) is a strategic document that corresponds to a geographic unit, such as a valley or a large urban area. It includes social, economic and environmental aims. The Local Town Plan (PLU) concerns a commune or a group of communes. It organises the development of the different urban functions and to preserve the rural and natural areas. The Concerted Planning Area defines the planning conditions of an area, related specifically to infrastructures and facilities.

Planning process and development control
Development control is exercised at the local level. Development proposals must comply with the determinations of the PLU in order to get a Planning Certificate or a Building Permit.

Sustainability and governance
The Grenelle de l'environnement is an open multi-party debate that brings together representatives of national and local government and organisations. It aims to define the key points of public policy on ecological and sustainable development issues. Citizen participation in the local planning process is wide and extensive.

Planning system in practice
The accumulation of an extensive amount of regulations and norms over time is one of the main weaknesses of the French planning system. This situation coupled with the lack of appropriate training on spatial planning and sustainable development issues, represents a major challenge for the professionals working in the field, in particular for those planners and architects working in small communes. In addition, the lack of appropriate monitoring of the development process renders the planning and implementation instruments inefficient.

FAST FACTS

- **Total Area:** 357,138km²
- **Total Population:** 80,500,000
- **Population Growth:** -0.08%
- **Unemployment Rate:** 6.8%
- **GDP:** $ 3,722 billion
- **GDP per capita:** $ 45,900
- **GDP growth rate:** 1.6%

SETTLEMENTS STRUCTURE

- **Capital City:** Berlin
  3,370,000 pop
- **Second City:** Hamburg
  1,730,000 pop
- **Density:** 225 pop/km²
- **Urban Population:** 76%

INSTITUTIONAL STRUCTURE

Federal Republic composed of 16 states subdivided into cities, towns and counties.

Read on: www.bbr.bund.de germanlawar-chive.iuscomp.org/

Administrative competence for planning

Planning competences lie primarily at the local level of 402 districts, with the municipal councils. At the federal level of this hierarchical system, the Ministries of Environment, Transport and Economics have framework responsibilities and no direct planning competence. At the level of the 16 states, the corresponding State Ministries have competence over their territory and the Regional Associations are responsible for sub-areas of each state.

Main planning legislation

The Federal Spatial Planning Act (2008) guides the regulation of state planning and regional planning. In addition, the Federal Building Code (1997) guides the regulation of planning and development at the municipal level.

Planning and implementation instruments

The latest reform of the Spatial Planning Act has meant that every tier of the planning system can prepare Spatial plans. Spatial Plans at the federal and state level are merely strategic whereas at the regional level facilitate inter-municipal coordination of urban development The three city-states (Berlin, Bremen, Hamburg) and the State of Saarland have waived this planning level completely. In any case, the main planning and implementation instruments are the Preparatory land use plans and the Legally binding land use plan, prepared by each municipal council.

Planning process and development control

The German planning system is ruled by two basic principles: municipal planning autonomy and mutual influence. As a result, the top tiers of the system have mainly coordinating tasks and powers, while direct competence for planning lies with the municipal councils. Accordingly, development control happens at this lower level.

Sustainability and governance

Sustainability is recognised as guiding principle of spatial development in the Federal Spatial Planning Act. In addition, the National Sustainable Development Strategy (2002) promotes the shift to renewable energy, the reduction of CO_2 emissions and sets up procedures, targets and indicators for monitoring sustainability across the country. Citizen participation in the planning process is open to everyone, regardless of their direct personal political or economic interest in it. Moreover, participation happens from inception to approval of plans and it is limited to the municipal level.

Planning system in practice

Decreasing population in Eastern areas, ageing population across the country and decreasing household size are challenging the existing planning system, which was adopted in a context of demographic growth. The German Reunification has increased the regional inequalities and the migration flow towards the Western parts of the country, leading to the shrinking cities phenomenon. Moreover, the transition towards a de-centralised planning system in East Germany has not fully happened yet, adding to these regional inequalities. Informal planning processes are emerging as a way of avoiding lengthy (and out of date) formal planning processes and ease coordination among actors.

GREECE

FAST FACTS

- **Total Area:** 131,957 km²
- **Total Population:** 10,815,197
- **Population Growth:** -1%
- **Unemployment Rate:** 27.3%
- **GDP:** $238 billion
- **GDP per capita:** $25,900
- **GDP growth rate:** 0.8%

SETTLEMENTS STRUCTURE

- **Capital City:** Athens
  3,089,698 pop
- **Second City:** Thessaloniki
  1,032,853 pop
- **Density:** 82 pop/km²
- **Urban Population:** 75.9%

INSTITUTIONAL STRUCTURE

Republic composed of 13 regions and 325 municipalities.

Read on: www.ypeka.gr

Administrative competence for planning
They mainly lie with the Ministry of Environment, Energy and Climate Change (EE&CC), which has decision making powers over spatial planning at national, regional and local levels. The Regional Councils share their planning competences at the regional level with the EE&CC, and with the local authorities at municipal level.

Main planning legislation
The Law 2742/1999 for sustainable spatial planning, with a national and a regional scope; the Law 2508/1997 for the sustainable development of cities and settlements, which has extended the boundaries of local plans up to their administrative border rather than their built up areas; and the Building Code, which sets the general rules for the construction of buildings.

Planning and implementation instruments
The Greek planning system has traditionally had an emphasis on the built environment, with a particular emphasis on urban architecture and building regulations. It includes strategic and framework plans at the national (National Plan, Special National Plans) and regional levels (Regional Plans), and regulatory urban plans and zoning plans at the local level – i.e. Master Plans (Athens and Thessaloniki); Local Structure Plans; Urban development Plans; and Implementation Plans.

Planning process and development control
Urban Control Offices are responsible for the development control through a combined system of planning, building control and monitoring of land-use changes in their municipality. However, development and building rights can still be implemented by individuals in areas outside the control of a local plan as long as the site complies with the minimal plot of land requirement (>0,4 Ha) and it has access to a municipal road.

Sustainability and governance
The protection of the environment is mainly regulated by the Law 1650/1986. Agenda 21 and its sub-programmes have had no actual results due to a lack of institutional capacity. Consultation and participation are foreseen at all levels by the Greek planning legislation. However, it is at the local level that the procedure of public participation is facilitated the most. The right to object before the Municipality can be enforced by individuals or institutions, regarding regulations imposed on their properties, or the Neighbourhood Planning Committee (NPC), regarding all matters raised by the Local and Urban Plans.

Planning system in practice
Preparation of plans happens at a very slow pace at all levels. This issue affects the coordination between the different planning instrument, which generates discontinuities in planning and development control across the territory. As for the implementation of plans, this is usually halted by the illegal construction resulting from the planning discontinuities. In addition insufficient financing and/or institutional capacity are also affecting the implementation of plans at all levels. The EE&CC is suggesting to reform and simplify the current planning system to tackle these issues.

HUNGARY

FAST FACTS

- **Total Area:** 93,030km²
- **Total Population:** 9,897,541
- **Population Growth:** -0.22%
- **Unemployment Rate:** 7.8%
- **GDP:** $246.4 billion
- **GDP per capita:** $24,900
- **GDP growth rate:** 3.6%

SETTLEMENTS STRUCTURE

- **Capital City:** Budapest
  1,714,000 pop
- **Second City:** Debrecen
  203,914 pop
- **Density:** 110 pop/km²
- **Urban Population:** 71.2%

INSTITUTIONAL STRUCTURE

Republic composed of 19 counties, 198 districts and 3,156 municipalities.

Read on: www.kormany.hu/en www.nth. gov.hu/en/activities/territorial-development

Administrative competence for planning
It is effectively split into three levels although the regional tier is acting on behalf of the central government and it was created in order to access the EU funds. At the national level, competence lies with the Prime Minister's Office and the Ministry of National Economy. At the regional level, it lies with the corresponding Regional Chief Architect. At the local level, it lies with the local councils. Budapest, the capital has a special two tier status as a municipality subdivided into districts which share planning competences.

Main planning legislation
The Act on the Formation and Protection of the Built Environment (1997) and the National Building Code (OTÉK) (1997).

Planning and implementation instruments
At the national level, there is the National Development and Regional Development Concept (2014). At the local level, there are the following instruments: Urban Development Concepts, Structure Plans (preparatory land use plan), Regulatory Plans (binding land use plan) and the Local Building Codes.

Development control
It is performed by the Building Authorities functioning as departments of local government offices in cities and bigger villages. For some building matters (i.e. heritage buildings, heritage areas, Natura 2000 districts) other state agencies function as first level building authorities and their full consent is needed for issuing a building permit.

Sustainability and governance
Hungary has adopted the EU Directive on Environmental Impact Assessment (EIA) and Strategic Environmental Assessment (SEA) which have direct relevance to spatial planning. The implementation of the sustainability concept, however, is rather weak in its social dimension.

Planning system in practice
The new Hungarian planning system is a real mixture of American and German planning tools. Although the initial idea was to introduce a flexible system with a (non-binding and long-range) Structure Plan, in reality urban planning started to function in the zoning mode. This has resulted in overprovision of building land under pressure of developers who had acquired land o secure their development rights. Moreover, although the municipalities have implementation instruments and competences to do so, most of them are unable to follow a really pro-active development policy. As a result of the privatisation process in the 1990s, they are inadequately provided with public land and public properties. Very few of them follow an efficient land policy and most are short of money for initiating larger infrastructural and building projects by themselves. Finally, even if they may be able to do so, they fear that they cannot claim back at least a share of the "betterment" resulting from their development activity because the Hungarian planning law does not include any legal measures for sharing expectation values or to work against speculation.

ICELAND

FAST FACTS

- **Total Area:** 103,000km²
- **Total Population:** 331,918
- **Population Growth:** 1.21%
- **Unemployment Rate:** 5%
- **GDP:** $16.69 billion
- **GDP per capita:** $43,600
- **GDP growth rate:** 1.8%

SETTLEMENTS STRUCTURE

- **Capital City:** Reykjavik
  183,000 pop
- **Second City:** Akureyri
  17,000 pop
- **Density:** 3.1 pop/km²
- **Urban Population:** 84.1%

INSTITUTIONAL STRUCTURE

Republic composed of 6 regions and 78 municipalities.

Read on: www.skipulagsstofnun.is/ www. smv.gl/Reg_seminar/thors_jan08.pdf

Administrative competence for planning

At the national level, spatial planning competences lie with the Ministry for the Environment and Natural Resources, and are implemented by the National Physical Planning Agency (NPPA). Local authorities have administrative competences at regional and municipal levels.

Main planning legislation

These are the Planning and Building Act (2008) and the Act No 123/2010, which provides concrete timeframes within which to perform the statutory obligations. Other Acts relevant to spatial planning are: Conservation Act 1999, Icelandic National Renewable Energy Action Plan, Act on Environmental Impact Studies 1993, Act on Information Distribution and Access to Information on Environmental Affairs 1993.

Planning and implementation instruments

It is a top-down system, hierarchically organised. At the top, the Sectoral Plans provide non-binding national guidelines. Regional Plans are legally binding documents formulated by two or more local authorities to agree on regional spatial strategies. However, there is no compulsory requirement for local authorities to produce these plans. At the lowest level of the system, there are two types of plans: Municipal plans, which detail the land use system for the entire municipality, and the Local plans, which provide detailed regulations for neighbourhoods and specific sites. The preparation and implementation of both plans is compulsory and they are also legally binding.

Planning process and development control

The planning committees of each municipality are responsible for controlling development in their territory. Planning and building permits are granted as long as the development proposal complies with the Municipal and Local plans.

Sustainability and governance

Iceland is committed to the sustainability principles and is a signatory to UN led initiatives proposed in Rio 1992. The adopted Agenda 21 has focused mainly on land preservation and soil erosion. Iceland also complies with EU directives on environmental matters. With regards to governance, public participation is still rather weak and self-selective, with a clear agency bias favourable to governmental institutions.

Planning system in practice

The voluntary nature of Regional plans and the lack of an administrative body with coordination powers to mediate between local authorities over land use disputes are the major weaknesses of the Icelandic planning system. The low level of citizen participation in the plan making process, particularly in the rural areas, is also a matter of concern.

IRELAND

FAST FACTS

- **Total Area:** 70,285km²
- **Total Population:** 4,588,252
- **Population Growth:** 7.59%
- **Unemployment Rate:** 11.3%
- **GDP:** $246.4 billion
- **GDP per capita:** $49,200
- **GDP growth rate:** 4.8%

SETTLEMENTS STRUCTURE

- **Capital City:** Dublin
  527,612 pop
- **Second City:** Cork
  119,230 pop
- **Density:** 62 pop/km²
- **Urban Population:** 63.2%

INSTITUTIONAL STRUCTURE

Republic composed of 3 regions, 94 municipalities and 31 cities.

*Read on: www.environ.ie www.pleanala.ie
www.myplan.ie*

Administrative competence for planning
At the national level, it lies with the Minister and Department of the Environment, Community and Local Government (DECLG). At the regional level, it lies with the Regional Assemblies. Finally, it lies with the Planning Authorities at the local level.

Main planning legislation
The Planning and Development Act (2000, 2002, 2010, 2012) and the Planning and Development (Strategic Infrastructure) Act (2006).

Planning and implementation instruments
The planning instruments are hierarchically divided according to the tiers of the system. At the national level, there is the National Spatial Strategy 2002-2020 (2002), currently under review. At the regional level, there are two sets of Regional Planning Guidelines (2004-2016 and 2010-2022). Finally, the City or County Development Plan is the key planning instrument at local level. In addition, the Local Area Plan (LAP) fills the void between the general objectives of the development plan and individual proposals at a local level. LAPs must be made for towns over 5,000 people; or for those areas that require economic, physical and social renewal; or for areas which are likely to be subject to considerable development.

Development control
The key process in relation to the control of development is the grant or refusal of planning permission. It lies with the Planning Authorities at the local level.

Sustainability and governance
Irish sustainability policy is outlined in the document Our Sustainable Future a Framework for Sustainable Development for Ireland 2012. In addition, coordination between the Environmental Protection Agency (EPA) and the Planning Authorities is ensured since planning permission must be obtained before the EPA makes a decision and grants licensing to any potentially polluting industry. Local Agenda 21, EIA (Environmental Impact Assessments) and SEA (Strategic Environmental Assessment) processes have also been implemented. Participation of the public happens at the local level throughout the plan-making process. More importantly, an independent appeals board - An Bord Pleanála – gives the right to third parties to appeal a decision made by a local planning authority. In these cases, the Planning Appeals Board considers the application anew. Finally, Myplan website (developed by DECLG) has brought together digitised information from all the planning authorities across the country.

Planning system in practice
The crash of the property market has left a legacy of unoccupied and unfinished housing developments in many rural towns and villages. In addition, the crisis in public finances and a dependence on the private sector has had a negative impact on the social housing constructed in recent years. In order to tackle these issues, reforms to the planning system with regards to zoning procedures, the role of regional governance and taxes on vacant or derelict land are being implemented.

ITALY

FAST FACTS

- **Total Area:** 301,401km²
- **Total Population:** 60,795,612
- **Population Growth:** 0.27%
- **Unemployment Rate:** 12.8%
- **GDP:** $2.148 trillion
- **GDP per capita:** $35,500
- **GDP growth rate:** -0.4%

SETTLEMENTS STRUCTURE

- **Capital City:** Rome
  2,753,000 pop
- **Second City:** Milan
  1,316,000 pop
- **Density:** 202 pop/km²
- **Urban Population:** 68,8%

INSTITUTIONAL STRUCTURE

Republic composed of 20 regions, 110 provinces and 8,1057 municipalities.

Read on: www.mit.gov.it/mit/site.php
www.beniculturali.it/mibac/export/
MiBAC/#&panel1-1

Administrative competence for planning
The Ministries of Infrastructure and Transportation, Culture and Environment, and Economic Development set out the legal framework for planning, which is then detailed further at the regional level. Regions have decision making powers and legal powers, which have led to an uneven planning picture across Italy. Provinces have plan-making powers but no legislative powers, which have been redirect towards the regions or the municipalities. Finally, Municipalities have full competences within their administrative area.

Main planning legislation
The Urban Planning Law 1150 (1942), and its subsequent modifications, regulates urban development. It is complemented by the D.M. 1444/1968, which establishes the planning standards (i.e. minimal shares per capita of space and public services in relation to urban dimension and population density).

Planning and implementation instruments
There is currently no National Plan. However, the appeal of EU structural funds has initiated the preparation of future Italian spatial arrangements. Regional Plans adapt the national directives to the specific regional contexts. Sectoral Plans are also elaborated at the regional level, according to the specific needs of each region. Provincial plans contain general guidelines about territorial organisation. Finally, Urban master plans (Metropolitan master plans and Municipal Master plans) organise the land use system at the local level.

Development control
Building permits and planning approvals are granted by the municipality as long as the development plans complies with the requirements of the Urban master plan. However, this process is becoming more discretional and negotiations between individuals and planning officers are more and more common. Although this has the positive effect of speeding up the extremely bureaucratic planning process, this incremental way of planning could seriously compromise the coherence of the Urban master plan.

Sustainability and governance
The tools for landscape control and governance had first been introduced by the Nature's Beauties Law in 1939. Nowadays, the state and the regions share the tasks concerning environmental protection. In addition, all plans and programmes must undergo strategic environmental assessment (SEA). Citizen participation is often reduced to the fulfilment of formal procedures and usually takes place at local level, only before the final approval of urban plans.

Planning system in practice
The current planning system encompasses four 'generations' of planning tools. Overlaps and discontinuities between them have never been addressed. This has resulted in an overly bureaucratic and complex planning system which is struggling to respond to the global economy changes and to the needs of a more complex society. More agile and flexible forms of urban plans are being explored to cope better with these fast evolving demands and changes.

FAST FACTS

- **Total Area:** 64,573 km²
- **Total Population:** 1,986,100
- **Population Growth:** -1.06%
- **Unemployment Rate:** 10.8%
- **GDP:** $31.97 billion
- **GDP per capita:** $23,700
- **GDP growth rate:** 2.4%

SETTLEMENTS STRUCTURE

- **Capital City:** Riga
    641,007 pop
- **Second City:** Daugavpils
    86,435 pop
- **Density:** 30.75 pop /km²
- **Urban Population:** 67.9%

INSTITUTIONAL STRUCTURE

Republic composed of 5 regions and 119 municipalities.

Read on: www.varam.gov.lv/eng www.lps. lv/About_LALRG/

Administrative competence for planning
At national level, these lie with the Ministry of Environmental Protection and Regional Development and it is steered by the Inter-sectoral Coordination Centre. Regional Councils, formed of representatives from the different municipal councils, exercise their competences through their executive development agencies. At the local level, competences fall within the remit of recently created municipalities, which have resulted from the abolition of district councils.

Main planning legislation
Spatial planning at the national level is currently regulated by the Spatial Development Planning Law (2011). In addition, strategic planning and physical planning at regional level are regulated by the Regional Development Law (2002) and the Physical Planning Law (2002). The territorial planning system, procedures and powers are determined by the Territorial Planning Law (2002).

Planning and implementation instruments
All the development planning documents should be coordinated with each other and they should correspond to Latvia's long-term conceptual document "Growth model of Latvia: man in the first place" (2008). According to it, the highest long-term development planning document is the Sustainable Development Strategy whereas the highest medium-term development planning document is the National Development Plan. Development strategies and Programmes regulate planning at the regional level. Finally, Territorial plans elaborate the principles of the regional instruments at the municipal level. Local plans, Detailed plans and Building regulations detail the implementation of the territorial plans.

Development control
Municipal councils are responsible for controlling development within their jurisdiction. In the absence of a valid plan, development proposals are assessed on a one-to-one basis, in a public hearing, by the corresponding municipal council.

Sustainability and governance
Latvia signed up to the Agenda 21 declaration on environment and development, which has led to the constitution of a national coordination body and to the formulation of the sustainable growth model for the country. However, Latvia is still one of the highest energy consumers per capita in Europe and its considerable CO2 emissions can be attributed to its transport system. Public participation in the plan making process is still quite limited although residents have the right to attend local council meetings and have free access to decisions.

Planning system in practice
The transformation of the formerly centralised planning system has followed the EU principles on spatial planning – i.e. competitiveness, territorial governance, polycentrism, territorial impact, and place making. However, more institutional capacity is needed to ensure their successful implementation. In addition, the increasing relevance of private property rights and the shift towards a free market economy are also major challenges for the public interest of the planning system.

BILATERAL
LICHTENSTEIN

FAST FACTS

- **Total Area:** 160km²
- **Total Population:** 37,129
- **Population Growth:** 0.84 %
- **Unemployment Rate:** 2.3%
- **GDP:** $5.113 billion
- **GDP per capita:** $89,400
- **GDP growth rate:** 1.8%

SETTLEMENTS STRUCTURE

- **Capital City:** Vaduz

  5,236 pop
- **Second City:** Schaan

  5,853 pop
- **Density:** 227,294 pop/km²
- **Urban Population:** 14.3 %

INSTITUTIONAL STRUCTURE

Constitutional monarchy composed
of 11 municipalities.

*Read on: www.llv.li/ www.regierung.li/
files/attachments/Energiestrategie_Kurz-
fassung.pdf?t=635582014477562293*

Administrative competence for planning

The Department of Building Permits and Subsidies and the Department of Construction and Infrastructure hold the competences at the national level. Regional planning competences also lie with the Department of Construction and Infrastructure since 2015. The Department for Local Planning, under direct control of the government, shares the administrative competences at the local level with the municipal councils.

Main planning legislation

There is no separate spatial planning law. The Building Law (2008) includes a brief description about the planning instruments of the planning system.

Planning and implementation instruments

The Land Structure Plan (2011) is a binding document that regulates spatial planning in the two regions. It also regulates cross-border planning of natural resources, transport infrastructures and settlements with Switzerland. At the local level, each municipality must prepare a series of planning documents that regulate the development planning in a hierarchical order. These are the following, from top to bottom: Community Structure Plan, a Building Code, a Zoning Plan, a Superstructure Plan and an Urban Design Plan.

Development control

The municipal councils have full competence over development control.

Sustainability and governance

The Land Structure Plan details the main principles to achieve a sustainable spatial development. These are: 1) Ensuring sustainable settlement development within existing building zones; 2) Streamlining settlement development and achieving the best possible connection with public transport to avoid urban sprawl. In addition, Lichtenstein has elaborated an Energy Strategy 2020 with the objective to reduce energy consumption by 20% and reduce CO_2 emissions by 20% as well. The "Mobile Liechtenstein 2015" document aimed to contribute to cross-border regional development, provide better access to the industrial area of Schaan, the second city and provide better mobility and accessibility for smaller settlements.

Planning system in practice

Due to the lack of spatial planning legislation and the high municipal autonomy, state and local authorities have to rely on constructive and well-coordinated communication about planning projects during the development process.

FAST FACTS

- **Total Area:** 65,302km²
- **Total Population:** 2,921,262
- **Population Growth:** -1.04%
- **Unemployment Rate:** 10.7%
- **GDP:** $48.23 billion
- **GDP per capita:** $27,100
- **GDP growth rate:** 2.9%

SETTLEMENTS STRUCTURE

- **Capital City:** Vilnius
   531,910 pop
- **Second City:** Kaunas
   301,357 pop
- **Density:** 44.7 pop/km²
- **Urban Population:** 66.5%

INSTITUTIONAL STRUCTURE

Republic composed of 10 counties and 60 municipalities.

Read on: www.tpdris.lt/lt_LT/web/guest/ home www3.lrs.lt/pls/inter3/dokpaieska. showdoc_l?p_id=343407

Administrative competence for planning

The Ministry of Environment is the main entity responsible for sustainable development, urban and climate change policy, land use planning issues, housing renovation, natural heritage protection and regulations of related matters. Municipal Councils have the administrative competences within the area of their jurisdiction.

Main planning legislation

The Territorial Planning Law (TPL 2013) sets out the planning goals, planning levels, arrangements and responsibilities for those who undertake planning initiatives. It also sets the hierarchy of plans and provisions for its preparations.

Planning and implementation instruments

Territorial planning documents can be Comprehensive or Special. These instruments exist at national (State Master Plan) and municipal (Municipal Master Plan) levels. Territorial documents determine the land uses, heritage conservation and infrastructure development guidelines within their jurisdiction. Local Area Master Plans, Detailed Plans and Special Plans set out the regulations for the functioning and the development of a concrete urban area within a municipality.

Development control

It is shared between the Building Inspectorate, at the national level, and the municipal planners at the local level.

Sustainability and governance

The Government of Lithuania approved a national sustainable development strategy in 2003. Although urban planning is not directly mentioned in this strategy, the document plays an important mutual role in achieving spatial sustainability and protecting natural and physical recourses. The recent strategy "Lithuania 2030" (2012) has renewed its efforts in making an effective use of energy resources and ensuring a neutral impact of economic activities on the environment. Public participation is open and democratic. It is regulated by the principles of the Aarhus convention – i.e. voluntarily participation of legal and natural persons or their groups in the preparatory process of territorial planning documents. The planning process and documents must be produced and made available via the electronic Territorial Planning Documents Register Information System (TPDRIS), which also monitors the time of planning procedures and processes.

Planning system in practice

Large-scale privatisation of many formerly state-owned enterprises as well as the availability of EU funds is creating continued improvement of infrastructures and modernisation of the urban areas. However, infrastructure development could increase regional development inequalities and urban sprawl. In this sense, the new TPL aims to streamline the plan making and development processes in order to provide up to date guidance and to monitor urban growth more effectively. To achieve this, it is necessary to change the existing planning mentalities of citizens and professionals around the issue of 'the public interest' to avoid unnecessary delays in the planning process.

LUXEMBURG ▬

FAST FACTS

- **Total Area:** 2,586km²
- **Total Population:** 563.000
- **Population Growth:** 2.13%
- **Unemployment Rate:** 6.9%
- **GDP:** $62.4 billion
- **GDP per capita:** $92,000
- **GDP growth rate:** 2.9%

SETTLEMENTS STRUCTURE

- **Capital City:** City of Luxembourg
  111,300 pop
- **Second City:** Esch-sur-Alzette
  33,300 pop
- **Density:** 217.7 pop/km²
- **Urban Population:** 90.2%

INSTITUTIONAL STRUCTURE

Constitutional monarchy composed of 3 districts and 12 cantons.

Read on: www.guichet.public.lu/entre-prises/en/urbanisme-environnement/in-dex.html www.dat.public.lu/publications/documents/broch_ivl/broch_ivl_en.pdf

Administrative competence for planning

The Department of Spatial Planning, under the direct control of the Minister of Sustainable Development and Infrastructure, is responsible for spatial development at the national level. Municipal councils have administrative competences at the local level and at the regional level – through agency of regional syndicates, which are formed of representatives from the municipal councils.

Main planning legislation

The Act of 30/07/2013 on spatial planning; and the amended Act of 19/07/2004 on the development of cities and other significant agglomerations.

Planning and implementation instruments

Guiding Sectoral Plans are the instruments for coordination of the spatial dimension in sectoral policies at the national level. National Land Use Plans are prepared for those areas with conflicts of interest between different kinds of land uses. Municipal Land Use Plans and Development Plans regulate land uses and development at the local level. In addition, concrete key projects are devised for particular areas and contain innovative concepts for showcasing exemplary developments in spatial, transport and landscape planning – e.g. the Southwest development of Luxembourg city on the basis of an interactive planning process or the 'Nordstad' development plan.

Development control

It lies in the hands of the municipal councils although the Minister has the right to evaluate those project proposals with a direct impact on the national goals of spatial development.

Sustainability and governance

The Act of 19/01/2004, on the protection of the environment and the natural resources, promotes a balanced management of the green zones. In accordance with EU directives, the law also requires an environmental impact assessment if a specific project is supposed to have large impacts on the green zones. The National Plan for Nature Protection (2007) evaluates the ecological potential of the green zones and defines proposals for their protection, restoration and management. Citizen participation is open to everyone and happens at all stages of the plan making process, both at national and local levels.

Planning system in practice

Poor mobility and urban sprawl are the main challenges for the current planning system. Daily commutes from all over the country to the City of Luxembourg have resulted in the congestion of the road network and the public transport. Moreover, the on-going "rurbanisation" of the rural environment – i.e. residential areas constructed along transport lines – is promoting traffic congestion of the road network even further. Better coordination between national and local planning bodies would help to minimise urban sprawl and traffic congestion. In addition, the reform of the municipal land use planning system, which will include new instruments such as building obligations and development, restructuring or regeneration areas, would also help to contain the rurbanisation phenomenon.

MALTA

Administrative competence for planning

The Malta Environment and Planning Authority (MEPA), directly accountable to the Parliamentary Secretariat for Planning and Administrative Simplification within the Office of the Prime Minister, is the authority responsible for spatial planning in the Maltese Islands.

Main planning legislation

The Environment and Development Planning Act (2010) sets out the main planning instruments and administrative setups that guide the development planning process. The law is currently under review and a series of added legislation, policy and guidance document (CAP.504) have been published for public consultation for approval and to be enacted shortly.

Planning and implementation instruments

The Strategic Plan for the Environment and Development (SPED) regulates the sustainable management of land and sea resources at the national level. The Local Plan is the main planning and implementation document at the local level. There are seven local plans covering the whole of the Maltese Islands, however, these are now being revised and it is intended to have three 'generic plans'. The local plans regulate land uses in each locality down to the design of each street, thus assisting deciding bodies in their assessment and final decision on development planning applications.

Development control

It lies with the state, in the Development Control Unit, within the Development Planning Directorate. The Development Notification Order (DNO) identifies what development is permitted without any form of application as well as those which require a simple notification. The rest require a full development application.

Sustainability and governance

The Environment and Planning Commission (EPC) evaluate and inform on every development application. Major projects, especially those requiring an Environmental Impact Assessment, are decided by the MEPA Board. The new policies that regulate development in Outside Development Zones areas (ODZ) have created an uproar amongst various environmental pressure groups since they may give rise to further urban sprawl in rural areas. All planning instruments are subject to public consultation exercises whereby the general public is invited to make their submissions on the various policies being proposed. The MEPA Board approves all the planning documents, which are then sent to the Minister for final approval.

Planning system in practice

The SPED highlights the main planning issues affecting the island, including the degradation of some localities as a result of inappropriate forms of development in the past. The high rate of vacant property, particularly in the old cities, is another concern. Planning policies have done very little in the past to ensure that such properties are put to proper use. Legal issues concerning multiple ownership of one same property have also played a part in the vacancy rate.

FAST FACTS

- **Total Area:** 2km²
- **Total Population:** 38,000
- **Population Growth:** 0.12%
- **Unemployment Rate:** 2%
- **GDP:** $6.063 billion
- **GDP per capita:** $78,700
- **GDP growth rate:** 9.3%

SETTLEMENTS STRUCTURE

- **Capital City:** Monaco
  38,000 pop
- **Second City:** ---

- **Density:** 19,000 pop/km²
- **Urban Population:** 100%

INSTITUTIONAL STRUCTURE

Constitutional monarchy composed of 8 districts.

Read on: www.gouv.mc/

Administrative competence for planning

There is no distinction between national and local levels. Accordingly, competences for planning lie with the state. The Department of Forward Studies, Urban Planning and Mobility, within the Minister of Public Works, Environment and Urban Development, are the government bodies directly responsible for planning.

Main planning legislation

The Sovereign ordinance (Ordonnance Souveraine n°4.816) Act (2014) sets out the legal framework ().

Planning and implementation instruments

The Urban regulations (Règlement d'Urbanisme - RU) define all the construction rules for the urban development of the Principality.

Development control

Once again, the Department of Forward Studies, Urban Planning and Mobility is directly responsible for the control of urban development in the country.

Sustainability and governance

Despite the scarcity of land and the high demand for new developments, there is a strong political focus on environmental protection and sustainable growth. For instance, the Climate and Energy Plan for the country aims to improve energy efficiency by 20% and achieve 20% of final energy consumption from renewable sources by 2020, in line with the Kyoto Protocol. In addition, the country is working on becoming carbon neutral by 2050. The country is also constantly working on the improvement of its green areas, which now cover 20% of the land. As for the transport system, numerous improvements are being made to the public transport, within the Principality and with the neighbouring countries, and to the soft transport modes.

Planning system in practice

The major challenge for the planning system is to reconcile the ambitious sustainable agenda with the demand for continuous development in such a constrained context. Land reclamation has been the way forward traditionally, with the earliest land reclamation works carried out in 1865 to create rail tracks. However, the increase of environmentally sensitive areas in the Principality is rendering this growth solution unviable. Consequently, development is now happening vertically, above and below ground, in order to allocate uses (e.g. residential, commercial) as well as main infrastructure (e.g. water, energy supply and wastewater treatment).

FAST FACTS

- **Total Area:** 41,500 km²
- **Total Population:** 16,919,139
- **Population Growth:** 0,39%
- **Unemployment Rate:** 7.4%
- **GDP:** $866.4 billion
- **GDP per capita:** $47,400
- **GDP growth rate:** 0.8%

SETTLEMENTS STRUCTURE

- **Capital City:** Amsterdam
  826,659 pop
- **Second City:** Rotterdam
  619,879 pop
- **Density:** 492,6 pop/km²
- **Urban Population:** 81.7%

INSTITUTIONAL STRUCTURE

Constitutional monarchy composed of 12 provinces and 393 municipalities.

Read on: www.government.nl/ministries/ministry-of-infrastructure-and-the-environment

Administrative competence for planning

The overall responsibility for spatial planning lies with the Ministry of Infrastructure and the Environment. At the regional level, the task falls within the remit of the 12 provincial governments. At the local level, it lies with the 339 municipal governments.

Main planning legislation

The Spatial Planning Act (WRO) 2008 focuses on achieving an efficient and transparent policy development with a strict law enforcement and more simple legal protection. The Crisis and Recovery Act (CHW) 2010 aims to accelerate the realisation of strategic projects in order to stimulate the national economy. The Environmental Planning Act (OW) 2018 is a bill which aims to renew the regulation of human activities with an effect on the physical environment.

Planning and implementation instruments

Structural visions are strategic policy documents which contain only policy statements with no (legally) binding elements towards lower levels of government. To implement these policies, there are the following instruments: (Digital) land use plans, which should facilitate spatial developments and control it at the same time; and project decisions, a procedure that is applied for large-scale complex projects and has to be followed by a revision of the particular land use plan. Governmental Decrees, provincial enactments, and guidelines are the other instruments to help the implementation of the structural visions at the three different levels of the planning system.

Development control

The municipal governments are responsible for development control unless the scale of the project requires a project decision procedure, in which case it will lie with the central/provincial government. When the OW is enforced, control will happen by means of Integrated environmental permits.

Sustainability and governance

The OW will remove divisions between the sectors that affect the physical environment and will unify all planning and decision-making procedures in one single Act with a single set of six uniform core instruments. It will also simplify the use of existing Environmental Impact Assessment (EIA) instruments, enhancing their use as a decision-making tool while easing the process for planning applicants. Finally, the OW will give responsibility for spatial planning back to the community and prescribe a general duty of care.

Planning system in practice

The former 'comprehensive integrated approach' that characterised the Dutch planning system until the 2000s has been replaced by a more decentralised and streamlined form of planning system. This change seems in tune with the re-structuring of the welfare state system into a more neoliberal state. Interestingly, the changes suggested in the new OW bring the relevance of the environment to the forefront and put forward a more 'integrated approach' to development again. The future implementation of the OW will reveal to what extent society is ready to take the powers that are being handed down to it.

NORWAY

Administrative competence for planning

At the national level, the responsibility for spatial planning lies with the Ministry of Local Government and Modernisation (MLGM). At the regional level, competences fall in the remit of 19 County councils. At the local level, planning competences lie with the 430 municipalities.

Main planning legislation

The Planning and Building Act (PBA 2008) is a comprehensive planning law with provisions for spatial planning at all levels of government, which overrules any other sectoral legislation related to spatial planning.

Planning and implementation instruments

National Planning Guidelines set up the major national objectives, determined in cooperation with other relevant ministries – e.g. Ministry of Transport. County Masterplans consist of long-term objectives and guidelines for regional development in a county and a four-year programme for coordinated actions by the county council, municipalities, state agencies concerned and the private sector. The Municipal Masterplan is a plan for local community development and services within the municipality. Area Zoning Plans and Detailed Zoning Plans regulate the use and protection of land, watercourses, sea areas, buildings and the outdoor environment in specific areas of the municipality. Local plans are the only legally binding documents but the whole system is hierarchically determined.

Planning process and development control

Development control happens mainly at the local level. In the Norwegian planning system there is no private building right. Therefore, building permits are granted only when the proposal is in accordance with the determinations of the local plans. Development control also happens at national level in the case of major alterations or construction of large buildings and installations. In this case, the corresponding municipality must notify the MLGM.

Sustainability and governance

Environmental Impact Assessment (EIA) and planning are coordinated processes. Not only does the PBA spell out EIA requirements but the Ministry of Environment has competence to intervene directly in the preparation of local plans with regards to the implementation of national or county council measures of development, construction or conservation. Citizen participation happens throughout the whole planning process at County and Local levels – from inception to publication.

Planning system in practice

Coordination of spatial planning across municipal boundaries is not sufficient. Municipalities are increasingly granting exemptions from their own enforced plans, which is causing a rather arbitrary spatial development and land use conflicts. Moreover, large municipalities with low and decreasing populations lack updated plans and many of them also lack planning competences. This situation poses a major challenge to compact urban development – one of central government's main aspirations – and the proper functioning of the Norwegian comprehensive planning system.

FAST FACTS

- **Total Area:** 324,000km²
- **Total Population:** 5,165,802
- **Population Growth:** 0.2%
- **Unemployment Rate:** 4.3%
- **GDP:** $500.2 billion
- **GDP per capita:** $66,900
- **GDP growth rate:** 2.2%

SETTLEMENTS STRUCTURE

- **Capital City:** Oslo
  634,463 pop
- **Second City:** Bergen
  271,949 pop
- **Density:** 16 pop/km²
- **Urban Population:** 75%

INSTITUTIONAL STRUCTURE

Constitutional monarchy composed of 19 counties and 428 municipalities.

Read on: www.regjeringen.no/en/dep/ kmd/id504/

FAST FACTS

- **Total Area:** 312,679km^2
- **Total Population:** 38,495,659
- **Population Growth:** -0,1%
- **Unemployment Rate:** 12,5%
- **GDP:** $546.6 billion
- **GDP per capita:** $25,100
- **GDP growth rate:** 3.3%

SETTLEMENTS STRUCTURE

- **Capital City:** Warsaw
  1,715,517 pop
- **Second City:** Cracow (Kraków)
  758,463 pop
- **Density:** 122 pop/km^2
- **Urban Population:** 60.6%

INSTITUTIONAL STRUCTURE

Republic composed of 16 provinces, 379 counties and 2,479 local communes.

Read on: www.mir.gov.pl/ www.tup.org.pl

Administrative competence for planning

Spatial planning is under control of the Ministry of Infrastructure and Development at the national level. At the regional level, competences are shared by the regional councils and the central government. At the local level, competences are shared as well between the county council and the municipal councils (cities or communes).

Main planning legislation

The Planning Act 1995 and its reform, the Planning Act 2003 were created to respond to the new need of managing the relationship between private interest and public good, due to the restitution of private ownership and the creation of private property markets. At present, there is a discussion on a general planning reform/ A draft of the new Code has been submitted for public consultation and review.

Planning and implementation instruments

The planning in communes is based on a two-tier system of Structure plans and Local area development plans. Structure plans are based on a study of conditions and directions of planning development at the local level. Once approved, it is a binding document for the Local area development plans. These local plans represent a local ordinance for a selected area. They regulate the size and volume of permitted development, define the permitted land uses, and specify the rules for division of property or heritage protection regulations. The Special tools introduce a simple administrative mechanism which allow for the development of areas subject which do not yet have a valid local development plan. Similarly, special planning procedures have been set up for other elements of infrastructure or to facilitate streamlined planning for special events (i.e. development of infrastructure for Euro Football Championships in 2012).

Development control

It lies with the county authority or the municipal authority in the case of large cities such as Warsaw.

Sustainability and governance

Many municipalities joined the Agenda 21 Programme at the beginning of the 1990s and have tried to include the concept of sustainable development in their strategic and planning documents. All members of the public have the right to participate in the planning process. However, public engagement in drafting the document comes late in the planning process and it does not normally exceed the statutory consultation procedures.

Planning system in practice

Not all municipalities have a valid Structure plan. This is one of the biggest challenges in terms of managing the urbanisation of Polish cities, particularly in their suburban zone, as the ordinances are the only legal way to establish permitted land uses and set up the development boundaries. In addition to the poor planning coverage, the incorporation of Special Tools in the Planning Act 2003, have undermined the functioning and regulatory role of the planning system, and thereby strengthened the unplanned urbanisation processes. The lack of coordination between metropolitan an urban areas is adding to the sprawling of suburbs.

PORTUGAL

FAST FACTS

- **Total Area:** 92,225.24km²
- **Total Population:** 10,427,301
- **Population Growth:** -0.57%
- **Unemployment Rate:** 13.9%
- **GDP:** $230 billion
- **GDP per capita:** $27,000
- **GDP growth rate:** 0.9%

SETTLEMENTS STRUCTURE

- **Capital City:** Lisbon

    547,733 pop
- **Second City:** Porto

    237,591 pop
- **Density:** 114,5 pop/km²
- **Urban Population:** 63.5%

INSTITUTIONAL STRUCTURE

Republic composed of 308 municipalities, 3,091 districts and 2 autonomous regions.

Read on: www.ccdrc.pt www.dgterritorio. pt www.dgotdu.pt/PNPOT/Default.html

Administrative competence for planning
Competences at national and regional levels lie with the central government, the former directly under the Minister of Environment, Spatial Planning and Energy, and the latter under the Regional Development Coordination Committee (CCDR) that are integrated in the Council of Ministers. At the local level, competences lie with the municipal councils or the municipal associations.

Main planning legislation
The Law no. 31/2014, establishes the public policies of land, spatial planning and urbanism. The Decree-Law no.380/99, and its modifications, establishes the legal framework for territorial management instruments.

Planning and implementation instruments
With a strategic nature, there are three different instruments for the organisation of the national territory: the National Spatial Planning Policy Programme; the Regional Spatial Plans; and the Inter-municipal plans. Of a regulatory nature are: the Municipal masterplan, which establishes the territorial development strategy, the municipal spatial planning policy and other urban policies; the Urban development plan, which defines the urban structure, the system of land use and the transformation of the territory criteria for a given area; and the Detailed plan, which develops and implements proposals for the occupation of an area of the municipal territory. Finally, the Special plans are complementary means for the central administration intervention to lay down objectives of national interest with a territorial impact (e.g. Coastal protection).

Development control
Municipal or Metropolitan councils are responsible for development control.

Sustainability and governance
The National Environment and Sustainable Development Council is a public body formed by government members and members from different sectors of the society. It holds a central role in the proposal and implementation of environmental and sustainable development policies. In addition, Local Agenda 21 programmes have been initiated across the country although from 2007, the funding for these was mainly coming from the EU. Public participation is open to everyone but only in the final stages of the plan-making process. On the other hand, planning documents and the land registry are freely accessible to the public through dedicated websites (National Territorial Information System and the National Land Registry Information System respectively).

Planning system in practice
The Spatial Planning and Urbanism Observatory evaluate the plans and spatial planning policies in Portugal. Their latest report, the Evaluation of the action programme of the national spatial planning policy programme (2014), identifies the lack of effective management of spatial and urban planning as the major challenge to tackle in the next period (2014-2020). On the other hand, the update of infrastructures is highlighted as the most successful outcome of the previous period.

ROMANIA

Administrative competence for planning

At national level, competences lie with the Ministry of Regional Development and Public Administration (MDRAP). At county level, the county council is the responsible authority for the coordination of spatial planning activities. At local level, the local councils are responsible for the coordination of all urban planning activities within their administrative area. There are no distinct competences in planning assigned to the regional level. However, the regional development councils and regional development agencies play an important part in the design and implementation of regional development strategies and plans.

Main planning legislation

The Law for Urban and Territorial Planning (no. 350/2001, with its subsequent modifications), which states the political aim of the spatial management of the territory.

Planning and implementation instruments

The main instruments specified in the planning legislation are the territorial and urban plans. The National Territorial Plan (PATN) represents a synthesis of the strategic sectoral programmes for the entire national territory. The County Territorial Plan (PATJ) represents the spatial expression of a county's social and economic development plan. The Territorial Zoning Plans (PATZ) are carried out in order to solve specific territorial issues. The General Urban Plan (PUG), has both a strategic character and a regulatory effect as it defines land use parameters for a city or a commune. Urban Zoning Plans (PUZ) are conducted for areas with specific problems within a city or commune. Finally, Detailed Urban Plans (PUD) contain only building regulations for one parcel, in relation to the neighbouring parcels.

Development control

It is implemented through the release of Urban Planning Certificates, overseen by the chief architects at local level. Furthermore, the application of these provisions is supervised by the State Building Inspectorate and county chief architects.

Sustainability and governance

Territorial planning documentations include environmental protection aspects. Moreover, all territorial and urban plans have to be subjected to the environmental impact assessment procedure. All urban planning documentation is produced in digital format and available on the INSPIRE Geoportal. In the last decade, efforts were made to ensure in the legal framework both decisional transparency and public participation. Public participation is, however, limited to statutory consultation and there is no real participation in the decision or plan making process.

Planning system in practice

The planning system in practice in Romania suffers from certain legislative gaps that haven't been covered yet by the successive changes in the planning legislation Therefore, the planning system needs to integrate better strategic elements, regulatory provisions and investment planning in territorial development from both national and EU sources and to avoid unnecessary overlaps between the different planning instruments.

SLOVENIA

FAST FACTS

- **Total Area:** 20.273 km²
- **Total Population:** 2,061,085
- **Population Growth:** -0.26%
- **Unemployment Rate:** 13.1%
- **GDP:** $49.51 billion
- **GDP per capita:** $29,700
- **GDP growth rate:** 2.6%

SETTLEMENTS STRUCTURE

- **Capital City:** Ljubljana
  277,554 pop
- **Second City:** Maribor
  114,487 pop
- **Density:** 101 pop/km²
- **Urban Population:** 49.6%

INSTITUTIONAL STRUCTURE

Republic composed of 12 statistical regions and 212 municipalities.

Read on: www.mop.gov.si/en/ www. geoportal.gov.si

Administrative competence for planning

At the national level, competences lie with the Ministry of the Environment and Spatial Planning (MESP), through the Directorate of Spatial Planning, Construction and Housing. There are no regional administrative authorities but Municipal councils have full competences for planning at the local level.

Main planning legislation

The Spatial Planning Act (SPA) (2002, 2007), the Spatial Management Act (2002) and the Construction Act (2003).

Planning and implementation instruments

At the national level, the Spatial Development Strategy of Slovenia (2004) sets guidelines for the long-term spatial development of Slovenia, while the Spatial Order of Slovenia (2004) sets general standards, instruments and planning regulations. The Detailed Plan of National Importance is an implementation document that determines planning conditions for the preparation of design projects of national relevance to obtain building permits. At the regional level, the Regional Spatial Plan is prepared jointly by the state and the interested municipalities according to the principle of partnership. It is a spatial (inter-municipal) land use plan for several interested municipalities. At the local level, the Municipal Spatial Plan contains long-term goals of spatial development within the municipality. It also sets the foundations for the Detailed Municipal Spatial plans, which plans in detail individual zones of land use in the municipality – i.e. towns and other settlements.

Development control

The MESP issues building permits for buildings of "national importance" directly, while territorial administrative districts (at the local level) issue building permits for all other buildings, e.g. construction activities in municipalities under their jurisdiction.

Sustainability and governance

Despite Slovenia's numerous environmental protection efforts, natural diversity has been in decline due to environmental pollution and degradation. The Spatial Development Strategy of the Republic of Slovenia draws on the international policies and recommendations (UN, Council of Europe, EU) to set out the concept and strategic guidelines for sustainable spatial development and the provisions and instruments for environmental protection. Participation in the plan making process happens in the final stages and it is limited to consultation about already given solutions. Spatial Information is still being gathered, digitalised and harmonised to ease the monitoring of development and its accessibility to the public.

Planning system in practice

The new planning system, which was established in 2001, is still being modified. This situation coupled with the absence of effective development control and monitoring of spatial development, and the absence of regional administrations, have increased the pressure on municipal administrations, the only ones with mandatory and comprehensive spatial planning powers. The main outcomes are uneven urban and regional development, inadequate local infrastructure provision and urban sprawl.

FAST FACTS

- **Total Area:** 49,036km²
- **Total Population:** 5,421,349
- **Population Growth:** 0.02%
- **Unemployment Rate:** -
- **GDP:** $99.97 billion
- **GDP per capita:** $28,200
- **GDP growth rate:** 2.4%

SETTLEMENTS STRUCTURE

- **Capital City:** Bratislava
  495,503 pop
- **Second City:** Košice
  240,164 pop
- **Density:** 110.56 pop/km²
- **Urban Population:** 53.6%

INSTITUTIONAL STRUCTURE

Republic composed of 8 regions, 79 districts and 2,890 municipalities.

Read on:www.build.gov.sk/mvrrsr/index. php www.zuups.sk

Administrative competence for planning

It is split in three levels. At the top level, it lies with the Ministry of Transport, Building and Regional Development (recently split into the Ministry of Construction and Regional Development and the Ministry of Transport, Communications and Public Works). Regional authorities have competences at the regional level and Municipal authorities have competences at the local level.

Main planning legislation

The Building Act No. 50/1976 Coll. on Physical Planning and Building Order (in short Building Code) and its modifications. The main changes to the law have to do with real estate ownership relations, decentralisation of planning powers, public participation and territorial information systems. A comprehensive new Building Code will be approved by the Slovak parliament in due course.

Planning and implementation instruments

At national level, there is the National Spatial Development Perspective (KURS). At regional level, the Regional Plan. At local (municipality) level, there are the Master Plans (for towns and villages) and the Zoning plans (for physical regulation of a part of a municipality). In addition, there is the Village Renewal Programme for the development of rural areas. .

Development control

It mainly lies with the local level – i.e. municipal authorities.

Sustainability and governance

Environmental principles of Agenda 21 will be an organic part of the new Building Code. More effective links between environmentally relevant documents, such as the EDoK (Ecological Document on Landscape), and spatial planning processes should be done to improve the sustainability of planning. At the moment, brownfield redevelopment has become one of the key ways for the country to bring about sustainable development. Public participation is still relatively low in Slovakia. It is limited to consultation in the final stages. In addition, there is a lack of awareness about the relevance of planning matters, partly due to the abolition of former research and professional institutions such as URBION or the City Chief Architect Boards.

Planning system in practice

After 1990, several institutions specialised in managing territorial development were abolished, which had a negative impact for settlement development and land use (URBION, City Chief Architect Boards, institutions for territorial development at district level, etc.). The absence of territorial development coordination, land use without clear rules and priorities and the diktat of developers and lobby groups brought negative impacts to territorial development. Professionals are permanently calling for the re-establishment of some of the former research planning institutions to provide the solutions for the problems which the planning system is facing. Some of these new challenges are the re-structuring of the settlement network (from utilitarian, isolated settlements into inter-linked network structures); the development and reconstruction of the technical infrastructure and transport system; and building the capacity of local authorities to be able to implement and monitor development effectively.

201

SPAIN

anary Islands are not shown.

FAST FACTS

- **Total Area:** 505,988km²
- **Total Population:** 47,129,783
- **Population Growth:** 1,93%
- **Unemployment Rate:** 25.9%
- **GDP:** $1.389 trillion
- **GDP per capita:** $30,100
- **GDP growth rate:** -1.3%

SETTLEMENTS STRUCTURE

- **Capital City:** Madrid
  3,207,247 pop
- **Second City:** Barcelona
  1,611,822 pop
- **Density:** 92.4 pop/km²
- **Urban Population:** 77.4%

INSTITUTIONAL STRUCTURE

Constitutional monarchy composed of 17 regions, 50 provinces, 8,111 municipalities and 2 autonomous cities.

Read on: www.ine.es/ www.fomento.gob.es/

Administrative competence for planning

The Unitary state with a constitutional monarchy and a parliamentary system of democracy has a two tier planning system. 17 Autonomous Communities (Comunidades Autónomas) at the upper level are enacting regional planning legislations and drawing up regional plans, while the municipalities at the lower level have full planning powers over plan making, development control and monitoring. The State and the 50 provinces have very few competences in urban and regional planning matters.

Main planning legislation

The current 2008 Land Act is the outcome of a continuous update of the first Land Use and Town Planning Act, enacted in 1956. With the devolution of planning powers to the Autonomous Communities in 1978, the different regions have subsequently produced their own regional Land Acts.

Planning and implementation instruments

There are a range of instruments, from strategic instruments at a National, Regional and Supra-Municipal levels, to detailed and concrete instruments at a Municipal level. All these planning instruments are hierarchically determined – the local instruments should be in accordance with the upper ones.

Planning process and development control

Local authorities have full planning powers of plan making, development control and monitoring. However, local plans must be compliant with regional plans. More importantly, local plans must be ultimately approved by the regional administration. Participation of society in the making of local plans is only compulsory during the consultation process, once the plan drafted by experts has been initially approved by the local authority. Conversely, statutory bodies have a say throughout the whole plan making process.

Sustainability and governance

The Local Agendas 21 (LA21) European initiative is the sustainable initiative most extensively followed across Spain. However, there are no records of how many local authorities have actually implemented these initiatives and to what extent. In addition, a comprehensive set of laws, guidelines and proposals affecting planning practice has also been promoted at national level. ICT has been successfully introduced in cities but this has not yet improved public participation in the planning process.

Planning system in practice

The lack of coordination among the different administrative bodies is the main hurdle for the implementation of the Spanish planning system. In addition, the relevance of the real estate sector in the plan making process at local level coupled with uneven access to information has usually resulted in high levels of corruption. However, the crisis seems to be encouraging more sustainable approaches to plan making at a local level, with a greater focus on urban regeneration instead of urban development

FAST FACTS

- **Total Area:** 447,412km²
- **Total Population:** 9,793,172
- **Population Growth:** 0,91%
- **Unemployment Rate:** 8.5%
- **GDP:** $570.1 billion
- **GDP per capita:** $46,000
- **GDP growth rate:** 2.1%

SETTLEMENTS STRUCTURE

- **Capital City:** Stockholm
  881,235 pop
- **Second City:** Göteborg
  525,089 pop
- **Density:** 21.5 pop/km²
- **Urban Population:** 85%

INSTITUTIONAL STRUCTURE

Constitutional monarchy composed of 21 counties and 290 municipalities.

*Read on:http://www.government.se/government-agencies/swedish-national-board-of-housing-building-and-planning/
http://www.government.se/government-of-sweden/ministry-of-the-environment/
https://openlibrary.org/publishers/Swedish Council for Building Research*

Administrative competence for planning

There are six ministers with their departments responsible for preparing and proposing government decisions regarding housing provision, national physical planning and building matters. They have no independent decision making power. The central supervisory body is the National Board of Housing, Building and Planning. It is responsible for producing technical rules and monitoring development planning. The 3 regions and 25 provinces do not have any planning competences. The 21 County Administration Boards with government appointed heads have competence over inter-municipal coordination planning issues and when national interests under the Environmental Code are at risk. They are also in charge of sectoral plans. The 290 Municipal Councils have competence for planning in their municipalities which are further divided into 2,512 parishes corresponding to church constituencies.

Main planning legislation

The Planning and Building Act (PBL 1987) concerns changes of land use; and The Environmental Code (1999) regulates how public interest is to be considered (by central and local governments) in the case of conflicting interests concerning land and water use. There is a two pillar system with spatial planning and environmental protection at equal level.

Planning and implementation instruments

The Swedish planning system remains top down in the public interest but favourable to market forces. It has to cope with growth concentrating in the south and decline in the much larger north. There are now national or county plans, except when a regional planning body has been set up. Plans at the local level are: Structure Plans and Detailed plans, and Property Regulations. Special Area Regulations at local level are produced by mandate of central government. The county may review municipal decisions.

Planning process and development control

Landowners have the right to build according to relevant plans and regulations. Local building committees grant building permission, change of use, etc. based on the requirements of the detailed plan. National and county government have deemed planning permission.

Sustainability and governance

Sweden has a long tradition of environmental protection (it hosted the first UN conference on the environment in 1972). The plan making process is very open and everyone can intervene at all stages of the planning process and appeal.

Planning system in practice

There is currently a discussion regarding if there should be only one municipal level instead of the two Sweden has today. Another discussion regards the extensive timeframe from idea to construction. Today there is a lack of dwellings in the three biggest cities. A common point of view is that the government is too passive and must intervene more in housing politics. The taxation rules should be changed and the planning process could be less complicated.

SWITZERLAND ✚

FAST FACTS

- **Total Area:** 41,277km²
- **Total Population:** 8,121,830
- **Population Growth:** 0.71%
- **Unemployment Rate:** 3.2%
- **GDP:** $712.1 billion
- **GDP per capita:** $58,100
- **GDP growth rate:** 2%

SETTLEMENTS STRUCTURE

- **Capital City:** Bern
   358,000 pop
- **Second City:** Zurich
   1,246,000 pop
- **Density:** 196.76 pop/km²
- **Urban Population:** 73.9%

INSTITUTIONAL STRUCTURE

Federal republic composed of 26 cantons and 2,396 municipalities.

Read on: www.are.admin.ch/ www.vlp-aspan.ch/de

Administrative competence for planning
At the national level, the Federal Office for Spatial Development, has the power to enact the fundamental legislation. At the canton level, each of the 26 Cantonal Planning Offices elaborate and coordinate their own planning and building laws. Large cantons often delegate supra-municipal spatial planning tasks to regional planning associations (e.g. Zurich). Finally, the Local Building Authority regulates land use planning at the communal (municipal) level.

Main planning legislation
The Federal Spatial Planning Act (1980) lays down the aims and principles of spatial planning for the whole of Switzerland. Its primary aim is the economical use of the limited land area.

Planning and implementation instruments
There is no overall national plan but Concepts and Sectoral Plans aimed at specific tasks of federal authorities. The Spatial Concept of Switzerland (2012) provides non-compulsory guidelines for physical planning at all levels. The Cantonal Structure Plans coordinate all activities with spatial impact in each canton. Regional Structure Plans, elaborated by regional planning associations, further specify the provisions of the Cantonal Structure Plan at the regional level (e.g. Zurich). At the local level, the Land Use Plans refer to the whole territory of the community and not only to the built up areas. Finally, the Agglomeration Programmes are an implementation-oriented tool designed to improve collaboration and coordination within conurbations or 'functional spaces'.

Development control
It happens at the local level, where the Local Building Authority controls development by means of building permits. The cantonal authorities have indirect responsibilities over development control since they approve the communal zoning plans and building regulations.

Sustainability and governance
The impact of climate change and the incidence of natural hazards which may threaten regional infrastructures are expected to grow in Switzerland. In this sense, Switzerland intends to reduce its domestic greenhouse gas emissions in 20% by 2020 (Kyoto protocol). In addition, the Sustainable Development Strategy of the Swiss Federal Council (1997) alongside the reviewed Federal Constitution (1997) promotes environmental protection and sustainable planning at all levels. Participation happens at the local level for all communal zoning and building regulations.

Planning system in practice
The development, regeneration, and more efficient use of existing settlement structures are now the main topics of spatial planning in Switzerland. Consequently, public transport has been improved (rail transport in particular) to minimise infrastructure impact on land. In addition, a number of initiatives such as the 'Second Homes Initiative' (2012) and the 'farmland initiative' (2012) limit the expansion of urban settlements and promote the re-use of existing urban land.

FAST FACTS

- **Total Area:** 244,000 km²
- **Total Population:** 64,100,000
- **Population Growth:** 0.63%
- **Unemployment Rate:** 5.5%
- **GDP:** $2,678 trillion
- **GDP per capita:** $41,787.47
- **GDP growth rate:** 1.7%

SETTLEMENTS STRUCTURE

- **Capital City:** London
  8,416,535 pop
- **Second City:** Birmingham
  1,073,000 pop
- **Density:** 4,351 pop/km²
- **Urban Population:** 81.5%

INSTITUTIONAL STRUCTURE

Constitutional monarchy composed of England, Northern Ireland, Scotland and Wales.

Read on:http://www.planningportal.gov.uk/ http://www.gov.scot/Topics/Built-Environment/planning http://www.planningni.gov.uk/

Administrative competence for planning

Four nations, England, Scotland, Wales and Northern Ireland constitute the UK, a unitary state and constitutional monarchy which all have their own planning system except for England. Planning is administered through central and local government. The Department for Communities and Local Government (DCLG), of the UK Government is responsible in England. National planning responsibilities in Scotland and Wales and Northern Ireland are with their Parliament or Assemblies. Some planning powers, drawing up plans, determination of planning applications and enforcement - are being devolved to local authorities in all four countries.

Main planning legislation

The broad principles of the 1947 Act have remained largely unchanged. In England and Wales subsequent amendments and acts strengthen presumption of development. Scotland: Town and Country Planning (Scotland) Act 1997! NI: the Planning (Northern Ireland) Order 1972, the Planning (Northern Ireland) Order 1991 and the Planning Act (NI) 2011.

Planning and implementation instruments

With the abolition of the Regional Spatial Strategies in England in 2011 the main planning instrument in the country is the Local Development Framework (LDF) produced at the local level, but they have to respect the National Planning Policy Framework (NPPF). London has managed to keep its own regional spatial strategy, the London Plan within a two tier system including 32 London Boroughs and the London City Corporation at the lower level. In Scotland, Wales and Northern Ireland, there are national policy frameworks, national spatial plans, and the local plans are drafted by local authorities.

Planning process and development control

Local authorities have powers of plan making and development control in England and regional issues due to the 'duty to cooperate' (Localism Act 2011). In Scotland, Wales and Northern Ireland, planning powers are with local authorities and national authorities. Participation at the local level is quite open.

Sustainability and governance

The UK Government sees sustainable development as the core principle underpinning planning. The social, environmental and economic principles entailed in this sustainable approach underlie the planning policy guidance and they cascade down to local levels in the planning and policy making.

Planning system in practice

Since the 1990s, UK governments have emphasised the need to streamline planning to make it more effective and efficient in delivering the development that is needed and planning has shifted to the presumption of development. The sustainable development approach of UK policies has promoted the re-use of brownfield land and a tighter protection of greenfield land and green belts. The combination of a changed control of land use development and the fast growing urban population is challenging the efficiency of planning in large urban areas and the provision of much needed affordable housing and other social facilities.

ALBANIA

Political ans administrative organisation

Democratic parliamentary republic. The country is divided into 12 administrative counties (qark), which include 36 districts (rreth) and 373 municipalities (bashki or komunë) from which 72 municipalities have city status (qytet).

Administrative competence for planning

Divided into 3 main levels: National Level; Local Level (municipalities) and the Inter-Local Level (counties). Planning has been traditionally administered by the central government. However, more and more powers are being transferred to the local level. The role of the regional level remains a point of contention due to the territorial reconfiguration required as part of the EU accession agreement.

Main planning legislation

The current Territorial Planning Law (2009) represents a noticeable shift from the previous "General Regulatory Plan". The current legal framework tries to balance the needs of local planning issues with the spatial planning vision for the country, as well as preventing informal settlements and uncontrolled infill developments.

Planning implementation instruments

Local planning authorities are responsible for controlling development in the territory under their jurisdiction and their metropolitan area, in accordance with the binding national planning instruments (Territorial Policies, Territorial Plans and Regulations), the national development control regulations, and the building regulations drawn up in their administrative territory.

Development control

Although local authorities have plan making and development control powers, these are strongly regulated from the central government. Information to society in the making of local plans happens from the outset, with initial studies being publicly available in the on-line register. However, key stakeholders have a say from the initial stages of the plan-making process while the wider public has inputs only once the plan has already been drafted.

Sustainability and governance

Environmental issues and energy efficiency remain some of the main and growing problems of the country, because of the new consumerist culture and the lack of basic infrastructure. As for the governance dimension, there is currently a growing consideration for capacity building, especially at the regional level, to achieve a more transparent and professional planning system. The implementation of a national ICT Register system, which aims to widen participation in the plan-making process, it is a step in this direction.

Planning system in practice

The work of organisations such as Co-PLAN Institute for Habitat development is worth mentioning since they are helping change mentalities and providing the institutional capacity that is desperately needed at central, regional and local levels.

ARMENIA

FAST FACTS

- **Total Area:** 29.743 km²
- **Total Population:** 3,017,100
- **Population Growth:** 4.8%
- **Unemployment Rate:** 17.6%
- **GDP:** $10.88 billion
- **GDP per capita:** $7,400
- **GDP growth rate:** 3.4%

SETTLEMENTS STRUCTURE

- **Capital City:** Yerevan
    1,068,300 pop
- **Second City:** Gyumri
    119,900 pop
- **Density:** 101 pop/km²
- **Urban Population:** 63.4%

INSTITUTIONAL STRUCTURE

Republic composed of 10 provinces.

*Read on: www.gov.am/en/structure/14/
www.minurban.am/am/*

Administrative competence for planning

Competences are shared between the Ministry of Urban Development and the Councils of Aldermen, which represent the national and local levels respectively.

Main planning legislation

The Law on Urban Development of the Republic of Armenia.

Planning and implementation instruments

The General Settlement Strategy lays out the territorial organisation of the whole country. The Plan of Territorial Development for Marzes determines the spatial development of a region (marze) or the territories of more than one community. Master Plans determine the directions of the spatial development of a community while the Zoning Plans lay down details for use, buildings, and planning conditions for existing and planned areas. Finally, there are Special Plans for the protection of the historical heritage, landscape and environment of the built up areas of communes and the land designated for development outside their borders.

Development control

Competences are shared between the national and the local level once again. The Ministry Urban Development implements state inspection and control of urban development activities through the State Urban Development Inspection agency. In urban and rural communes, Councils of Aldermen are in charge of development control.

Sustainability and governance

The Armenia Development Strategy (ADS) (2014) is mainly focused on the social and economic dimensions of the sustainable development concept. On the environmental dimension, Armenia is producing a new integrated energy strategy, which contemplates the introduction of nuclear and geothermal powers. The strategy also addresses the process of energy generation, distribution and consumption in order to improve its sustainability. In addition, new building regulations to improve earthquake resistance are being introduced. Participation in the plan and decision making process is being promoted and improved to make it more open, transparent and accessible.

Planning system in practice

The new situation in the country after the post-Soviet period has led to a fundamental review of its spatial development policy. In this sense, the country is adapting the methods of spatial planning and territorial management in accordance to the guiding principles of sustainable spatial development adopted by the United Nations and the Council of Europe. The main challenges to achieve this transformation are the improvement of the monitoring of the urban development activities and the creation of an up-to-date spatial information system. The other major challenge is capacity building in the planning process. At the moment, many Master Plans are elaborated by the state due to the lack of capacity in the communes. Therefore, the state is promoting professional training for its officials in Europe, to gain knowledge in terms of spatial planning and landscape sustainability.

AZERBAIJAN

FAST FACTS

- **Total Area:** 86,600 km^2
- **Total Population:** 9,593,000
- **Population Growth:** 1.29%
- **Unemployment Rate:** 6%
- **GDP:** $74.15 billion
- **GDP per capita:** $17,600
- **GDP growth rate:** 2.8%

SETTLEMENTS STRUCTURE

- **Capital City:** Baku
  2,204,200 pop
- **Second City:** Ganje
  1,240,800 pop
- **Density:** 105.8 pop/km^2
- **Urban Population:** 53.2%

INSTITUTIONAL STRUCTURE

Republic composed of the Nakhchivan Autonomous Republic, 66 administrative regions, 70 towns and 4,272 villages.

Read on: www.arxkom.gov.az/ www.unece.org/ fileadmin/DAM/env/eia/documents/EaP_GREEN/ Round_Table_Azerbaijan_28-08-2014/AZ_SEA_ review_2nd_draft_forroundtable.pdf

Administrative competence for planning

All administrative competences for planning lie with the national level. The State Town Planning and Architecture Committee is the central executive body carrying out state policy and regulation on town-planning, projecting, designing and architecture.

Main planning legislation

The Urban Planning and Construction Code (2012).

Planning and implementation instruments

At the national level, there are a series of strategic documents (i.e. State programmes and Action plans). These strategic documents have no definition in the legislation at all, whereas the spatial planning documents are subject to detailed legislative provisions (see section above). The main spatial planning instruments are Regional broad plans, City general plans and City Detailed plans. Finally, the capital city of Baku has a special planning status due to the level of uncontrolled growth happening there. The Housing Code of Azerbaijan (2013) was enacted to specifically tackle illegal construction taking place in the city.

Development control

Lower tier planning levels are responsible for development control. However enforcement of building regulations is weak.

Sustainability and governance

Azerbaijan adopted the "Complex Action Plan 2006-2010 for the improvement of ecological conditions in the Azerbaijan Republic". The government has also proposed measures to fight pollution, such as the oil lakes around Baku and the dense smoke fog covering the capital, resulting from burning household waste. Alternative and renewable energy sources, such as solar panels and wind farms, are being fostered by the Ministry of Industry and Energy (2009, 2011). Azerbaijan has also adopted EIA (Environmental Impact Assessment) and SEA (Strategic Environmental Assessment) and has applied them to the Greater Baku Regional Development Plan (2004). The Code on Urban Planning and Construction sets the requirements for public participation in spatial planning. The SEA for Greater Baku Regional Development Plan showed that participation worked to some extent but there is still room for improvement – e.g. number of consultations held during the process.

Planning system in practice

The main challenges that the planning system faces today are related to the high number of migrants and refugees present in the country; the serious levels of air and water pollution; and the lack of institutional capacity at the local level to take up the planning powers handed down to them by the central government. With reference to the environmental concerns, the UNECE is assisting Azerbaijan to develop appropriate legislation that will help to implement and enforce the already adopted EIA and SEA processes. As for the institutional capacity, the solution is to provide adequate financial and human resources, as well as adequate training, at the local level. Finally, the migration problem requires a wider approach that demands a strong coordination between the economic, spatial and environmental dimensions, which is lacking at the moment.

FAST FACTS

- **Total Area:** 207,560 km²
- **Total Population:** 9,485,300
- **Population Growth:** -0.2%
- **Unemployment Rate:** 0.7%
- **GDP:** $76.14 billion
- **GDP per capita:** $18,200
- **GDP growth rate:** 1.6%

SETTLEMENTS STRUCTURE

- **Capital City:** Minsk
  1,939,800 pop
- **Second City:** Gomel
  1,424,000 pop
- **Density:** 46.74 pop/km²
- **Urban Population:** 76.8%

INSTITUTIONAL STRUCTURE

Republic composed of 6 regions and 1 municipality with special status (Minsk).

Read on: http://mas.by/ru www.irup.by/ en/

Administrative competence for planning

Competences lie with the President and the Council of Ministers (State Committee on Property, the Ministry of Architecture and Construction, the Ministry of Economy, and the Ministry of Natural Resources and Environment Protection) at the national level. At the local level, competences lie with the District or Cities' Executive Committees.

Main planning legislation

The law on Architectural, Urban Planning and Building Activity in the Republic of Belarus (2005). Technical regulation of spatial and urban planning is implemented through the building norms, standards, rules, regulations, guidance.

Planning and implementation instruments

There are two types of spatial planning: Comprehensive planning and Specialised Planning. The former sets priorities and articulates main directions for the development strategy. The latter is reserved for those particular instances in which the content and the borders of the planning object are not set by the legislative act. Within the first type of planning there are the following instruments: the National Plan of Spatial Development of the Republic of Belarus; the Plans (schemes) of Spatial Development of Regions; and the Master Plans of Urban and Other Settlements and the Detailed Plans. Within the Specialised Planning, there are Specialised Schemes and Projects at national level and Detailed Plans at the local level.

Development control

It lies with the local authorities through the granting of building permits, in accordance with the determinations of the Master Plan or the Detailed Plan.

Sustainability and governance

The sustainable development strategy is defined in the National Strategy of Sustainable Development of the Republic of Belarus (NSDS-2020) following the recommendations and principles of the UN Conference on Environment and Development (Rio de Janeiro, 1992). In addition, the National Plan of Spatial Development of the Republic of Belarus proposes the distinction between urbanised and natural areas, in order to improve the protection of the latter. Participation in the planning process is imbalanced, with a very little presence of small businesses or individuals due to the lack of accessible information.

Planning system in practice

The planning profession is trying to adapt to the complexity of working within the realm of multiple stakeholders – different to the centralised nature of the system in the past. But there is a lack of professionals who can address the challenge. Another issue is the lack of adequate funding and collaboration between the different bodies with planning competences, which has increased the mismatch between the determinations in the plans and the reality on the ground (the plans themselves do not include adequate implementation strategies). Finally, there is a huge need for developing the interface between professionals and the general public in order to make the planning process more accessible and increase citizen engagement.

BOSNIA & HERZEGOVINA

FAST FACTS

- **Total Area:** 51,197 km²
- **Total Population:** 3,875,723
- **Population Growth:** 0.1%
- **Unemployment Rate:** 43.6%
- **GDP:** $17.98 billion
- **GDP per capita:** $9,800
- **GDP growth rate:** 0.8%

SETTLEMENTS STRUCTURE

- **Capital City:** Sarajevo
  310,410 pop
- **Second City:** Banjaluka
  199,191 pop
- **Density:** 75.5 pop/km²
- **Urban Population:** 56.8 %

INSTITUTIONAL STRUCTURE

Republic composed of the Federation of Bosnia & Herzegovina and the Republic of Srpska and Brcko District.

Read on: www.fmpu.gov.ba/ www.vladars. net/eng/vlada/ministries/MSPCEE/Pages/ default.aspx

Administrative competence for planning
At the national level, competences are divided between the Federation of BiH, with the Federal Ministry of Physical Planning, and the Republic of Srpska, with the Ministry for Spatial Planning, Civil Engineering and Ecology holding competences for the latter. At the local level, it lies with the municipal authorities.

Main planning legislation
Constitution of the Federation of Bosnia and Herzegovina (1997); Law on Spatial Planning and Land Use at the level of the Federation of BiH (2002); and the Law on Spatial Planning and Construction in the Republic of Srpska (2013).

Planning and implementation instruments
At the strategic level, the instruments in the Federation of BiH include the Spatial Plan of the Federation of BiH, spatial plans of the cantons, spatial plans of the municipalities and spatial plans for the areas with special characteristics in the Federation. At the urban planning level, the instruments are urban plans and detailed plans, regulation plans, zoning plans and urban projects. As for the Republic of Srpska, the strategic instruments are the Spatial Plan of the Republic of Srpska (1996, 2007), Spatial plans of Municipalities, Urban plans and Regulation plans. It is worth mentioning that both the Federation of BiH and the Republic of Srpska exchanged spatial data during the preparation of their Spatial plans.

Development control
It lies with the municipal level although the central government monitors their activity very closely through the Inspectorate departments, for the Federation of BiH, and the Minister and competent commissions, for the Republic of Srpska.

Sustainability and governance
Sustainable development is one of the principles included in the legal regulations of Bosnia and Herzegovina. However, the country faces serious challenges, such as air pollution in the BiH due to the use of highly polluting cars, or the protection and recovery of the built environment, particularly difficult in cities such as Mostar, severely damaged during the war and without a local government. As for public participation, it is still weak despite the efforts to make the planning process open and accessible – e.g. with public debates and ICT platforms – mainly due to a lack of education of the citizens in terms of information related to spatial planning. Finally, ICTs are taking over the central position in strategies aimed at improving the countries' competitiveness worldwide. For that reason, the Information Society Development Policy, Strategy and Action Plan, adopted at state level, represents a relevant achievement.

Planning system in practice
Development issues of Bosnia and Herzegovina are mainly illegal constructions, lack of coordination between the different tiers of planning, and lack of development control. This situation is especially striking in the city of Mostar. In the Republic of Srpska, planning seems to have been more successful in the development of its cities. However, the private sector has increasingly gained control over the planning process.

GEORGIA

FAST FACTS

- **Total Area:** 69,700 km²
- **Total Population:** 3,729,500
- **Population Growth:** -0.3%
- **Unemployment Rate:** 14.9%
- **GDP:** $16.54 billion
- **GDP per capita:** $7,700
- **GDP growth rate:** 4.7%

SETTLEMENTS STRUCTURE

- **Capital City:** Tbilisi
  1,118,300 pop
- **Second City:** Kutaisi
  149,100 pop
- **Density:** 53.51 pop/km²
- **Urban Population:** 57.5%

INSTITUTIONAL STRUCTURE

Republic composed of 2 autonomous republics (Abkhazia and Ajara) subdivided into municipalities.

Read on: www.economy.ge/en/home

Administrative competence for planning

At the national level, it lies with the Ministry of Economy and Sustainable Development. At the local level, it lies with the corresponding authorities of the Abkhazia and Ajara Autonomous Republics and the rest of the municipalities. 20% of Georgia is under Russian occupation since 2008.

Main planning legislation

Georgia still lacks the proper legislation, normative documents and technical regulations for full-scale coverage of the spatial planning sector. At the moment of writing, the legislation dealing with planning matters is contained in the Code of Local Self-Government (2014) and the Law of Georgia on Spatial and Territorial Arrangement and Fundamental City-planning (2005).

Planning and implementation instruments

There is no unified set of planning instruments. According to the 'Main Statements', contained in the by-law "Main Principles of the regulation for use and construction on the territories of settlements" (2008), the local governments elaborate the regulation rules of land use and construction of their respective territories, which will then be used to produce the appropriate spatial planning documents. The documents covering the zones of cultural heritage are adopted in agreement with the Ministry of Culture and Monument Protection. Some local governments have not been able to produce their specific planning regulations. In these cases, they use the Main Statements contained in the by-law as the guiding principles for the spatial planning arrangements.

Development control

The local authorities are responsible to issue the permissions for construction and supervise the construction on their territories.

Sustainability and governance

Although the legislation on environmental protection has been reasonably well developed - Law on Environmental Permits (2007) and Law on Ecological Expertise (2008) – the implementation of their standards and regulations is not as successful. Public participation and involvement in urban decision making is not a widespread practice in Georgia. Low levels of awareness on environmental issues, planning matters and upfront opposition to development prevails among the population.

Planning system in practice

The lack of strong institutional support from the state, the absence of an established body of planning legislation and the absence of research institutions are hindering the transformation of Georgia's planning system. As a consequence, the general public has little contact with, and interest in the planning processes. State policy now favours a liberal market economy with a minimal participation of the state. Due to a high level of corruption among civil servants and the lack of master plans and land use plans, cities are being developed chaotically by the private sector and illegal construction is widespread. Finally, it is notable that the country lacks relevant statistical information/data in the urban development sector which prevents a clear diagnosis and development vision of the settlement system.

KOSOVO

FAST FACTS

- **Total Area:** 10,908 km²
- **Total Population:** 1,804,944
- **Population Growth:** 0.9%
- **Unemployment Rate:** 30.9%
- **GDP:** $7.318 billion
- **GDP per capita:** $8,000
- **GDP growth rate:** 2.7%

SETTLEMENTS STRUCTURE

- **Capital City:** Prishtina
  207,477 pop
- **Second City:** Prizren
  182,449 pop
- **Density:** 165.47 pop/km²
- **Urban Population:** 49 %

INSTITUTIONAL STRUCTURE

Republic composed of 37 municipalities and 1,467 settlements.

Read on: mmph-rks.org/en-us/Home
www.unhabitat-kosovo.org

Administrative competence for planning
At the national level, it lies with the Assembly of Kosovo; the Government of Kosovo and the Ministry of Environment and Spatial Planning (MESP). At the local level, it lies with Municipal Assemblies and municipal authorities responsible for spatial planning and management (MArSPM).

Main planning legislation
The Law on Spatial Planning (LSP) (2013).

Planning and implementation instruments
There are two levels of planning and planning instruments. At the national level, the instruments are the Spatial Plan of Kosovo, the Zoning Map of Kosovo and the Spatial Plans for Special Zones (e.g. National Parks, industrial areas). At the local level, municipalities are regulated through Municipal Development Plans, Municipal Zoning Maps and Detailed Regulatory Plans (non-mandatory).

Development control
The responsibility is shared between the central level, managed by the Inspectorate of spatial and urban planning of MESP and Construction Inspectorate, and the local level, managed by the Municipal Inspectorate of Construction. The main concern in this regard is the limited capacities at both levels, to undertake tasks related to monitoring and supervision of plan implementation and control of developments.

Sustainability and governance
Spatial planning documents are compatible with the principle of sustainable development and drafting a report on the Strategic Environmental Assessment (SEA) for these documents is a legal requirement. Practical application of the SEA reports started in 2010, whereby some issues in relation to harmonisation of the legal and the planning frameworks with the SEA itself have been identified. Spatial planning processes in Kosovo seek to involve a wide range of stakeholders. However, participation is still relatively weak partly because of the period of transition that Kosovo is still experiencing, but also because of lack of public participation culture. Despite this, some Kosovo municipalities have shown good examples of public participation by adopting visioning as a participatory planning toolkit.

Planning system in practice
The Kosovo planning system is undergoing a second cycle of transformation. The main issue within both cycles (2003 and 2013) relates to the mismatch between the requirements introduced by the legal frameworks and the local capacities to implement them. This has indirectly had an impact on the degradation of the physical environment. Secondly, the legislation does not provide a clear mechanism for monitoring and evaluating the implementation of planning documents. In practice, this may result in developments that are not in line with the planning instruments. Taking these reasons into consideration, it is necessary to increase political awareness about the importance of spatial planning as a coordinated and interrelated policy; and to establish a formal education in planning, which would be the key element of capacity building for the system.

MACEDONIA

FAST FACTS

- **Total Area:** 25,713 km²
- **Total Population:** 2,022,547
- **Population Growth:** 0.21%
- **Unemployment Rate:** 28,6%
- **GDP:** $11.34 billion
- **GDP per capita:** $13,300
- **GDP growth rate:** 3.8%

SETTLEMENTS STRUCTURE

- **Capital City:** Skopje
  444,800 pop
- **Second City:** Bitola
  74,550 pop
- **Density:** 78.7 pop/km²
- **Urban Population:** 58%

INSTITUTIONAL STRUCTURE

Republic composed of 84 municipalities.

Read on: www.moepp.gov.mk/?lang=en

Administrative competence for planning

At the national level, it lies with the Ministry of Environment and Physical Planning (RMEPP). At the local level, it lies with the City Advisory Boards and the Communes Advisory Boards.

Main planning legislation

The Law on Local Self Government (2002) and the Spatial and Urban Planning Act (2005).

Planning and implementation instruments

There are two types of planning instruments: spatial planning ones, at national level, and urban planning ones, at local level. Within the first group, there are the Spatial Plan of the Republic of Macedonia (2004); 3 Spatial Plans for Regions; Spatial Plans for an area of special interest for the Republic, prepared for a national park or other category of protected area; and Spatial Plans for Municipalities, with just one proposed for the City of Skopje. Within the second group, there are General (Master) Urban Plans, with one already adopted for the City of Skopje; Urban plans for part of a city, prepared for a quarter with an area of at least 30 hectares; Detailed urban plans; Urban Plans for Villages, adopted for settlement area in the municipality of rural character; and Urban plan outside a populated place, adopted for planning coverage not covered by the general urban plan and the urban plan for the village.

Development control

It lies mainly with the local authorities, which use traditional instruments such as land use and construction diagrams, urban projects and building (location) permits in this activity. These instruments are more or less inefficient because the principles of allocation and distribution of different land categories have changed rapidly since the fall of former Yugoslavia. Uncontrollable urban expansion better known as "urban sprawl" has becomes one of pressing issues and this context.

Sustainability and governance

The National Strategy for Sustainable Development (NSSD), developed as part of the requirements for the country to join the EU, describes the country's vision until 2030. Public participation in the plan making process is not possible at the spatial planning level. It only happens at the urban/local level where it is still weak. Although the country has already recognised the importance of having a solid spatial and urban planning system of information, the introduction and use of GIS in some planning offices and institutions is in its infancy.

Planning system in practice

The main problems are: rigid and centralised planning system; absence of necessary municipal plans due to lack of financial resources; public participation is weak, since the citizens are not well informed about the significance of the planning process. In light of these, the reform of local self-government and decentralisation should continue; more resources should be put into building capacity of, and providing technical assistance to the central and local departments; and transparency and openness of the planning process should be adopted to improve public participation.

MOLDOVA

FAST FACTS

- **Total Area:** 33,851 km²
- **Total Population:** 3,546,847
- **Population Growth:** -1.03%
- **Unemployment Rate:** 4%
- **GDP:** $7.944 billion
- **GDP per capita:** $5,000
- **GDP growth rate:** 4.6%

SETTLEMENTS STRUCTURE

- **Capital City:** Chișinău
  725,000 pop
- **Second City:** Tiraspol
  148,900 pop
- **Density:** 107.83 pop/km²
- **Urban Population:** 45 %

INSTITUTIONAL STRUCTURE

Republic composed of 32 districts, 3 municipalities, 1 autonomous territorial unit and 1 territorial unit.

*Read on: www.mdrc.gov.md/ www.undp.
md/publications/doc/RAPORT_21.pdf*

Administrative competence for planning

At national level, it lies with the Ministry of Construction and Regional Development. At the regional level, it still lies with the central government handled by the Regional Development Councils. At the local level, the different local authorities have the administrative competences over their territories (i.e. Rayonal Councils over the rayons, City, Town or Commune councils over the municipalities, villages and communes).

Main planning legislation

The Law on the Principles of Urbanism and Territorial Arrangement no. 835/1996 (1997).

Planning and implementation instruments

The instruments for spatial planning are the National Spatial Plan, the Regional Spatial Plans (Spatial Zoning Plans, Spatial Plans of the Municipality of Chisinau, Rayonal Spatial Plans) and the Local Spatial Plans. The latter can refer to both spatial plans of the inter-city or inter-communal territory and spatial plans of the municipal, city or commune territory. The instruments for the detailed regulation of Local Spatial Plans are the General Urban Plan, Urban Zoning Plan and Detailed Urban Plan.

Development control

It lies with the local public authorities, who issue Urban Planning Certificates and Building Permits as long as the proposals are compliant with the requirements of the planning documentations.

Sustainability and governance

The planning system has incorporated the concept of sustainable development as part of the requirements for spatial development. The National Strategy for Sustainable Development sets out the objectives of a balanced development that should be materialised through the territorial spatial plans. The planning process is open to a wide variety of stakeholders, including the general public. Participation of citizens happens throughout the decision and plan making process and at organised public hearings. If the documentation is more complex, the consultation of the population is also done through research about urban sociology, interviews, questionnaires, etc.

Planning system in practice

One of the key problems is the fact that the legal framework on urban planning does not correlate with other laws in the field of local public administration, which has led to many contradictions. This adds to the fact that the regulations regarding the content of urbanism documentations and their adoption remain unclear. Moreover, the decentralisation of competencies does not go hand in hand with the adequate provision of financial resources, which undermines the ability of local authorities to take up full responsibility for their new planning powers and competences. The Association Agreement signed with the European Union and the future prospect of European integration can become a great factor in the improvement of planning legislation in Moldova. Economic viability of plans, a better inclusion of environmental protection issues and regulation of GIS systems for spatial data management are all elements that could appear in the legislation related to planning in the near future.

MONTENEGRO

FAST FACTS

- **Total Area:** 13,812 km²
- **Total Population:** 620,029
- **Population Growth:** -0.5%
- **Unemployment Rate:** 18.5%
- **GDP:** $4.462 billion
- **GDP per capita:** $15,000
- **GDP growth rate:** 1.1%

SETTLEMENTS STRUCTURE

- **Capital City:** Podgorica
  (the Old Royal Capital is Cetinje,
  mentioned in the constitution)

  150,977 pop
- **Second City:** Nikšić

  50,970 pop
- **Density:** 45 pop/km²
- **Urban Population:** 63.2%

INSTITUTIONAL STRUCTURE

Republic composed of 21 municipalities.

*Read on: www.mrt.gov.me/en/
ministry?alphabet=lat*

Administrative competence for planning

At national level, it falls with the Ministry of Sustainable Development and Tourism. At local level, it lies with the municipalities. Despite the division of the country into three regions, there are no real planning competences at the regional level.

Main planning legislation

Law on spatial development and construction of structures (2008) and the Law on physical planning and development (2008).

Planning and implementation instruments

There are two types of planning instruments: spatial planning instruments and physical planning instruments. Within the first group, there is the Spatial Plan of Montenegro (SPM); the Special Purpose Spatial Plans (SPSP), prepared for specific and unique spaces designated by SPM; Detailed Spatial Plans, prepared particularly for public/government projects of general importance; State Study of Locations, prepared for the locations/areas/zones within the scope of the SPSP. Within the second group, there are the Spatial and Urban Plan (SUP) of a local self-government unit, which combine both general master and detailed urban design plans; Detailed Urban Plans, which contains a detailed definition of public buildings and spaces; Urban design documents, for a smaller area that will be subject to a significant and more complex development; and Local studies of locations, for areas where a neither a detailed urban plan nor urban design have been planned.

Development control

The main instruments are planning/building permits. All development control matters at national and local level fall under the remit of urban development and spatial protection inspectors who work alongside building inspectors.

Sustainability and governance

The current legal framework requires Strategic Environmental Impact Assessments (SEA) and Environmental Impact Assessments (EIA) as part of the plan making process. In addition, the Strategy for Regional Development introduces sustainable development with emphasis on the socio-economic dimensions and it aspires to establish a more balanced development pattern and reduce socio-economic inequalities. Participation is open to the public but only at the final stages of the planning process and in a consultative manner. Moreover, there is a lack of horizontal and vertical coordination, facilitation, negotiation amongst different stakeholders and actors involved in planning.

Planning system in practice

The majority of buildings constructed over the last decades is estimated to have been illegally developed. To tackle this issue, the government has signed up the Vienna Declaration on National and Regional Policy and Programmes, regarding Informal Settlements in South Eastern Europe. In addition, the lack of real planning powers at the regional level have made it almost impossible to tackle regional development inequalities. As a matter of urgency, regional planning should be included in the Law on Spatial Planning and Territorial Organisation.

Administrative competence for planning

It is split between the state level (Ministry of Economy and Ministry of Construction), the regional level for federal republics, and the local level for local communities. A reform of the Federal legislation (2014) has shifted all planning processes to the upper level of governance. Thus, many regions are encuraging municipalities to centralise the planning process upwards.

Main planning legislation

The Federal Strategic Planning Law (2014), the Urban Planning Code (2005) and the Land Code (2001).

Planning and implementation instruments

At the national level, there are Spatial Planning Strategies and Spatial (or Territorial) Plans for regions. At the local level, there are regional Spatial (or Territorial) plans for Rayons, General Plans and Zoning rules, for Urban Okrug, Urban and Rural Settlements. Municipalities may introduce their own planning norms and regulations in order to work out in detail but not in contradiction with the regional ones. The Land Use Plan is an obligatory planning document at local level of the sub-city (building block or micro-rayon or a group of plots) level. Both Land Use Plan and Zoning Rules define spatial, functional and some quantitative restrictions for any development, construction or reconstruction project.

Development control

Planning documents are not subject to obligatory controls and monitoring. The only really effective control mechanism is Litigation whereby citizens or enterprises apply for compliance to General Plans or Zoning Rules. The role of planning councils and their ability to affect the planning and development processes varies among regions.

Sustainability and governance

The term sustainability is not really embedded in the planning system, which mainly focuses on nature protection. Participatory planning is comparatively new and limited in Russia. It was introduced with the Town Planning Code, which places the participatory stage at the end of planning process. These changes are changing mind sets and the general public is gradually getting more interested and are demanding a greater scope for citizen engagement in the planning process. The Ministry of Construction will launch a new informational system to support planning and construction activities, which will replace the current Federal state information system of territorial planning (FGIS TP).

Planning system in practice

A specific characteristic of the Russian planning system is unevenness of application of the law across the country, because planning implementation procedures are currently outside urban planning legislation. Coupled with a lack of planning and development control this has led to urban sprawl and inefficient transport and social infrastructure. Moreover, planning activity in Russia does not require licensing or any other type of permission by State or public bodies. As a result, planning is mainly in the hands of private companies that are taking advantage of the lack of public control and the current growth-led agenda in the country.

FAST FACTS

- **Total Area:** 17,098,246 km^2
- **Total Population:** 143,700,000
- **Population Growth:** -4,3%
- **Unemployment Rate:** 5.1%
- **GDP:** $1.857 trillion
- **GDP per capita:** $24,800
- **GDP growth rate:** 0.6%

SETTLEMENTS STRUCTURE

- **Capital City:** Moscow
  12,111,194 pop
- **Second City:** St. Petersburg
  5,131,967 pop
- **Density:** 8.4 pop/km^2
- **Urban Population:** 74 %

INSTITUTIONAL STRUCTURE

Federation composed of 21 republics, 9 krais, 46 oblast, 2 federal cities, 1 autonomous oblast and 4 autonomous okrugs.

Read on: http://en.ngup.ru/ fgis.economy. gov.ru/fgis/

216

SERBIA

FAST FACTS

- **Total Area:** 8,8361 km²
- **Total Population:** 7,176,794
- **Population Growth:** -0.46%
- **Unemployment Rate:** 21%
- **GDP:** $43.87 billion
- **GDP per capita:** $13,300
- **GDP growth rate:** -1.8%

SETTLEMENTS STRUCTURE

- **Capital City:** Belgrade
  1,182,000 pop
- **Second City:** Novi Sad
  335,701 pop
- **Density:** 82.7 pop/km²
- **Urban Population:** 55.6%

INSTITUTIONAL STRUCTURE

Republic composed of provinces, regions, administrative areas, the city of Belgrade, cities and municipalities.

Read on: www.srbija.gov.rs/?change_lang=en www.rapp.gov.rs/en-GB/content/cid310/spatial-plan-for-the-republic-of-serbia

Administrative competence for planning

At the national level, it lies with the Ministry of Natural Resources Mining and Spatial Planning. At the local level it lies with the Municipal Councils. However, their activity is monitored by the Republic Agency for Spatial Planning, which is an independent agency, directly responsible to the Government of Serbia and not to the Ministry.

Main planning legislation

The Law of Self-governance (2002), the Planning and Construction Law (2009).

Planning and implementation instruments

There are two types of instruments: spatial plans and urban plans. Within the first group there is the Spatial Plan of the Republic of Serbia (2010) at the national level; and the Regional Spatial Plans, the Spatial Plan of a Unit of Local Government and the Spatial Plan for Special Purpose Areas at the local level. Within the second group, there are General Urban Plans, General Regulation Plans and Detailed Regulation Plans at the local level.

Development control

It lies with the local administration responsible for issuing licenses and building permits to those proposals that comply with the requirements of the local plans – both spatial and urban.

Sustainability and governance

The Ministry of Environment, Mining and Spatial Planning is responsible for environmental issues as well as in charge of defining policies concerning environmental protection. The Spatial Plan of Serbia provides the foundation for all regional and local plans and programmes to be based on sustainable development and environmental protection. It also includes the Environmental Impact Assessment (EIA) and Strategic Impact Assessment (SIA) as compulsory requirements of the plan making process. Professionals usually criticise that citizens lack proper understanding of the 'public interest' and 'common good' and their solutions because they are guided by their narrow interest. The development of a spatial information system for monitoring the spatial and urban development is one of the key priorities included in the Spatial Plan of Serbia (2010). The National Agency for Spatial Planning is responsible for carrying the project forward.

Planning system in practice

The quality of urban and spatial plans in many municipalities are of low quality or do not exist at all. This is caused by a lack of standardised technical requirements, low capacity in municipalities, insufficient stakeholder participation in the planning process, monopolisation of the planning market, and under-qualified urban planners. This situation illustrates a wider problem for the planning system and its practice: they have not been developed in accordance with the ideal of a democratic, participative and emancipatory-modernising model, but instead manipulation, clientelism and paternalism dominate in practice. In sum, planning practice represents a mixture of elements from different "models": planning as crisis management; planning as a mechanism for support of "uncontrolled privatisation"; and, to a lesser extent, planning as a way to meet the 'public interest'.

TURKEY

FAST FACTS

- **Total Area:** 814,578 km²
- **Total Population:** 76,667,864
- **Population Growth:** 1.4%
- **Unemployment Rate:** 9.9%
- **GDP:** $806.1 billion
- **GDP per capita:** $19,600
- **GDP growth rate:** 2.9%

SETTLEMENTS STRUCTURE

- **Capital City:** Ankara
  5,013,667 pop
- **Second City:** Istanbul
  14,160,467 pop
- **Density:** 94.12 pop/km²
- **Urban Population:** 73.4 %

INSTITUTIONAL STRUCTURE

Republic composed of 7 regions and 81 provinces.

Read on: www.csb.gov.tr/english/

Administrative competence for planning

It lies with the Ministry of Environment and Urbanisation, at the national level. At the local level, it lies with the municipal councils.

Main planning legislation

The Law No 3194 on Land Development Planning and Control (1985), and the Spatial Planning Regulation (2014).

Planning and implementation instruments

It is a two-tier system with larger scale plans and local scale plans. Within the top tier, there are the following instruments: the National Development Plan (reviewed every five years), Regional Plans (carried out only if deemed necessary), Strategic Spatial Plans, Environmental Plans (for areas that constitute administrative, spatial or functional areas), and Metropolitan Area Plans (for areas that fall within multiple municipal authorities). At the local scale, there are the following instruments: Land Use Plans (mandatory only in settlements above 10,000 population), Area Land Use Plans (for settlements under 10,000 population) and Urban Improvement Plans (which detail the full extent of the physical built up area).

Development control

Development control lies mainly with the local authorities.

Sustainability and governance

Although legislation and implementation measures for sustainable development (Environmental Impact Assessments, EIA and Local Agenda 21) have been adopted in Turkey since 1993, Turkey has not met the EU targets for environment and sustainability. The main issue has been the implementation of the various laws and regulations and in the reporting of required environmental indicators. The EU has also raised concerns regarding the dual role of the Environment and Urbanisation Ministry, which entails difficulties in balancing the development pressures with environmental regulations. Participation in the planning process is weak. There was no regulation about the process until the Spatial Planning Regulation came into force in 2014.

Planning system in practice

The most contested planning related legislation in Turkey is Law 6306 "The Act on the Transformation of Areas under Disaster Risk" that was enacted in 31/5/2012. This law has changed power dynamics within the planning system. According to this law any area that is deemed under risk from a particular disaster falls under the jurisdiction of the national government and all planning activities are conducted through the Ministry of Environment and Urbanisation. Between September 2012 and June 2013, 73 areas and 20,069 buildings were declared 'under risk', 136 buildings demolished and 1,067 dwelling units demolished. There have been objections to the implementation of these urban transformation projects from affected residents, academics and non-governmental organisations. However, such a repeated demolition process forms part of Turkey's settlement history.

FAST FACTS

- **Total Area:** 603,628 km²
- **Total Population:** 42,876,243
- **Population Growth:** -0.6%
- **Unemployment Rate:** 10.5%
- **GDP:** $130.7 billion
- **GDP per capita:** $8,700
- **GDP growth rate:** -6.8%

SETTLEMENTS STRUCTURE

- **Capital City:** Kiev
  2,889,244 pop
- **Second City:** Kharkiv
  2,726,979 pop
- **Density:** 74 pop/km²
- **Urban Population:** 69.7%

INSTITUTIONAL STRUCTURE

Republic composed of 24 regions, the Autonomous Republic of Crimea and the cities of Kiev and Sebastopol.

Read on: www.kmu.gov.ua/control/en/publish/officialcategory?cat_id=247605901 city-institute.org/en/

Note: The Republic of Crimea and the City of Sebastopol were occupied by Russian Federation in February of 2014. Several rayons of Donetsk and Lugansk regions were occupied by Russian Federation in May-October of 2014.

Administrative competence for planning
It is split between the Minister of Regional Development, Building and Housing and Communal Services at the national level; the Regional and Rayon Councils at the regional level; and City, Township and Rural Councils at the local level.

Main planning legislation
The Constitution of Ukraine (1996) and the Law on Planning and Development of territories (2000).

Planning and implementation instruments
There are different instruments according to the different administrative levels. In this sense, the General Settlement Strategy of Ukraine is the instrument at the national level; Regional and Rayon plans for the regional level; and Master Plans, Zoning Plans and Detailed Plans for the local level - for towns up to 50,000 inhabitants, Master Plans can be combined and developed with Detailed Plans in the same document.

Development control
It lies with the local authorities.

Sustainability and governance
The government is trying to promote the development of renewable energies such as wind energy, solar energy or biomass energy. Ecological evaluation and forecast of pollution impacts is still performed by very rough obsolete methodology without precision. This led to plenty of cases of pollution and local ecological disasters. There are different channels for public participation in the plan making process – i.e. traditional general public hearings and the more recent hearings at Public Councils and Architectural and Urban Planning Councils. However, participation is not genuinely accessible to the general public because they are required to submit formal proposals in order to be heard at these hearings. However, there are different public organisations such as the City Institute or the Urban Rada, that are making participation in planning matters more accessible for citizens. Finally, the introduction of a new public cadaster, GIS-based, unveiled plenty of overlaps and uncertainties that have not been solved yet.

Planning system in practice
The urban planning system is obsolete and ineffective because: it does not use sociological, environmental and urban studies for designing; ignores demands of communities; the impact of locals in decision making on urban planning is quite weak; masterplans are not dynamic and cannot manage urban changes in time; zoning plans and detailed plans are duplicated documents for the same stage because they were borrowed from different systems – European and soviet; there is a lack of a legal strategy stage in urban designing. Corruption in urban planning endorsements still exists in 2015.

Acuña, Jorge Daniel	PARAGUAY
Adamu, Ahmed	NIGERIA
Adilova, Lyudmila	UZBEKISTAN
Ahou, Bernard K.	BENIN
Ajanović, Asim	BOSNIA & HERZEGOVINA
Al-Hathloul, Saleh	SAUDI ARABIA
Al Khani, Roudaina	SYRIA
Alvarez, Royee	COSTA RICA
Alleyne, Yolanda	BARBADOS
Antonov, Alexander	RUSSIA
Arefian, Farnaz	IRAN
Aubert, Bernard	FRANCE
Babarinde, Jacob Adejare	PAPUA NEW GUINEA
Bahreldin, Ibrahim Zakaria	SUDAN
Baires, Sonia	EL SALVADOR
Banteyakandi, Ambroise	BURUNDI
Bardauskiene, Dalia	LITHUANIA
Barrell, Hamish	UNITED KINGDOM
Beltran Uran, Haydee del Socorro	COLOMBIA
Bishop, Andrew	GUYANA
Caballero Zeitún, Elsa Lily	HONDURAS
Camprubi, Alex	CHINA
Castellanos, Grethel	DOMINICAN REPUBLIC
Cavric, Branko	BOTSWANA CROATIA, MACEDONIA, MONTENEGRO
Constantinides, Glafkos	CYPRUS
Córdova, Marco	ECUADOR
Cravid e Sousa, Estêvão Gloria	SAO TOME & PRINCIPE
Crawford, Jan	NEW ZEALAND
Chang, Jung-Ying	TAIWAN
Chephethe, Ralph	BOTSWANA
Chipungu, Lovemore	ZIMBABWE
Dayaram, Tanya	SOUTH AFRICA
Delgado, Marcelo	BOLIVIA
de Kock, Johan	NAMIBIA
Demires Ozkul, Bazak	TURKEY
Demirović, Senada	BOSNIA & HERZEGOVINA
de Monseignat Lavrov, Marie Isabel	MONACO
Dhamo, Sotir	ALBANIA
Dimitriu, Sabina	MOLDOVA, ROMANIA
Dobrucká, Anna	SLOVAKIA
dos Santos, Cleon Ricardo	BRAZIL
Droege, Peter	LIECHTENSTEIN
Durán, Gustavo	ECUADOR
El Adli, Khalid	EGYPT
El-Atrash, Ahmad	PALESTINE
Elgendy, Hany	GERMANY
Elisei, Pietro	ROMANIA, MOLDOVA
Ellul, Toni	MALTA
Enemark, Stig	DENMARK
Eser, Thiemo	LUXEMBURG
Fernández Maldonado, Ana María	PERU
Ferrer, Mércedes	VENEZUELA
Fetahagic, Maida	BOSNIA & HERZEGOVINA
Finegan, Jack	MYANMAR
Franchini, Teresa	SPAIN
Fraser, Adam	SAMOA
Galland, Daniel	DENMARK
Gargoum, Ammar	LIBYA
Garon, Meir	ISRAEL
Gashi-Shabani, Lumnije	KOSOVO
Gilbert, Craig	MYANMAR
Goedman, Jan	NETHERLANDS
Goguen, Adam	SIERRA LEONE
Goldie, Stephen	UNITED ARAB EMIRATES
Golubeva, Yana	BELARUS
Golubovic Matic, Darinka	SERBIA
Gómez, Nersa	VENEZUELA
Greene Castillo, Fernando	MEXICO
Hafiane, Abderrahim	ALGERIA
Halim, Deddy	PHILIPPINES
Hithnawi, Anjad	PALESTINE
Hvingel, Line	DENMARK
Hyde, Janet	JAMAICA
Ilmonen, Mervi	FINLAND
Ingabire, Bernice	BURUNDI
Inkoŏm, Daniel Kweku Baah	GHANA
Islam, Muḣammad Ariful	BANGLADESH
Ivanic, Luka	SLOVENIA
Jamakovic, Said	BOSNIA & HERZEGOVINA
Janku, Eranda	ALBANIA
Jerguš, Martin	SLOVAKIA
Jokhadze, Natia	GEORGIA
Junussova, Madina	KAZAKHSTAN
Juvara, Martina	CYPRUS

Kammeier, H. Detlef — CAMBODIA THAILAND
Kamrowska-Załuska, Dorota — POLAND
Karunathilake, A. V. G. C. — SRI LANKA
Kassahun, Samson — ETHIOPIA
Liu, Thai-Ker — SINGAPORE
Khanh, Duong Quoc — VIETNAM
Khanlarov, Azer — AZERBAIJAN
Kostrzewska, Małgorzata — POLAND
Kovachev, Atanas — BULGARIA
Kreuzberg, Elena — KYRGYZSTAN
Krishnadath, Lilian — SURINAME
Kublacovs, Andis — LATVIA
Kyessi, Alphonce G. — TANZANIA
Lamzah, Assia — MOROCCO
Ledo, Carmen — BOLIVIA
Ledwon, Slawomir — QATAR
Lim, Seo Hwan — SOUTH KOREA
Lin, John Chien-Yuan — TAIWAN
Lloyd, Greg — UNITED KINGDOM
Lombardini, Giampiero — ITALY
Lorens, Piotr — POLAND
Lyubenov, Yordan — BULGARIA
Maier, Karel — CZECH REPUBLIC
Maissa, Jean Pierre — GABON
Makathy, Tep — CAMBODIA
Mäntysalo, Raine — FINLAND
March, Alan — AUSTRALIA
Martineau, Yann — HAITI
Matsumoto, Tadashi — JAPAN
Md Dali, Melasutra Binti — MALAYSIA
Mekvichai, Banasopit — THAILAND
Mendes Correia, Maria Alice — ANGOLA
Merce, Miquel — ANDORRA
Merlo Robles, Lilian Regina — GUATEMALA
Milojevic, Brankica — BOSNIA & HERZEGOVINA
Miloševic, Predrag — ZIMBABWE
Miller, Nikola — UNITED KINGDOM
Møller, Jørgen — DENMARK
Moreira, Inês — PORTUGAL
Morgado, Sofia — PORTUGAL
Moussali, Simon — LEBANON
Mozambique Working Group,
Development Cooperation in Basic

Habitability Group,
Madrid Technical School of
Architecture, Spain — MOZAMBIQUE
Muldagalieva, Karlygash — KAZAKHSTAN
Munir, Syed Rizwa — PAKISTAN
Murphy, Patricia — MALDIVES
Mycoo, Michelle — TRINIDAD AND TOBAGO
Nada, Mohamed — EGYPT
Nghi, Duong Quoc — VIETNAM
Oderson, Derrick — BARBADOS
Olufemi, Olusola — LESOTHO, SWAZILAND, CANADA
Omwenga, Mairura — KENYA
Osman, Salah Mahmoud — SUDAN
Palmér, Karl — SWEDEN
Pallai, Katalin — HUNGARY
Pancewicz, Łukasz — POLAND
Papageorgiou, Marilena — GREECE
Pavlovic, Dubravka — MACEDONIA, MONTENEGRO
Paz, Diana — ECUADOR
Peel, Deborah — UNITED KINGDOM
Perea, Luis — SIERRA LEONE
Pettang, Chrispin — CAMEROON
Pichler-Milanovic, Nataša — SLOVENIA
Pleho, Jasna — BOSNIA & HERZEGOVINA
Pomazan, Roman — UKRAINE
Poppleton, Richard — UNITED KINGDOM
Preem, Martti — ESTONIA
Qerimi, Rudina — KOSOVO
Rassam, Sahar — IRAQ
Raymond, Patrick — MONACO
Razafindrazaka, Ravo Lalaina — MADAGASCAR
Reyes, Ramón — VENEZUELA
Ribeiro, Edgard F. — INDIA
Rizwan, Fauzia — PAKISTAN
Robinson, Peter — SOUTH AFRICA
Roig, Angels — ANDORRA
Russell, Paula — IRELAND
Rydén, Ewa — SWEDEN
Sangare, Ahmed — COTE D´IVOIRE
Seraj, Toufiq M. — BANGLADESH
Stephens, Richard — UNITED STATES OF AMERICA
Suhono, Andreas — INDONESIA
Sabukunze, Dieudonné — BURUNDI

Scornik, Carlos Osvaldo	ARGENTINA
Schloeth, Lukas	SWITZERLAND
Schrøder, Lise	DENMARK
Shaafi, Enhened	LIBYA
Sihlongonyane, Mfaniseni	LESOTHO, SWAZILAND
Silvan, Juraj	SLOVAKIA
Simonyans, Armine	ARMENIA
Slaev, Aleksandar	BULGARIA
Sørensen, Esben M.	DENMARK
Stober, Dina	CROATIA
Suleiman, Moh'd Nageeb	SUDAN
Summers, Bob	PHILIPPINES
Suraji, Akhmad	INDONESIA
Terrazas Febres, René Zaide	NICARAGUA
Thors, Stefan	ICELAND
Tillner, Silja	AUSTRIA
Topchiev, Hristo	BULGARIA
Tse, Janice Ching Yu	HONG KONG
Turki, Sami Yassine	TUNISIA
Vansteenkiste, Frank	LUXEMBURG
Vardosanidze, Vladimer	GEORGIA
Viana, Isabel	URUGUAY
Vicente Sola, Félix	ANDORRA
Vicuña, Magdalena	CHILE
Vloebergh, Guy	BELGIUM
Wang, Liang Huew	HONG KONG
Watson, Barrie	NAMIBIA
Wirén, Erik	SWEDEN
Wøhni, Arthur	NORWAY
Yunusa, Mohammed-Bello	NIGERIA
Zeleza Manda, Mtafu A.	MALAWI
Zonneveld, Wil	NETHERLANDS

AFRICA

NORTH AFRICA

ALGERIA	Hafiane, Abderrahim
LIBYA	Gargoum, Ammar
	Shaafi, Enhened
EGYPT	El Adli, Khalid
	Nada, Mohamed
MOROCCO	Lamzah, Assia
TUNISIA	Turki, Sami Yassine

EAST AFRICA

BURUNDI	Banteyakandi, Ambroise
	Ingabire, Bernice
	Sabukunze, Dieudonné
ETHIOPIA	Kassahun, Samson
KENYA	Omwenga, Mairura
MADAGASCAR	Razafindrazaka, Ravo Lalaina
MALAWI	Zeleza Manda, Mtafu A.
MOZAMBIQUE	Mozambique Working Group, Development Cooperation in Basic Habitability Group, Madrid Technical School of Architecture, Spain
SUDAN	Bahreldin, Ibrahim Zakaria
	Osman, Salah Mahmoud
	Suleiman, Moh'd Nageeb
TANZANIA	Kyessi, Alphonce G.
ZIMBABWE	Chipungú, Lovemore
	Miloševic, Predrag

MIDDLE AFRICA

ANGOLA	Mendes Correia, Maria Alice
CAMEROON	Pettang, Chrispin
GABON	Maissa, Jean Pierre
SAO TOME & PRINCIPE	Cravid e Sousa, Estêvão Gloria

SOUTH AFRICA

BOTSWANA	Cavric, Branko
	Chephetzhe, Ralph
LESOTHO	Olufemi, Olusola
	Sihlongonyane, Mfaniseni

NAMIBIA	de Kock, Johan
	Watson, Barrie
SOUTH AFRICA	Dayaram, Tanya
	Robinson, Peter
SWAZILAND	Olufemi, Olusola
	Sihlongonyane, Mfaniseni

WEST AFRICA

BENIN	Ahou, Bernard K.
COTE D´IVOIRE	Sangare, Ahmed
GHANA	Inkoom, Daniel Kweku Baah
NIGERIA	Adamu, Ahmed
	Yunusa, Mohammed-Bello
SIERRA LEONE	Goguen, Adam
	Perea, Luis

ASIA & PACIFIC

MIDDLE EAST

IRAN	Arefian, Farnaz
IRAQ	Rassam, Sahar
ISRAEL	Garon, Meir
LEBANON	Moussali, Simon
PALESTINE	El-Atrash, Ahmad
	Hithnawi, Anjad
QATAR	Ledwon, Slawomir
SAUDI ARABIA	Al-Hathloul, Saleh
SYRIA	Al Khani, Roudaina
UNITED ARAB EMIRATES	Goldie, Stephen

CENTRAL ASIA

BANGLADESH	Islam, Muhammad Ariful
	Seraj, Toufiq M.
INDIA	Ribeiro, Edgard F.
KAZAKHSTAN	Junussova, Madina
	Muldagalieva, Karlygash
KYRGYZSTAN	Kreuzberg, Elena
MALDIVES	Murphy, Patricia
PAKISTAN	Munir, Syed Rizwa
	Rizwan, Fauzia
SRI LANKA	Karunathilake, A. V. G. C.
UZBEKISTAN	Adilova, Lyudmila

EAST ASIA

CAMBODIA	Kammeier, H. Detlef
	Makathy, Tep
CHINA	Camprubi, Alex
HONG KONG	Tse, Janice Ching Yu
	Wang, Liang Huew
INDONESIA	Suhono, Andreas
	Suraji, Akhmad
JAPAN	Matsumoto, Tadashi
MALAYSIA	Md Dali, Melasutra Binti
MYANMAR	Finegan, Jack
	Gilbert, Craig
PHILIPPINES	Halim, Deddy
	Summers, Bob
SINGAPORE	Liu, Thai-Ker
SOUTH KOREA	Lim, Seo Hwan
TAIWAN	Chang, Jung-Ying
	Lin, John Chien-Yuan
THAILAND	Kammeier, H. Detlef
	Mekvichai, Banasopit
VIETNAM	Khanh, Duong Quoc
	Nghi, Duong Quoc

AUSTRALASIA & PACIFIC

AUSTRALIA	March, Alan
NEW ZEALAND	Crawford, Jan
PAPUA NEW GUINEA	Babarinde, Jacob Adejare
SAMOA	Fraser, Adam

AMERICA

CENTRAL AMERICA & PACIFIC

COSTA RICA	Alvarez, Royee
EL SALVADOR	Baires, Sonia
GUATEMALA	Merlo Robles, Lilian Regina
HONDURAS	Caballero Zeitún, Elsa Lily
NICARAGUA	Terrazas Febres, René Zaide

CARIBE

BARBADOS	Alleyne, Yolanda
	Oderson, Derrick
DOMINICAN REPUBLIC	Castellanos, Grethel
TRINIDAD & TOBAGO	Mycoo, Michelle
HAITI	Martineau, Yann
JAMAICA	Hyde, Janet

NORTH AMERICA
CANADA   Olufemi, Olusola
MEXICO   Greene Castillo, Fernando
UNITED STATES OF AMERICA   Stephens, Richard

SOUTH AMERICA
ARGENTINA   Scornik, Carlos Osvaldo
BOLIVIA   Delgado, Marcelo
                        Ledo, Carmen
BRAZIL   dos Santos, Cleon Ricardo
CHILE   Vicuña, Magdalena
COLOMBIA   Beltran Uran, Haydee del
                        Socorro
ECUADOR   Córdova, Marco
                        Durán, Gustavo
                        Paz, Diana
GUYANA   Bishop, Andrew
PARAGUAY   Acuña, Jorge Daniel
PERU   Fernández Maldonado,
                        Ana María
SURINAME   Krishnadath, Lilian
URUGUAY   Viana, Isabel
VENEZUELA   Ferrer, Mercedes
                        Gómez, Nersa
                        Reyes, Ramón

EUROPE
EUROPEAN UNION, EUROPEAN ECONOMIC AREA AND
BILATERAL
ANDORRA   Merce, Miquel
                        Roig, Angels
                        Vicente Sola, Félix
AUSTRIA   Tillner, Silja
BELGIUM   Vloebergh, Guy
BULGARIA   Kovachev, Atanas
                        Lyubenov, Yordan
                        Slaev, Aleksandar
                        Topchiev, Hristo
CROATIA   Cavric, Branko
                        Stober, Dina
CYPRUS   Constantinides, Glafkos
                        Juvara, Martina
CZECH REPUBLIC Maier, Karel
DENMARK   Enemark, Stig
                        Galland, Daniel

                        Hvingel, Line
                        Møller, Jørgen
                        Schrøder, Lise
                        Sørensen, Esben M.
ESTONIA   Preem, Martti
FINLAND   Ilmonen, Mervi
                        Mäntysalo, Raine
FRANCE   Aubert, Bernard
GERMANY   Elgendy, Hany
GREECE   Papageorgiou, Marilena
HUNGARY   Pallai, Katalin
IRELAND   Russell, Paula
ITALY   Lombardini, Giampiero
LATVIA   Kublacovs, Andis
LIECHTENSTEIN   Droege, Peter
LITHUANIA   Bardauskiene, Dalia
LUXEMBURG   Eser, Thiemo
                        Vansteenkiste, Frank
MALTA   Ellul, Toni
MONACO   de Monseignat Lavrov,
                        Marie Isabel
                        Raymond, Patrick
NETHERLANDS   Goedman, Jan
                        Zonneveld, Wil
NORWAY   Wøhni, Arthur
POLAND   Kamrowska-Załuska, Dorota
                        Kostrzewska, Małgorzata
                        Lorens, Piotr
                        Pancewicz, Łukasz
PORTUGAL   Moreira, Inês
                        Morgado, Sofia
ROMANIA   Dimitriu, Sabina
                        Elisei, Pietro
SLOVAKIA   Dobrucká, Anna
                        Jerguš, Martin
                        Silvan, Juraj
SLOVENIA   Ivanić, Luka
                        Pichler-Milanović, Nataša
SPAIN   Franchini, Teresa
SWEDEN   Palmér, Karl
                        Rydén, Ewa
                        Wirén, Erik
SWITZERLAND   Schloeth, Lukas
UNITED KINGDOM Barrell, Hamish
                        Lloyd, Greg

Miller, Nikola
Peel, Deborah
Poppleton, Richard

NON EUROPEAN UNION
ALBANIA   Dhamo, Sotir
                 Janku, Eranda
ARMENIA   Simonyans, Armine
AZERBAIJAN   Khanlarov, Azer
BELARUS   Golubeva, Yana
BOSNIA & HERZEGOVINA   Ajanović, Asim
                 Demirović, Senada
                 Fetahagić, Maida
                 Jamaković, Said
                 Milojević, Brankica
                 Pleho, Jasna
GEORGIA   Jokhadze, Natia
                 Vardosanidze, Vladimer
KOSOVO   Gashi-Shabani, Lumnije
                 Qerimi, Rudina
MACEDONIA   Cavric, Branko
                 Pavlovic, Dubravka
MOLDOVA   Dimitriu, Sabina
                 Elisei, Pietro
MONTENEGRO   Cavric, Branko
                 Pavlovic, Dubravka
RUSSIA   Antonov, Alexander
SERBIA   Golubovic Matic, Darinka
TURKEY   Demires Ozkul, Bazak
UKRAINE   Pomazan, Roman

COLLABORATORS/ACKNOWLEDGMENTS
IMPP 2015

ANGOLA. Hélder da Conceição José, António Pedro Bunga, Julião Webba, Victor Daniel, Eliude Marculino. Sara Vilas Boas, Feuder Caetano and D,forAll
BELGIUM. Bruno Clerbaux and Pierre Cox

CAMEROON. Joseph Tedou, Georges Kouamou and Eric Kowa

CHINA. Huszar Brammah and Associates

GREECE. Elias Beriatos

INDONESIA Hendro P. Suselo, Budhy Tjahyati, Maurits Pasaribu, Ruchyat Deni D, Max H. Pohan, Tatag Wiranto, Budi Sitomurang, Kawik Sugiana, Tetti Armiati Argo and Ernan Rustiadi

NICARAGUA. Luis Zúñiga, Leonardo Icaza and Iara Terrazas

NORWAY. Jensen, Rolf

PARAGUAY. María Milagros Aquino Casco, Daniela Leonor Bloch Stelnicki, Evelin Ester Campañoli Lorer, María Belén Candia Cañiza, Francisco Centurión Vargas, Karen Mariela Endler Dickel, Aldrin Oliver Iriarte Venialgo, Adela Kim, Miguel Mathias Trussy Chilupa, Rolando Javier Valdez Villalba, Katia Marcela Acosta Condoretty, Claudia Tatiana Chaparro Ibarra, Luis Alberto Fariña Chudyk, Lucia Mabel Ganchozo Llano, Alexander Ariel Nikolaus Frans, Héctor Alcides Villalba Ortiz, Fabio Armando López Curtido, Eric Javier López, Ryoma Alan Komatsu Funada, Dahiana Medina Dávalos, Víctor Daniel Giménez, Benito Marcelo Ibarra Mauro, Luis María Brizuela and Alejandra María Sipiliuk Lopoja.

SURINAME. Rashni Soerdjlal, Prevind Punwasi, Anjanidewi Natha, Manisha Jiawan, Bianca de Bats and Ravin Bhawan

TUNISIA. Sabrine Ben Hassen, Morched Chabbi, Hatem Kahloun and Henda Gafsi

ZIMBABWE. F. Chapisa

LIST OF AUTHORS A-Z AND COUNTRIES 2008

Adilova, Lyudmula	Uzbekistan	Ferrer, Mercedes	Venezuela
Ajanovic, Asim	Bosnia	Ferro Lozano, Ricardo	Colombia
Ahmed, Adamu	Nigeria	Fetahagic, Maida	Bosnia
Alaverdyan, Ruzan	Armenia	Figueroa, Jonas	Chile
Al-Hathloul, Saleh	Saudi Arabia	Fookes, Tom	New Zealand
Alleyne, Yolanda	Barbados	Franchini, Teresa	Spain
Anderton, Christopher	Netherlands	Garay, Gonzalo	Paraguay
Ankrah, Alexander	UK (Scotland)	Gargoum, Ammar	Lybia
Arana, Vladimir	Peru	Garon, Meir	Israel
Arroyo C., Víctor	Costa Rica	Gashi, Lumnije	Kosovo
Aubert, Bernard	France	Goedman, Jan C.	Netherlands
Bahreldin, Ibrahim Zakaria	Sudan	Golubovic Matic, Darinka	Serbia
Baires, Sonia	El Salvador	Goodman, Robin	Australia
Bardauskiene, Dalia	Lithuania	Gossop, Chris J.	United Kingdom
Bertran, M.	Chile	Green Castillo, Fernando	Mexico
Besio, Mariolina	Italy	Guet, Jean-Francois	France
Bishop, Andrew	Guyana	Hafiane, Abderrahim	Algeria
Brieva, A.	Chile	Halim, Deddy	Philipines
Brenes A., Daniel	Costa Rica	Ilmonen, Mervi	Finland
Burra, Marco	Tanzania	Inkoom, Daniel K. B.	Ghana
Butt, Abdul Manan	Pakistan	Islam, Muhammad Ariful	Bangladesh
Cace, Lolita	Latvia	Jamakovic, Said	Bosnia
Causarano, Mabel	Paraguay	Jokhadze, Natia	Georgia
Cavric, Branko I.	Botswana; Macedonia	Joergensen, Lars O.	Denmark
Crawford Jan	New Zealand	Junussova, Madina	Kazakhstan
Chabbi, Morched	Tunisia	Jurkovic, Sonja	Croatia
Chipungu, L.	Zimbabwe	Karunathilake, A. V. G. C.	Sri Lanka
Chowdhury, Tufayel Ahmed	Bangladesh	Khanlarov, Azer T.	Azerbaijan
da Costa Lobo, Manuel	Portugal	Kudryavtsev, Fedor	Russia
de Kock, Johan	Namibia	Kumata, Yoshinobu	Japan
Davies, John	United Kingdom (Wales)	Kyessi, Alphonce G.	Tanzania
Demires Ozkul, Basak	Turkey	Ledo, Carmen	Bolivia
Dhamo, Sotir	Albania	Lehzam, Abdellah	Morocco
Editors	Egypt; Greece	Leven, Rosie	United Kingdom (Scotland)
Elgendy, Hany	Germany	Lim, Seo-Hwan	Korea South
Ellul, Tony	Malta	Lin, John Chien-Yuan	Taiwan
Enotiades, Phaedon	Cyprus	Liu, Thai Ker	Singapore
Eser, Thiemo	Luxembourg	Lusigi, Roswitha	Kenya

Magalhaes, Fernanda	Brazil	Sapatu, Fiona	Samoa
Maier, Karel	Czech Republic	Scholl, Bernd	Germany
March, Alan	Australia	Seraj, Toufiq M	Bangladesh
Mayo, Shaker Mehmood	Pakistan	Schloeth, Lucas	Switzerland
Merlo Robles, Lilian Regina	Guatemala	Schrenk, Manfred	Austria
Milosevic, Pedrag V.	Zimbabwe	Scornik, Carlos Osvaldo	Argentina
Moeller, Joergen	Denmark	Shaafi, Emhemed	Lybia
Molina, Nixon	Venezuela	Sihlongonyane, Mfaniseni	Lesotho; Swaziland
Murphy, Patricia	Maldivas	Snaggs, Keneth	Trinidad Tobago
Movahed, Khosrow	Iran	Soemoto, Sugiono	Indonesia
Nghi, Duong Quoc	Vietnam	Somova, Victoria	Kazakhstan
Niemczyk, Maria	Poland	Spiridonova, Julia	Bulgaria
Nollert, M.	Germany	Srinivas, Hari	Japan
Obregon Hartleben, Oliver	Guatemala	Stephen, Richard	USA
Odendaal, Nancy	South Africa	Suleiman, Moh'd Nageeb	Sudan
Oderson, Derrick	Barbados	Summers, Bob	Philipines
Olufemi, Olusola	Lesotho; Swaziland	Thors, Stefan	Iceland
Osman, Salah Mahmoud	Sudan	Trusins, Jekabs	Latvia
Osorio, María del Socorro	Honduras	ur Rahman, M. Atiq	Pakistan
Pacheco, Paola	Portugal	Van den Broeck, Jef	Belgium
Palmer, Karl G.	Sweden	van Ypersele, Joel	Belgium
Pallai, Katalin	Hungary	Viana, Isabel	Uruguay
Paskova, Miloslova	Slovakia	Vilas, Sara	Angola
Phiri, Daniel	Zambia	Wagener, Carmen	Luxembourg
Pichler-Milanovic, Natasa	Slovenia	Wang, Chi-Hsien	Taiwan
Pleho, Jasna	Bosnia	Wang, Liang Huew	Hong Kong
Preem, Martti	Estonia	Watson, Barrie	Namibia
Rassam, Sahar	Iraq	Wiren, Erik	Sweden
Ribeiro, Edgard	India	Wohni, Arthur	Norway
Ricardo dos Santos, Cleon	Brazil	Wolfe, Jeanne	Canada
Ringli, Helmut	Switzerland	Wyporek, Bogdan	Poland
Robinson, Peter	South Africa	Yunusa, Mohammed – Bello	Nigeria
Ross, Peter	China	Zeleza Manda, Mtafu A.	Malawi
Rubicki, Irene	Austria		
Russell, Paula	Ireland		
Ryden, Ewa	Sweden		
Ryser, Judith	Azerbaijan		
Sakano, T.	Japan		

COLOPHON

Published by ISOCARP (International Society of City and Regional Planners)
P.O. Box, 2501 CZ, The Hague, The Netherlands
Email:isocarp@isocarp.org www.isocarp.org

First edition 1992, 2nd edition 1995, 3rd edition 1996, 4th edition 2001
5th extended edition 2008

6th new extended and restructured edition 2015
Editors: Judith Ryser & Teresa Franchini
Copyright © with the authors (editors: Creative Commons Copyright Conditions)
All rights reserved

A catalogue record for this book is available from the British Library
ISBN: 978-94-90354-40-4

Book, cover design and production by TEAM TEAM (Paula Blanco Ballesteros,
Marina Lorenzo, Elena Herrero, Mario Larra, Mónica Beltrí, Teresa Casamayor,
Ismael Martín and Claudia Pfannes)
Digital device design, coding and typeset managed by Dino Juloya
Research collaboration by Sonia Freire-Trigo
Logistic support by ISOCARP Secretariat

Printed in the EU
ARTIX PLUS SRL
Bukarest, December, 2015